Beginning Axum

Learning Modern Web Development
With Rust

Indo Yoon

Apress®

Beginning Axum: Learning Modern Web Development With Rust

Indo Yoon
Seoul, Korea (Republic of)

ISBN-13 (pbk): 979-8-8688-2630-6   ISBN-13 (electronic): 979-8-8688-2631-3
https://doi.org/10.1007/979-8-8688-2631-3

Managing Director, Apress Media LLC: Welmoed Spahr
Acquisitions Editor: Anandadeep Roy
Editorial Assistant: Jessica Vakili

Cover designed by eStudioCalamar

Cover image designed by Freepik (www.freepik.com)

Distributed to the book trade worldwide by Springer Science+Business Media New York, 1 New York Plaza, New York, NY 10004. Phone 1-800-SPRINGER, fax (201) 348-4505, e-mail orders-ny@springer-sbm.com, or visit www.springeronline.com. Apress Media, LLC is a Delaware LLC and the sole member (owner) is Springer Science + Business Media Finance Inc (SSBM Finance Inc). SSBM Finance Inc is a **Delaware** corporation.

For information on translations, please e-mail booktranslations@springernature.com; for reprint, paperback, or audio rights, please e-mail bookpermissions@springernature.com.

Apress titles may be purchased in bulk for academic, corporate, or promotional use. eBook versions and licenses are also available for most titles. For more information, reference our Print and eBook Bulk Sales web page at http://www.apress.com/bulk-sales.

Any source code or other supplementary material referenced by the author in this book is available to readers on GitHub. For more detailed information, please visit https://www.apress.com/gp/services/source-code.

If disposing of this product, please recycle the paper

Table of Contents

About the Author

 **Indo Yoon** is a software engineer at SAP Labs Korea specializing in Python, Rust, and Go. A Seoul National University alumnus, he extends his impact beyond code as a frequent speaker and technical author. With a strong focus on web services, Indo is dedicated to advancing the developer community through his lectures and written works.

About the Technical Reviewer

 **Joshua Mo** is a software engineer and technical writer specializing in Rust, AI infrastructure, and web development. He is currently the project lead for Rig, an open-source Rust framework for building agentic and AI-driven systems, where he focuses on system design, reliability, and developer ergonomics.

Previously, Joshua worked at Shuttle, where he wrote many articles on using Axum, helped drive Rust adoption across companies, and supported developers learning async Rust and modern Rust web frameworks. He is known for translating real-world engineering experience into practical, production-focused guidance.

Acknowledgments

I am deeply grateful to my wife for her unwavering support and patience throughout the writing of this book. The countless late nights and weekends I spent at my desk were made possible only by her understanding, encouragement, and the extra responsibilities she quietly shouldered at home. This book would not exist without her.

Introduction

This book introduces Axum, a modern Rust web framework. Through practical code examples, you'll learn to build production-ready backend applications—from basic routing and database integration to middleware and real-time WebSocket communication. Whether you're new to Rust or an experienced developer exploring new frameworks, this book provides a hands-on path to mastering Axum.

About This Book

This book covers Axum, a Rust backend framework. Axum is developed by the Tokio project, Rust's most prominent project, and is the fastest-growing Rust framework. Currently, no books specifically focus on the Axum framework, either domestically or internationally. We wrote this book to promote Axum, which has tremendous growth potential, and to help more people adopt it.

We explain Axum's unique user-friendly approach through actual code examples. We've focused on features essential in real-world development and structured the book so you can build a complete backend application simply by following along.

We provide concise explanations of Rust programming basics and backend technologies while covering each functional component in detail, helping you naturally understand Axum's architecture.

Through this book, we hope you'll fully experience the appeal of Rust and Axum, and we look forward to seeing many more projects adopt this powerful combination.

Target Audience

This book will be especially helpful for the following readers.

Readers Who Want to Learn Rust

If you want to learn Rust through this book, you'll master core concepts and important syntax in each chapter. We cover many examples where you can actually apply each concept, giving you an opportunity to learn Rust quickly.

Readers Who Want to Try a New Project

If you've learned Rust and want to create your own project, especially web-related projects, this book is ideal. Since Axum actively utilizes Rust's strength in asynchronous programming, you'll get an opportunity to learn new things while reviewing Rust's core concepts.

Readers Who Want to Write a High-Performance Web Server

This book covers various practical techniques including database configuration, middleware construction, and implementing Server-Sent Event (SSE) endpoints. Whether you're building high-performance servers for work or side projects, this book will help you achieve your goals more quickly.

Prerequisites

We recommend having some background knowledge of Rust to read this book, though it's not required. For readers encountering this content for the first time, we've included brief background information and related explanations at the beginning of each chapter.

For Rust basics, familiarity with the following concepts is helpful. If you're new to Rust, we recommend first studying *Learning Rust by Comparing with Python* (J-Pub, 2024), which clearly explains Rust's fundamental syntax and concepts.

- **Ownership**: Ownership transfer/borrowing, references

- **Asynchronous programming**: Arc, Mutex, async/await (tokio knowledge is helpful but not required)

- **Other**: Structs, closures

For backend server fundamentals, understanding the following is helpful. Don't worry if you're unfamiliar—we've included plenty of examples and detailed explanations to help you understand easily.

- **Relational Database Management System (RDBMS)**: This book uses PostgreSQL. Experience with other relational databases (MySQL, MariaDB, etc.) transfers easily.

- **SQL**: Basic queries for table definition, data retrieval, and modification.

- **HTTP**: Concepts like query parameters, path parameters, and request bodies needed for REST API design.

Book Structure

Each chapter covers the following:

- **Chapter 1**: Introduces Rust backend development characteristics and performs environment setup for practice exercises.

- **Chapter 2**: Examines Axum's core components—routing HTTP requests, processing query parameters and JSON bodies through Extractors, and sharing state across the app through State.

- **Chapter 3**: Integrates PostgreSQL with SeaORM, explores schema and migration management, completes all necessary endpoints, and modularizes the project.

- **Chapter 4**: Examines tower middleware essentials like logging, timeouts, and authentication and applies them to the application.

- **Chapter 5**: Explores WebSocket, a protocol for real-time bidirectional communication between clients and servers, and implements single-connection and multi-connection WebSocket handlers.

- **Chapter 6**: Builds a complete chat service project with SSE-based real-time messaging, a React frontend, automated testing, and Docker deployment.

The book is structured for easy follow-along with code and screenshots. All code is available on GitHub. If you encounter problems or have questions, please use the repository's Discussion section. Example code can be found at

- REST API example: `https://github.com/Indosaram/axum-book-code`

- Chat service example: `https://github.com/Indosaram/axum-react-chat-app`

The Docker image built in Chapter 6 is available at `https://hub.docker.com/repository/docker/indosaram/axum-chat-app/general`.

CHAPTER 1

Rust and Server Development

Backend servers are the core of web applications. They connect frontends to databases, process and deliver data, and handle essential service operations like security, logging, and monitoring.

Today, companies use many different programming languages and frameworks for backend development. What makes Rust stand out among them? Which companies are actually using Rust for their production backends?

Learning Points

- Why Rust excels at backend development

- Real-world case studies of Rust backends in production

- Essential components for Rust server development

1.1. Why Rust?

To understand why Rust excels at server development, we need to first examine what makes Rust itself so powerful.

1.1.1. Advantages of Rust

Rust is a modern programming language that makes it easy to build fast, reliable programs. It delivers performance nearly identical to C/C++ (about 99%), but catches memory leaks and thread race conditions at compile time—problems that have plagued

I. Yoon, *Beginning Axum*, https://doi.org/10.1007/979-8-8688-2631-3_1

1

C/C++ developers for decades. This combination of high performance and high safety has made Rust the most desired language among developers for eight consecutive years in Stack Overflow's global developer surveys [1].

Beyond performance and safety, Rust's popularity stems from its excellent developer experience. As a modern language, it features elegant syntax and clear style guidelines that help you write correct code. Features like pattern matching and closures let you express complex logic concisely and efficiently.

The compiler acts like a pair programmer—it not only identifies problems but also suggests solutions, helping you write the code you want faster. Rust also provides a convenient toolchain. A single toolchain called `cargo` handles everything from building and deploying to installing and updating dependencies. Additionally, `rust-analyzer` analyzes your source code in real time and provides immediate feedback as you write. It provides code completion, references to the code, type hints, and inline error messages in IDEs such as Visual Studio Code. Detailed instructions will be covered later.

1.1.2. Advantages of Developing Backends with Rust

The advantage of developing backend servers with Rust is that you can easily build servers with both high performance and safety. For example, developing servers with JavaScript or Python often means hitting language-imposed performance limitations or spending significant time resolving thread race conditions and other concurrency issues. Even Java, widely used in Korea, can experience delays in server response times due to garbage collection pauses.

In short, Rust is the ideal language for developing large-scale servers that require heavy CPU computation.

1.2. Rust Server Development Case Studies

Leading tech companies like Microsoft, Cloudflare, Facebook, and Amazon are already actively adopting Rust for their backends. In Korea, companies like Kakao and Korbit have also adopted Rust as their backend language. Let's examine some famous cases where companies used Rust to solve problems like concurrency limitations and performance degradation from garbage collection.

1.2.1. Figma

Figma is a browser-based UI prototyping tool. Reflecting design shapes and functionality to users in real time is crucial. However, as the service grew, increased user load caused the existing TypeScript server's CPU and memory usage to spike, leading to longer response times. To solve this, they decided to rewrite the server in Rust. The results were dramatic: compared to the TypeScript server, memory usage improved by up to 3.8x and response times improved by up to 16.4x [2].

1.2.2. Discord

Discord is a messenger service for text and video chat. As the service grew, they discovered periodic performance drops in their existing Go-based backend server. In the graph in Figure 1-1, the sections with periodic spikes represent the original server written in Go. You can see CPU usage spiking periodically, temporarily overloading the server and causing response times to increase cyclically. This was caused by Go's garbage collector—while it periodically removes unused objects from memory, all other operations must pause. After rewriting the server in Rust, CPU usage stabilized and response times became much shorter.

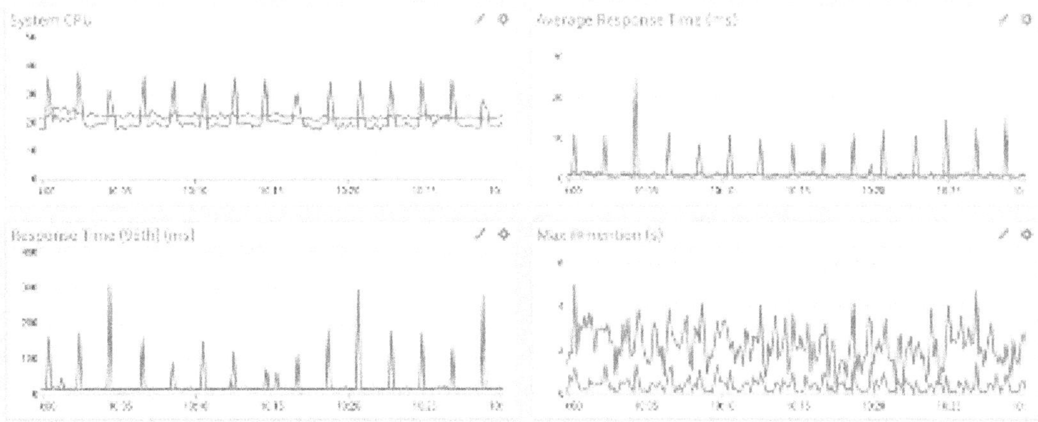

Figure 1-1. *Discord Server Performance*

1.2.3. Dropbox

Dropbox is a leading cloud storage service with millions of users worldwide. One of Dropbox's core features is rapidly synchronizing files and folders on local computers with remote storage. However, as the service scaled, they faced difficulties maintaining and improving the C++-based synchronization logic.

To solve this problem, Dropbox decided to rewrite the synchronization logic in Rust. This enabled the Dropbox team to develop high-performance concurrent programs more productively.

1.2.4. npm

npm is the package repository for Node.js, a JavaScript runtime environment. Developers can easily install and manage libraries and tools through npm. However, as more users and packages were registered, npm faced performance degradation and stability issues.

To resolve server bottlenecks, the development team considered various programming languages and even attempted actual implementations. Node.js, Go, and Java were candidates, but Rust was ultimately chosen. With the introduction of Rust, both server performance and stability improved significantly.

1.3. Comparing Rust Backend Frameworks

Thanks to Rust's many advantages, many people have become interested in Rust server development. As a result, numerous Rust backend frameworks are being developed. Since each framework has its own philosophy, design patterns, and coding approach, you should choose a framework appropriate for your environment. Especially in production, it's advisable to select a popular, well-maintained framework.

The following are the four most widely used among famous Rust frameworks:

- **Rocket**: Rocket is often used with Diesel ORM. It's designed with a focus on safety, flexibility, and security, but may not be suitable for large-scale or high-performance projects. It's developed by individual developers and has a history of development pauses.

- **Actix-web**: Actix-web has the highest performance among Rust frameworks. However, since most functionality must be handled within the framework, it has a high barrier to entry and requires implementing many features yourself. It's well-suited for small-scale web apps like microservices.

- **Axum**: Axum focuses on both usability and performance. It uses Rust asynchronous programming patterns and has high compatibility with third-party crates, making it relatively simple to build high-performance servers with various features.

- **Warp**: Warp is known for its filter system. It's relatively less popular than the other frameworks.

Looking at various benchmarks, Axum, Actix-web, and Warp show no significant performance differences. Rocket is slower in some cases, but overall shows similar performance to the other frameworks. Therefore, when choosing a Rust backend framework, usability should be prioritized over performance.

1.3.1. Why You Should Use Axum

1.3.1.1. Good Flexibility and Scalability

Rust doesn't provide an async runtime at the language level. An async runtime is what executes and manages asynchronous functions. For Rust, you must choose between tokio and smol. Each runtime has slightly different purposes and implementations, so you can choose one appropriate for your situation, but generally you should use tokio, which supports everything from embedded systems to large-scale programs.

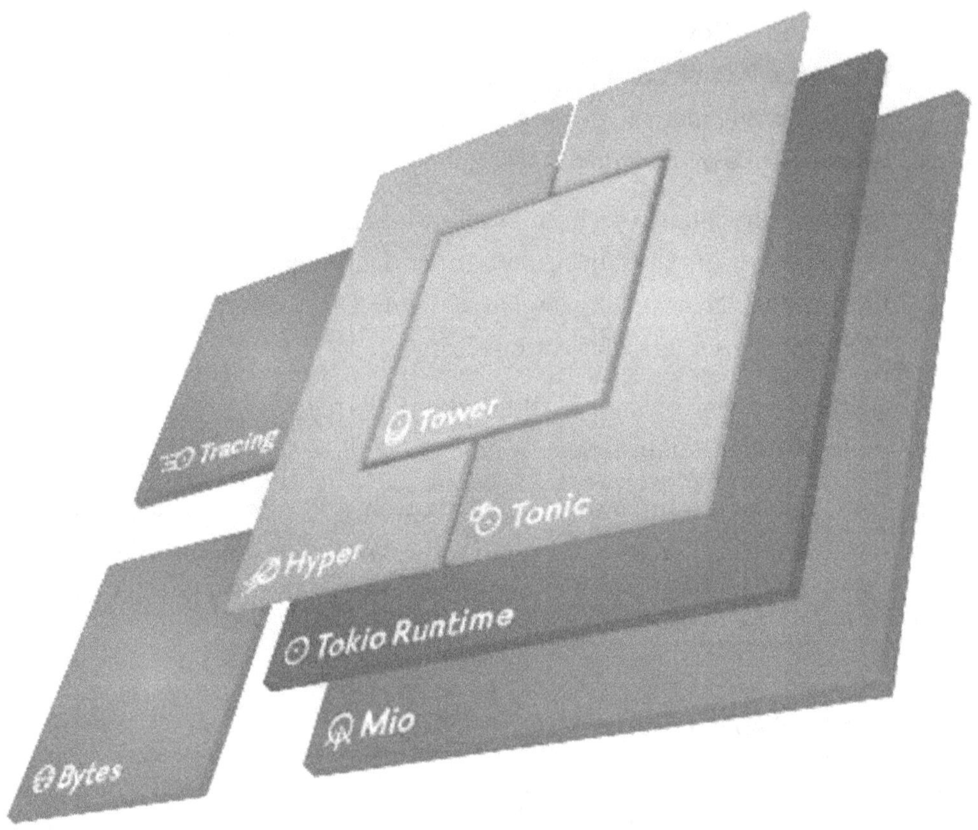

Figure 1-2. *Tokio Ecosystem*

The Tokio project to which tokio belongs forms one massive ecosystem built from libraries for creating fast and reliable network applications. It includes many libraries such as tokio for creating async runtimes, tracing for logging systems, and hyper for HTTP servers.

Axum is a server framework created specifically to properly use tokio and hyper, so it integrates smoothly with other libraries in the Tokio ecosystem. In particular, it integrates very conveniently with tower, a middleware crate that's widely used in other frameworks and has various middleware functionality pre-implemented. For these reasons, Axum is the most suitable choice if you want to easily integrate and use the various features provided by the Tokio ecosystem.

1.3.1.2. Excellent Developer Experience

Axum is designed to let you implement desired functionality with minimal code, making it very convenient compared to other frameworks. It supports all modern protocols including WebSocket, SSE (Server-Sent Event), and HTTP/2.

It also allows developers to quickly learn and apply patterns through consistent APIs. For example, you can consistently extract various types of inputs coming into the server through Extractors. It also has intuitive patterns like easily defining APIs using macros and routing requests to handlers using routers.

In summary, Axum is a framework developed by the Tokio project, the largest project in Rust's ecosystem, so it will continue to grow into an even more powerful and flexible framework with more features and improvements.

1.4. Setting Up the Development Environment

Let's explore how to set up a development environment for developing backend servers using Axum. First, you need to install the tools necessary for writing Rust code. Since installation methods differ slightly by operating system, please install according to your environment.

As of Axum 0.7.4, at least Rust version 1.66 (MSRV, Minimum Supported Rust Version) is required. You can check your Rust version by entering `rustc --version` in the terminal. If you want to upgrade your installed Rust version, enter `rustup update`. If Rust isn't installed yet, you can find installation instructions at `https://www.rust-lang.org/tools/install`.

1.4.1. Installing the Rust Toolchain

Install the Rust compiler `rustc` and system manager `cargo`. Since these two tools are included in a toolchain called `rustup`, you only need to install `rustup`.

You can install more simply by visiting the official homepage at `https://rustup.rs/#`.

1.4.1.1. macOS/Linux

macOS or Linux users can install with the following command:

```
$ curl --proto '=https' --tlsv1.2 https://sh.rustup.rs -sSf | sh
```

1.4.1.2. Windows

Windows users should download the 32-bit or 64-bit installation file from the official homepage.

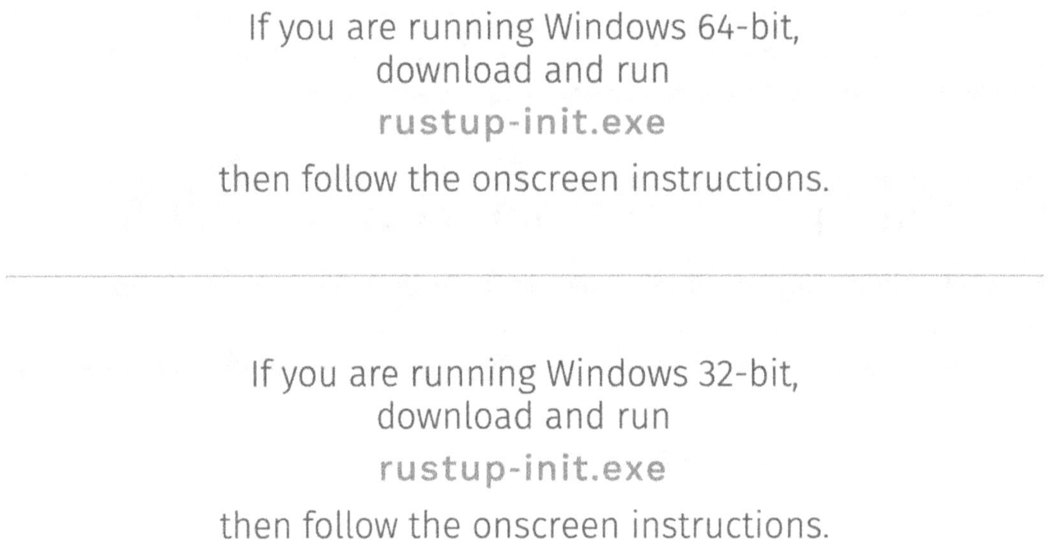

If you are running Windows 64-bit, download and run

rustup-init.exe

then follow the onscreen instructions.

If you are running Windows 32-bit, download and run

rustup-init.exe

then follow the onscreen instructions.

Figure 1-3. *Windows Rust Installation Page*

1.4.2. Installing and Setting Up Visual Studio Code

You can write Rust code with any type of text editor, but this book uses Visual Studio Code (VSCode) as the integrated development environment. We recommend using VSCode because it makes it easy and convenient to use Rust's compilation, debugging, and language server features.

We also recommend trying Zed, a very fast code editor built with Rust.

1.4.2.1. VSCode Installation

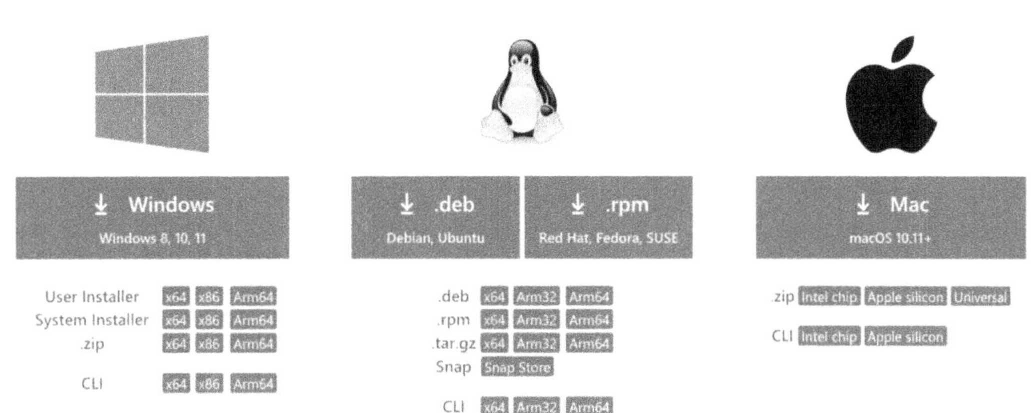

Figure 1-4. *VSCode Installation Page*

Go to the Visual Studio Code download page [3], then download and install the installation file for your operating system.

1.4.2.2. Installing Extensions

Now launch VSCode. In VSCode, you only need to install one extension: `rust-analyzer`. Click the block-shaped icon on the left, then search for the extension name.

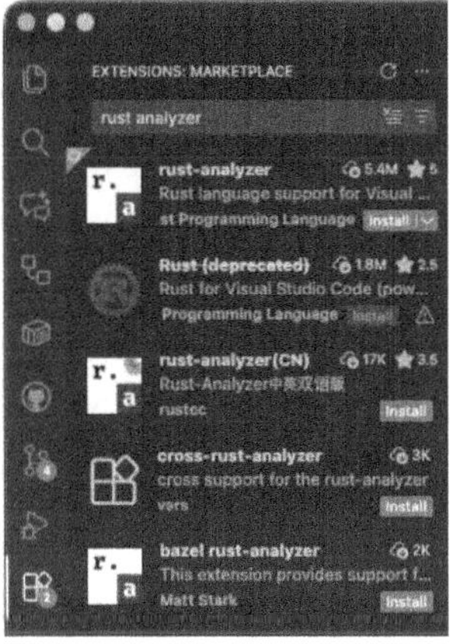

Figure 1-5. *rust-analyzer Extension Installation*

`rust-analyzer` provides various features like code auto-completion, error display, and related documentation display. Among many features, the best one is inferring and displaying variable types on screen. We'll revisit the details when writing source code later.

1.4.3. Creating a Project

In programming, projects are always managed in folder units. Folders contain all project-related documents, configuration files, and source code. Similarly, VSCode uses a method of selecting and opening folders rather than individual files when creating new projects or continuing work on existing projects. Let's create a new folder and create a project.

Click [File] ➤ [Open Folder] in VSCode's top menu. Create a new folder named `rust_project`, then select that folder. The window will refresh and show an empty project screen. From now on, projects created in this book will be created by making new folders under this folder.

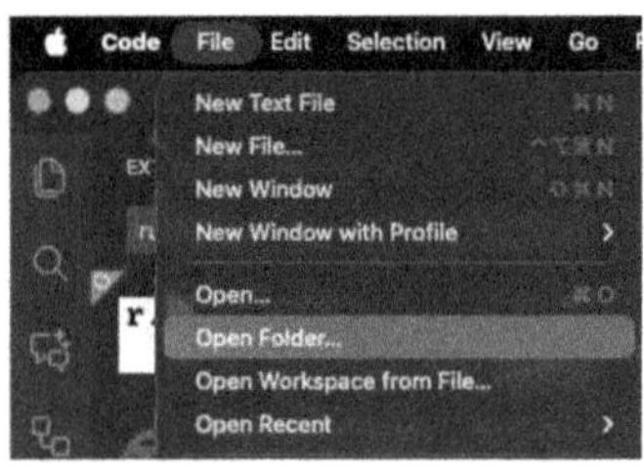

Figure 1-6. *How to Open Folders*

1.4.4. Installing the PostgreSQL Database

The PostgreSQL database is a widely used database (pronounced "post-gres"). PostgreSQL is a relational database that stores data in tables and defines relationships between tables. PostgreSQL is open source and free to use, making it usable for everything from small personal projects to large enterprise projects. Also, most of the cloud service providers offer managed Postgres services, so you can start your service more easily and quickly. It's a high-performance database that pairs well with Rust's fast processing capabilities. In particular, PostgreSQL supports a wide variety of data types including text, numbers, arrays, JSON, XML, UUID, and IP addresses, making it useful from a general web service perspective. It was also selected as the most popular database with 45.55% of all responses in the 2023 Stack Overflow survey. Even if you haven't used PostgreSQL but have only used other relational databases like MySQL or MariaDB, you'll be able to understand without much difficulty since the basic usage methods and SQL syntax are similar.

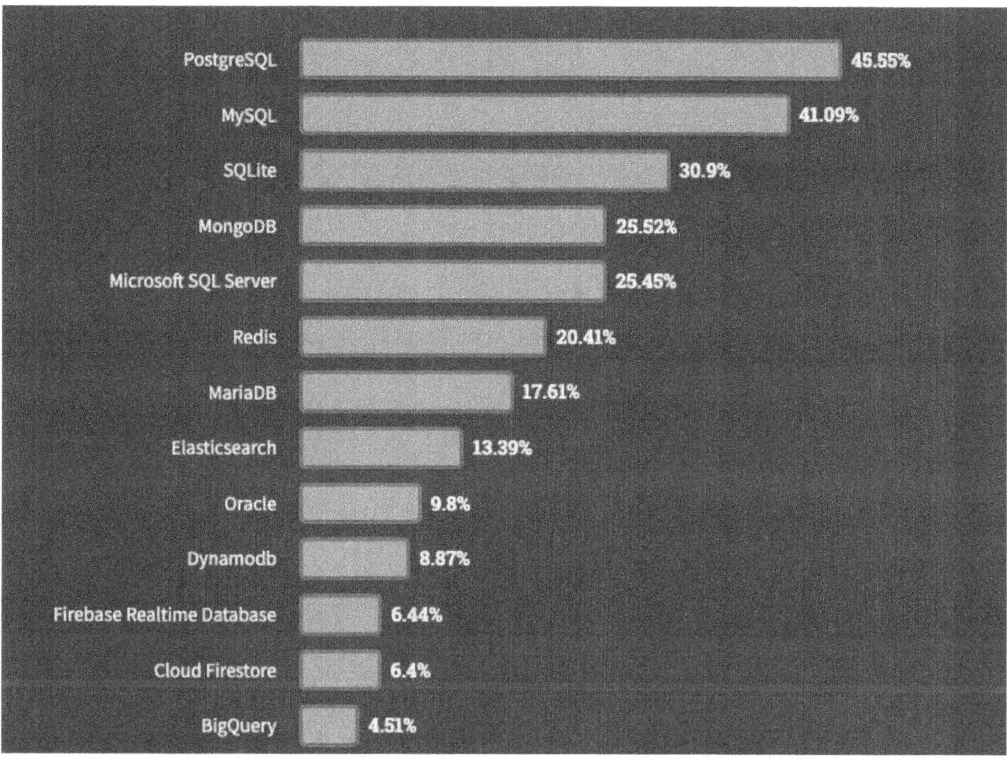

Figure 1-7. *Database Rankings*

To install PostgreSQL, go to the following address, download the installation file for your operating system, and proceed with installation. For Linux, follow the guided installation script.

```
https://www.postgresql.org/download/
```

This book recommends PostgreSQL version 15 or higher, but if PostgreSQL is already installed, version 13 or higher is fine.

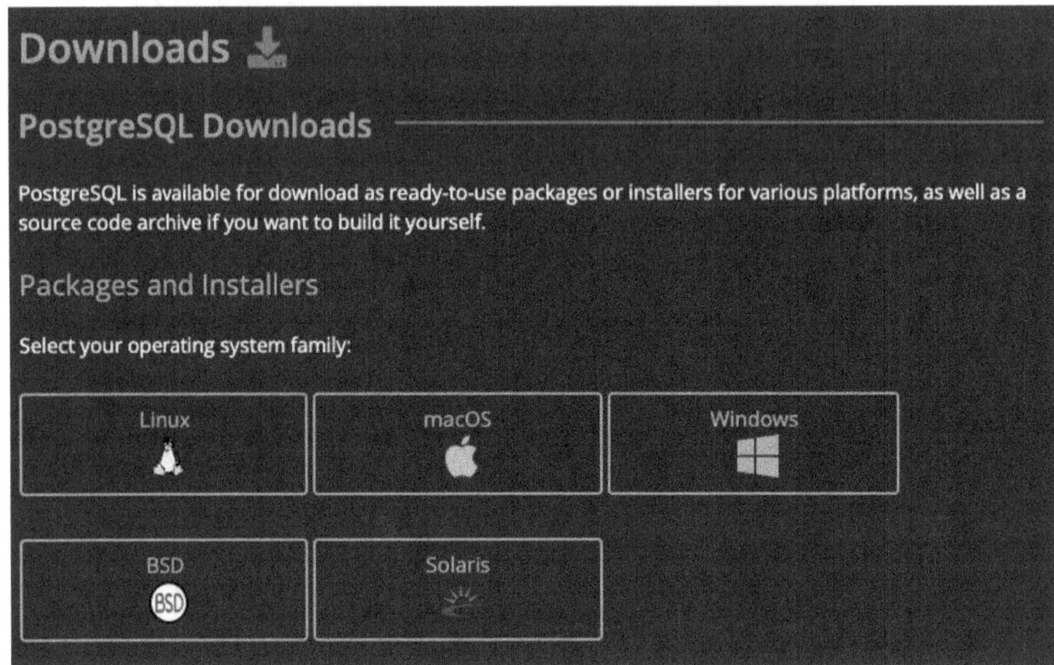

Figure 1-8. *PostgreSQL Installation Page*

For Mac users, you need to additionally install the CLI:

```
brew install postgresql
```

Once PostgreSQL is installed, let's try using `psql` from the terminal. `psql` is a tool for connecting to PostgreSQL from the terminal to manage databases or send queries. Use the following command from the terminal to log in as the default user `postgres`:

```
psql -U postgres
```

If you successfully log in, you should see the following screen:

```
psql (15.0)
Type "help" for help.

postgres=#
```

The default user is the `postgres` user created when PostgreSQL is installed. This user has permission to create and delete all databases. Using this user in actual services is not recommended because it could unintentionally delete other databases or tables in use.

Therefore, we'll create a new user axum for our backend service. Use the following commands to create the new user axum in the database and change the password to '1234':

```
postgres=# CREATE USER axum;
CREATE ROLE
postgres=# ALTER USER axum PASSWORD '1234';
ALTER ROLE
```

Here, we've set the password to '1234' for convenience in this tutorial, but in actual services you should use encrypted keys or random strings.

Next, create the axum database. All tables we create will be stored as schemas in this database.

```
postgres=# CREATE DATABASE axum;
CREATE DATABASE
```

Then change the database owner to the axum user. Now you can create tables and modify data when logged in as the axum user.

```
ALTER DATABASE axum OWNER TO axum;
```

Now you can log in as the axum user and use the axum database. To log in as a different user, use the \q command to log out from the postgres user.

```
postgres=# \q
```

Then log in as the axum user. Previously, you saw postgres=# on screen, but now you see axum=#. This shows which user you're currently logged in as.

```
$ psql -U axum axum
psql (15.0)
Type "help" for help.

axum=#
```

From Chapter 3 onward, we'll learn how to handle databases using SeaORM without writing SQL directly, so actually you'll rarely use the psql shell from here on. Therefore, don't panic if you're not familiar with the shell environment. Just understanding that we created a user called axum and a database called axum, and that we'll use them to complete the application going forward, is sufficient.

1.4.5. Installing DBeaver

DBeaver (pronounced "dee-beaver") is a powerful integrated development environment (IDE) that can manage multiple relational and non-relational databases. DBeaver supports connections to various databases like MySQL, PostgreSQL, SQLite, Oracle, and SQL Server. DBeaver provides an intuitive graphical interface where users can explore database structures, execute SQL queries, and visualize data. It also makes it easy to perform tasks like comparing database schemas and creating, modifying, and deleting database objects.

DBeaver includes various features to efficiently assist database administrators in their work. For example, the SQL editor provides syntax highlighting, and the auto-completion feature makes the query-writing process faster and more accurate. It's currently developed as open source and provided in two versions: community and commercial. This book will use the free community version.

To install DBeaver, go to the DBeaver homepage [4], scroll to the bottom, and click the [Download] button under the Community Edition.

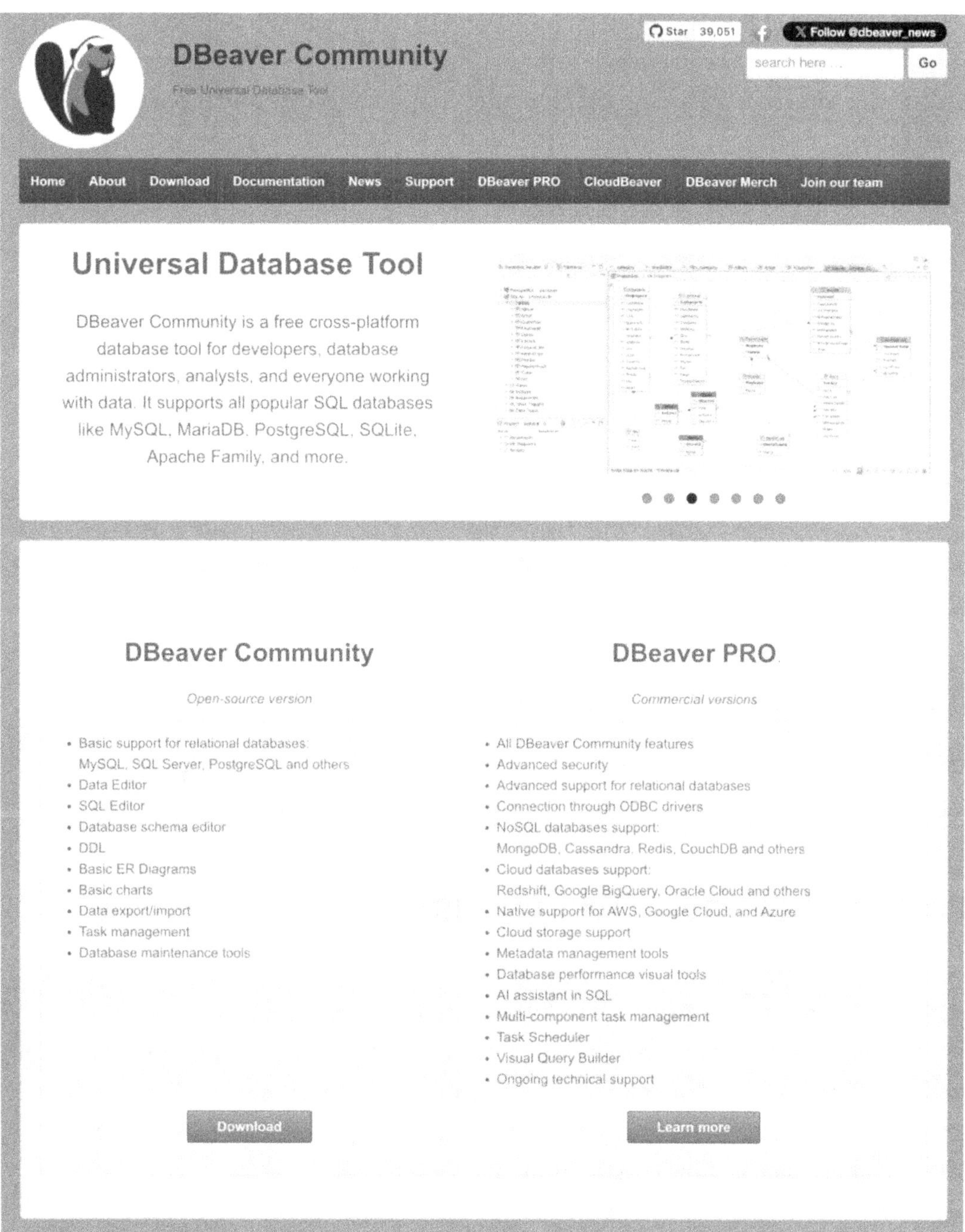

Figure 1-9. *DBeaver Homepage*

After moving to the download page, download the installation file for your operating system. Windows users can click [Windows (installer)] to download the installation file. On Mac, download the dmg file matching your architecture and proceed with installation.

Windows

- **Windows (installer)**
- Windows (zip)

- Chocolatey (`choco install dbeaver`)
- Install from Microsoft Store

Mac OS X

- **MacOS for Apple Silicon (dmg)**
- **MacOS for Intel (dmg)**

- Brew Cask (`brew install --cask dbeaver-community`)

Figure 1-10. *DBeaver Installation Page*

We'll examine how to actually connect to the database and perform queries in detail in Chapter 3.

1.4.6. Installing API Testing Tools

When building applications that interact with APIs, it's important to use appropriate tools for testing and debugging those APIs. It's especially convenient during development because you can immediately test whether specific endpoints are working properly. This method of directly communicating and testing between API clients and API servers is called End-to-End Testing. During development, end-to-end testing is convenient because it allows you to immediately test code.

Let's look at some tools widely used for such API testing. Since there are various testing tools besides the following three, you can use tools that suit you well.

- **cURL**: cURL is a command-line tool that can send all types of HTTP requests. It's installed by default on most systems and provides various control features through flags and options. cURL commands can be saved in scripts to automate testing. However, it can be difficult for beginners to use since it lacks a GUI.

- **Postman**: Postman is a user-friendly graphical tool for API testing. It provides an intuitive UI where you can build requests, inspect responses, and automate test workflows. Postman can help with mock servers, importing API definitions, and request monitoring. It's currently the most popular, but has the disadvantage that companies and institutions must have licenses to use it.

- **Insomnia**: Insomnia is an open-source API client that provides a native app experience on various platforms like Linux, Mac, and Windows. It provides a beautiful UI for intuitive test workflows. Insomnia can import OpenAPI/Swagger definitions and provides excellent support for GraphQL APIs. Flexible environments, global variables, and scripting help with complex scenarios. It supports authentication and integration features for end-to-end testing.

Compared to cURL, Postman and Insomnia are much more convenient because they allow you to save tests and run them repeatedly through a GUI. Between Postman and Insomnia, we most recommend Insomnia as the API testing tool to use in this book because of its intuitive and fast UI and the advantage of being usable without a license.

If you sign up for the Insomnia service, you have the advantage of synchronizing and storing tests created in Insomnia to the cloud, but you can also download directly without signing up. You can download at the following link:

```
https://insomnia.rest/download
```

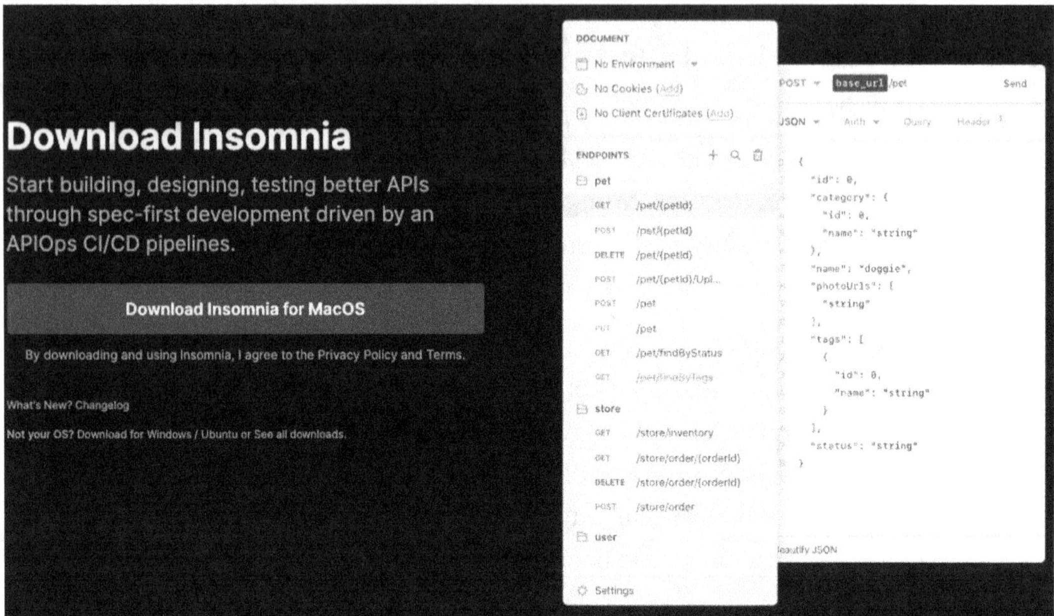

Figure 1-11. *Insomnia Installation Page*

If you want to sign up, go to the following address to proceed with Insomnia registration:

```
https://app.insomnia.rest/app/authorize
```

Select your desired method from Google, GitHub, or email login. Additional authentication procedures may be required depending on the login method.

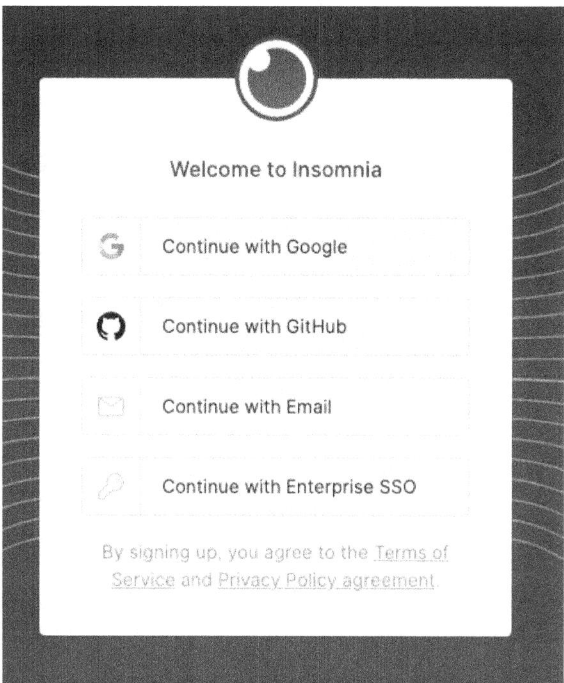

Figure 1-12. *Login Method Selection*

E2EE is a feature that protects data sent to Insomnia by encrypting it. Enter the password to use for encryption in the Passphrase. Once you create a passphrase, you can't check the value again or change it, so you must save it in a safe location.

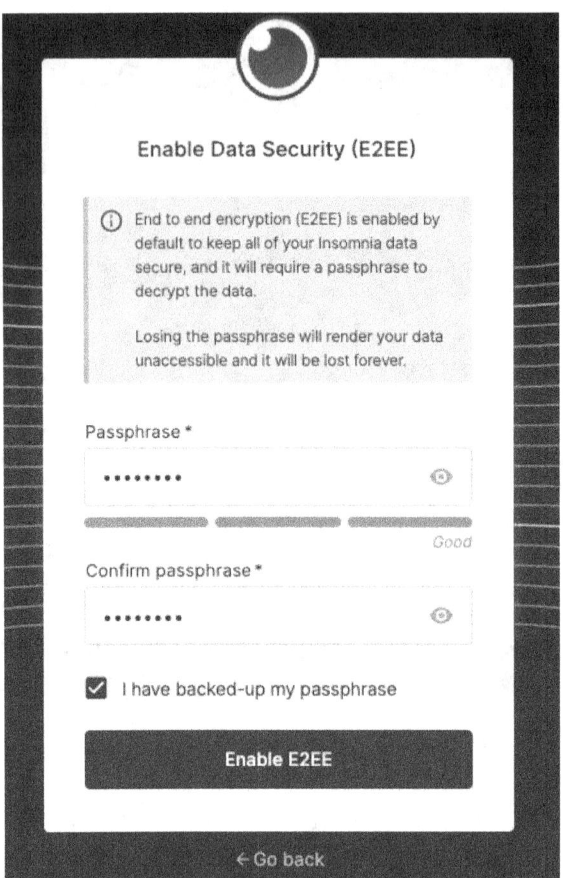

Figure 1-13. *Data Security Settings*

You can use most features even if you select the Free plan, so don't worry.

Choose your personal subscription

You are one step away from improving your API productivity, please choose your subscription to continue.

Pricing plan	≡ View all plans	Review payment	
Free	⌄	Free Plan	$0.00 / user / year
Subscribe		Total	$0.00

By subscribing you agree to Insomnia, by Kong Inc. terms and conditions and privacy policy

Figure 1-14. *Pricing Plan Selection*

After registration is complete, you can see the following dashboard screen. Click the [Download for …] button on the right to install Insomnia. The button text may differ slightly depending on the operating system.

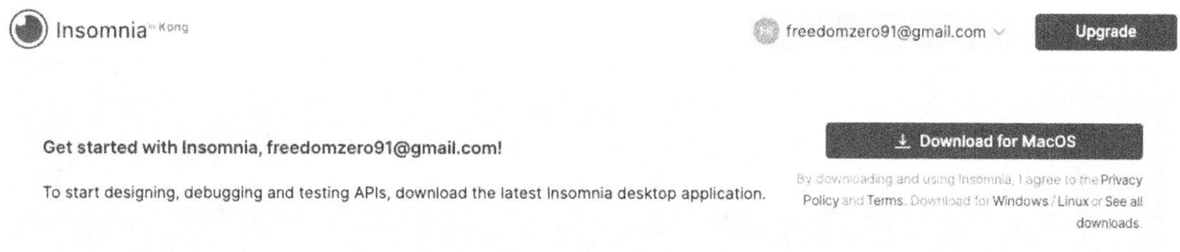

Figure 1-15. *Program Download*

Once installation is complete, launch Insomnia. When you run it, you can see the following screen:

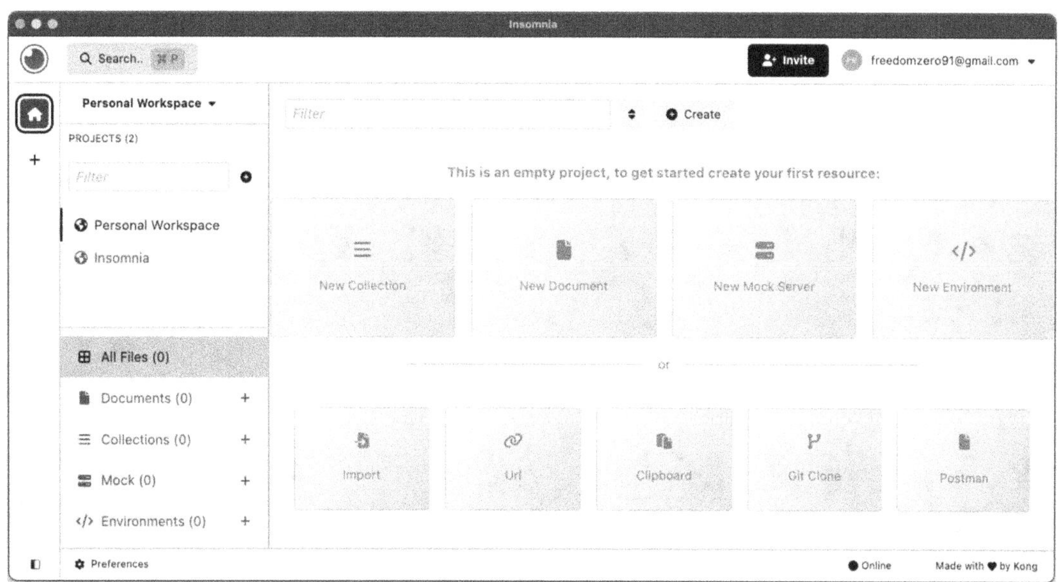

Figure 1-16. *Main Screen*

Now click [New Collection] here. Set the collection name to **My Collection**.

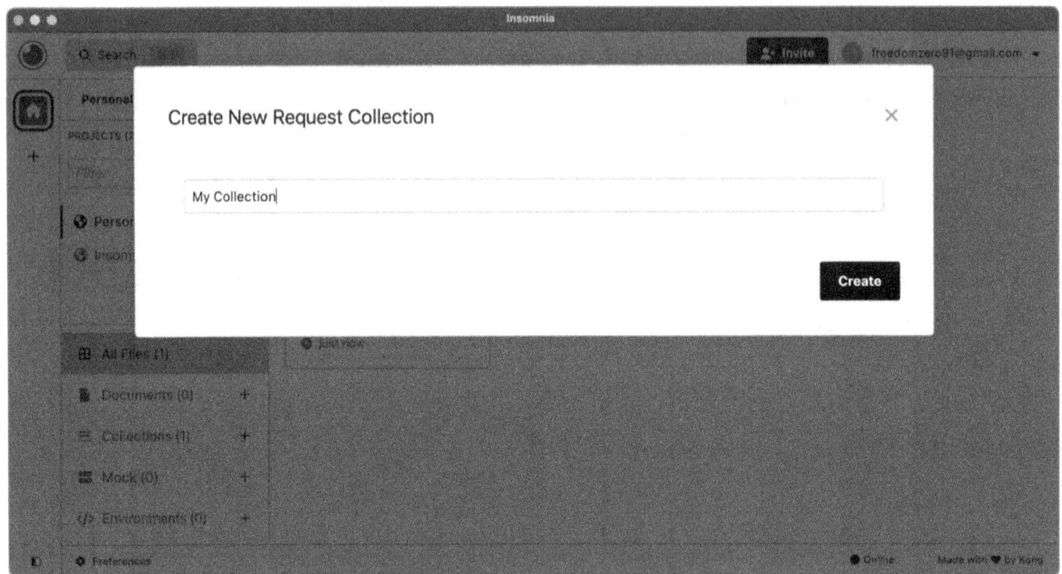

Figure 1-17. *Creating Request Collection*

For reference, Insomnia's color theme is set to High Contrast in this book. If you want to change the theme, enter the Themes tab from Preferences in the lower left and select your desired theme.

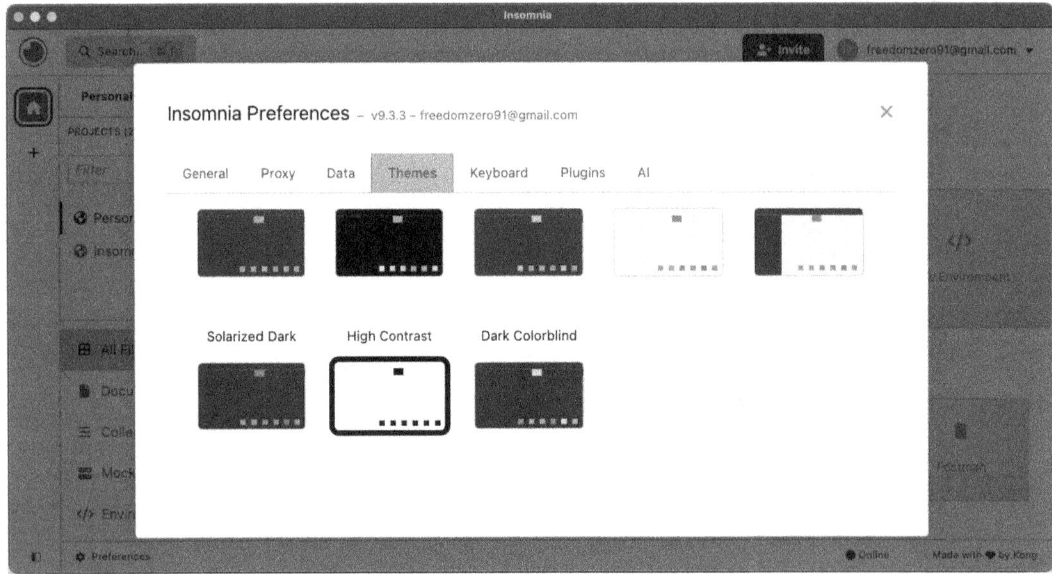

Figure 1-18. *Theme Selection*

Double-click the created collection to enter the collection page. Then click the [+] button on the left side of the screen to create a new HTTP request.

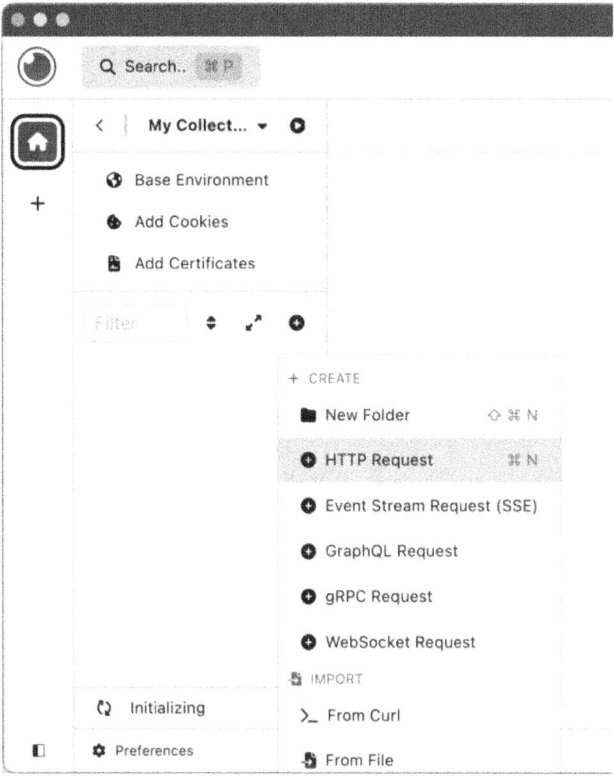

Figure 1-19. *Creating Requests*

In the center of the screen are a dropdown menu for selecting HTTP methods and an input field for entering addresses. Enter your desired method and address here and click the [Send] button, and the HTTP request results will appear on the right side of the screen. We'll cover testing APIs using Insomnia in detail in Chapter 2 when we actually create endpoints.

Figure 1-20. *URL Input Field*

1.5. Reviewing Rust Core Concepts

Here we'll systematically review the core Rust concepts needed to understand this book. If you're already familiar with Rust syntax, feel free to skip this section.

1.5.1. Ownership

Every program uses the computer resource called memory, which stores data used by the program. When you assign a value to a variable in code, that value is stored in memory. However, since memory is a limited resource, each programming language makes efforts for efficient memory management in its own way.

Rust manages memory through a concept called ownership. Thanks to ownership, Rust programs are guaranteed both memory safety and thread safety.

- **Memory Safety**: In Rust, only one piece of code can access a value at a time, so unexpected value changes don't occur. In languages like C/C++, bugs and memory leaks can occur from incorrect pointer usage or memory access, but in Rust you don't need to worry about these problems.

- **Thread Safety**: Rust detects race conditions and deadlock problems that occur when multiple threads access values simultaneously at compile time, guaranteeing stable program execution. Since race conditions and deadlocks—very difficult problems in multi-threading program development—can be prevented in advance in Rust, writing stable code is easy.

Ownership can be summarized with the following three rules:

- Every "value" has an Owner that "owns" that value.

- Only one owner can exist at a time. Two owners cannot exist simultaneously for one value.

- When the owner goes out of scope in the current code, the value is deallocated from memory.

1.5.2. Ownership of Values

In Rust, every value is assigned an owner, and when the owner of that value disappears, the value is immediately deallocated from memory. Let's look at the following example:

```rust
fn main() {
    let x = 1;
    // x is deleted
}
```

In this example, the value 1 contained in variable x is no longer used when it exits the main() function. Therefore, x is immediately deleted from memory. Similarly, even within the same function, values disappear immediately when they go out of scope.

```rust
fn main() {
    let x = 1;
    {
        let y = x;
        println!("{} {}", x, y);
        // y is deleted
    }
    println!("{} {}", x, y); // This line won't compile
                             // x is deleted
}
```

This time, a scope was added by {} in the middle of the code, and y was declared inside it. When this scope is exited, y is no longer used so it's immediately deallocated from memory. Similarly, the same principle applies when passing variables as parameters to functions. Here String::from("Hello") is a way to declare strings in Rust—detailed content about strings will be explained in the next chapter.

```rust
fn dummy(x: String) {
    println!("{}", x);
    // x is dropped
}
```

```rust
fn main() {
    let x = "Hello".to_string();
    dummy(x);
    println!("{}", x); // This line won't compile
}
```

After the string is passed to function dummy, x is deleted immediately when exiting the function. But since x, which was already deleted from memory, is being referenced on line 9, an error occurs. So does this mean all values can never be used again once passed to other functions? There are two methods you can use in such cases.

1.5.3. Returning Ownership

First, there's a method where the function can return ownership of that variable. Let's look at the following example:

```rust
fn dummy(x: String) -> String {
    println!("{}", x);
    x
}

fn main() {
    let x = "Hello".to_string();
    let x = dummy(x);
    println!("{}", x);
}
```

Execution result:

```
Hello
Hello
```

In function dummy, input variable x is used inside the function and then returned. Then ownership returns to x by assigning the function's return value to the redeclared variable x. To make it easier to understand, let's change the variable names as follows. In conclusion, only the variable owning the value "Hello" changes in order x → y → z, and the value remains the same. However, this method has the disadvantage of reduced code readability because you must redeclare the function's return value as a variable every time, and it's difficult to know which variable the value moves to.

```rust
fn dummy(y: String) -> String {
    println!("{}", y);
    y
}

fn main() {
    let x = "Hello".to_string();
    let z = dummy(x);
    println!("{}", z);
}
```

Execution result:

```
Hello
Hello
```

1.5.4. References and Borrowing Ownership

Rust has a concept called borrow where you can temporarily lend ownership of a value. You use the & keyword before a variable, which means declaring a reference to that variable. A reference is a way to refer to a value without taking ownership. Let's look at the following example:

```rust
fn main() {
    let x = "Hello".to_string();
    let y = &x;

    println!("{} {}", x, y);
}
```

Execution result:

```
Hello
Hello
```

Even when declared as let y = &x;, ownership of the string "Hello" value still belongs to x, and y simply refers to the value. Therefore, no error occurs even when printing both variables x and y at the end.

In the following example, the parameter type of dummy function is &String, which means a reference type to a string. When executing dummy in the main function, &x, which is a reference to variable x, was passed. This means temporarily lending ownership to the y parameter inside the function. When the variable that borrowed ownership exits the scope of the dummy function, ownership immediately returns to the original owner x. Therefore, even after using the string value stored in x in the dummy function, you can continue using x afterward. So printing x at the end doesn't cause errors and compiles well.

```rust
fn dummy(y: &String) {
    println!("{}", y);
    // ownership returns to x
}

fn main() {
    let x = "Hello".to_string();
    dummy(&x);
    println!("{}", x);
}
```

Execution result:

```
Hello
Hello
```

1.5.5. Mutable References

To change the value of the original variable using a reference to that variable, you must declare the original variable as mutable. In the following example, we pass variable x to function dummy as a reference. And we're using the push_str function to add the string "world!" to the end of x. But when you run the code, an error occurs.

```rust
fn dummy(y: &String) {
    y.push_str(" world!");
    println!("{}", y);
    // ownership returns to x
}
```

```rust
fn main() {
    let x = String::from("Hello");
    dummy(&x);
    println!("{}", x);
}
```

Execution result:

```
Compiling rust_part v0.1.0 (/Users/code/temp/rust_part)
error[E0596]: cannot borrow `*y` as mutable, as it is behind a `&`
reference
 --> src/main.rs:2:5
  |
1 | fn dummy(y: &String) {
  |             ------- help: consider changing this to be a mutable
                       reference: `&mut String`
2 |     y.push_str(" world!");
  |     ^^^^^^^^^^^^^^^^^^^^^^ `y` is a `&` reference, so the data it refers
                              to cannot be borrowed as mutable
```

According to the error, we borrowed ownership from y, but can't modify the value because it's not a mutable reference. Let's make y a mutable reference as the compiler advised. Here we modified three places in total:

1. Change dummy function parameter y's type to &mut String

2. Declare variable x as a mutable variable

3. Pass x as mutable reference &mut x when calling dummy function

```rust
fn dummy(y: &mut String) { // 1) mutable reference
    y.push_str(" world!");
    println!("{}", y);
    // ownership returns to x
}
```

```rust
fn main() {
    let mut x = "Hello".to_string();    // 2) mutable variable
                                        //    declaration

    dummy(&mut x);                      // 3) mutable reference
    println!("{}", x);
}
```

Execution result:

```
Hello world!
Hello world!
```

When using mutable references, you must be careful about the second rule of
ownership: "Only one owner can exist at a time." For example, let's try creating two
mutable references to one value. Variables y and z are both mutable references to
variable x.

```rust
fn main() {
    let mut x = "Hello".to_string();
    let y = &mut x;
    let z = &mut x;

    println!("{} {}", y, z);
}
```

Execution result:

```
Compiling rust_part v0.1.0 (/Users/code/temp/rust_part)
error[E0499]: cannot borrow `x` as mutable more than once at a time
 --> src/main.rs:4:13
  |
3 |     let y = &mut x;
  |             ------ first mutable borrow occurs here
4 |     let z = &mut x;
  |             ^^^^^^ second mutable borrow occurs here
5 |
6 |     println!("{} {}", y, z);
  |                       - first borrow later used here
```

A compile-time error occurs saying "cannot borrow ownership of variable x more than once." If multiple variables could borrow one ownership, bugs could occur because multiple places could access one memory location.

For example, if some mutable reference changes a value while another place needs the pre-change value, unexpected results could occur. Therefore, Rust doesn't allow multiple mutable references to one value. However, creating multiple simple references is no problem.

```rust
fn main() {
    let x = "Hello".to_string();
    let y = &x;
    let z = &x;

    println!("{} {}", y, z);
}
```

Execution result:

```
Hello Hello
```

The compiler generates errors when ownership rules are violated and suggests solutions, always enabling safe code creation.

1.5.6. Crates

A crate is the smallest unit that can bundle Rust code. There are two types of crates: binary and library. Generally, when you create a project using cargo, a folder is created, and the crate type is determined based on the name of the file that serves as the crate's standard.

1.5.6.1. Binary Crates

A binary crate is a crate that is compiled to generate a binary file. Create a project with the cargo new <crate name> command, and a main.rs file is created. The project folder structure is as follows:

```
├── Cargo.toml
└── src
    └── main.rs
```

1.5.6.2. Library Crates

A library crate is a crate that is not compiled. Since it's not compiled, it doesn't generate binaries. It's a crate provided so that other crates or packages can reference code.

Create a project with the `cargo new --lib <crate name>` command, and a `lib.rs` file is created. The project folder structure is as follows:

```
├── Cargo.toml
└── src
    └── lib.rs
```

1.5.6.3. Crate Root

A crate root means the entry point where compilation starts. For binary crates, the `src/main.rs` file, and for library crates, the `src/lib.rs` file becomes the crate root.

1.5.7. Modules

In Rust, you can distinguish modules by file units and define multiple modules in one file.

Let's create two files as follows:

```rust
// main.rs
fn main() {}
// my_module.rs
mod dummy1 {}
mod dummy2 {}
```

At this time, since there are two files inside the crate, each file is basically recognized as a module, and `dummy1` and `dummy2` additionally declared inside `my_module.rs` are also recognized as modules.

1.5.7.1. Public and Private

All modules and objects in Rust are private by default. That is, it's impossible to access that module or object from outside the module. Therefore, to allow external access to modules or objects inside modules, you must use the `pub` keyword to make that object public. Struct fields, associated functions, and methods are also private by default.

```rust
pub mod module {
    // module
}

pub fn function() {
    // function
}

pub struct Struct {
    // struct
    private_field: i32,
    pub public_field: i32,
}

impl Struct {
    // methods
    pub fn public_method(&self) {}
    fn private_method(&self) {}
}
```

We'll explain how public and private are actually distinguished with actual code right after this.

1.5.8. Using Modules

The use keyword serves to bring a specific path into the current scope. Note that paths always start from the crate root.

The mod keyword serves to declare that you'll use that module. For example, when mod new_module is used, the compiler looks for that module in the following locations:

1. The module definition should come after mod new_module.

```rust
mod new_module {
    fn new_func() {
        ...
    }
    ...
}
```

2. Look for the `src/new_module.rs` file.

3. Look for the `mod.rs` file in the `src/new_module` folder.

```
pub mod new_module;
```

Just like defining regular modules, you can also define submodules, which are modules within modules. Modules declared in modules other than the crate root become submodules, and the rules for the compiler finding these submodules are the same as above.

Access to specific modules can be done using absolute paths based on the crate root. For example, modules can be accessed from anywhere in the code as follows:

```
// src/new_module.rs -> MyType
use crate::new_module::MyType;
```

Sometimes relative paths are used, in which case the `self` and `super` keywords are used. First, here's how to reference functions based on the current module using `self`:

```
mod mod2 {
    fn func() {
        println!("mod2::func()");
    }

    mod mod1 {
        pub fn func() {
            println!("mod2::mod1::func()");
        }
    }

    pub fn dummy() {
        func();
        self::func();
        mod1::func();
        self::mod1::func();
    }
}
```

```rust
fn main() {
    mod2::dummy();
}
```

Execution result:

```
mod2::func()
mod2::func()
mod2::mod1::func()
mod2::mod1::func()
```

super means the parent module of the current module. Therefore, using super in mod2 means the main module, so you can reference mod1 belonging to the main module. Of course, it's also possible to reference with absolute paths like use crate::mod1; instead of use super::mod1;.

```rust
mod mod1 {
    pub fn dummy() {
        println!("Hello, world!");
    }
}

mod mod2 {
    // same as `use crate::mod1;`
    use super::mod1;
    pub fn dummy() {
        mod1::dummy();
    }
}

fn main() {
    mod2::dummy();
}
```

Execution result:

```
Hello, world!
```

1.5.9. Packages

A package is a collection of multiple crates. Packages have a `Cargo.toml` file. When we first create a project with the `cargo new` command, a `Cargo.toml` file is created, so that project becomes a package.

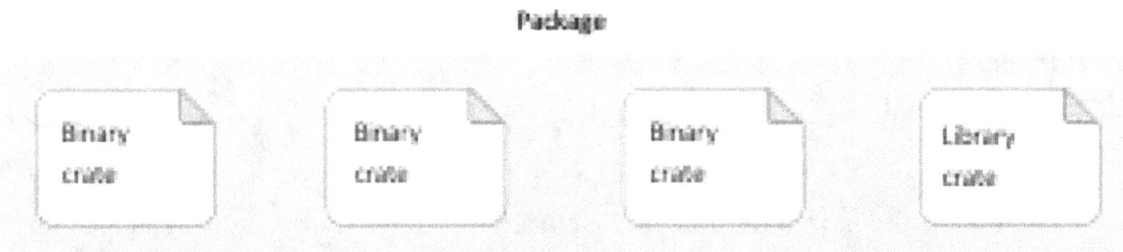

Figure 1-21. *Packages and Crates*

One package can contain only one library crate. However, it can contain multiple binary crates. Generally, having `main.rs` in the crate root makes it a binary crate, but you can explicitly specify the entry point of a binary crate with a different name by specifying the path in the `[[bin]]` section of the `Cargo.toml` file.

```
[package]
name = "my_package"
version = "0.1.0"
edition = "2018"

[lib]
name = "my_library"
path = "src/lib.rs"

[[bin]]
name = "my_binary1"
path = "src/bin/binary1.rs"

[[bin]]
name = "my_binary2"
path = "src/bin/binary2.rs"
```

The folder structure in this case is as follows:

```
my_package
├── Cargo.toml
└── src
    ├── bin
    │   ├── binary1.rs
    │   └── binary2.rs
    └── lib.rs
```

Summarizing the content so far:

Name	Description
Package	Collection of multiple crates
Crate	Collection of modules that create libraries or binaries
Module	Collection of structs, functions, etc.

1.5.10. Traits

Rust doesn't have struct inheritance like other object-oriented languages. You can't pass fields and methods from one struct to another. However, you can define one property that allows different structs to share functions, which is traits. There are two ways to share functions through traits—let's examine the first approach. In traits, you define the prototypes of methods to share.

```rust
trait Greet {
    fn say_hello(&self) {}
}
```

When declared like this, say_hello is an empty function that doesn't execute anything, so you must implement the actual content in each struct's methods.

```rust
struct Person {
    name: String,
    age: i32,
    alive: bool,
}
```

```rust
impl Person {
    fn new(name: &str, age: i32) -> Person {
        Person {
            name: name.to_string(),
            age: age,
            alive: true,
        }
    }
    fn get_older(&mut self, year: i32) {
        self.age += year;
    }
}

impl Greet for Person {}

struct Student {
    name: String,
    age: i32,
    alive: bool,
    major: String,
}

impl Student {
    fn new(name: &str, age: i32, major: &str) -> Student {
        Student {
            name: name.to_string(),
            age: age,
            alive: true,
            major: major.to_string(),
        }
    }
}
```

```rust
impl Greet for Student {
    fn say_hello(&self) {
        println!("Hello, I am {} and I am studying {}", self.name,
        self.major)
    }
}
```

Now let's create instances of Person and Student structs in the main function and call the say_hello method for each.

```rust
fn main() {
    let mut person = Person::new("John", 20);
    person.say_hello(); // 😶
    person.get_older(1);
    println!("{} is now {} years old", person.name, person.age);

    let student = Student::new("Jane", 20, "Computer Science");
    student.say_hello();
}
```

Execution result:

```
John is now 21 years old
Hello, I am Jane and I am studying Computer Science
```

You can see that person.say_hello() outputs nothing because it uses the trait Greet's method as is.

The second method is to define the default implementation of say_hello when declaring the trait. Going back to the trait declaration, the say_hello function receives &self as a parameter, but functions defined in traits cannot access instance properties. If you modify the function prototype as follows and try to compile, an error will occur.

```rust
trait Greet {
    fn say_hello(&self) {
        println!("Hello, Rustacean!");
    }
}
```

Therefore, when you want to share the function prototype itself created in traits, you can only define associated functions that don't access `self`. So the following code compiles normally. For brevity, some unused code has been modified.

```rust
trait Greet {
    fn say_hello() {
        println!("Hello, Rustacean!");
    }
}

struct Person {
    name: String,
    age: i32,
    alive: bool,
}

impl Greet for Person {}

struct Student {
    name: String,
    age: i32,
    alive: bool,
    major: String,
}

impl Greet for Student {}

fn main() {
    let person = Person {
        name: "Bob".to_string(),
        age: 20,
        alive: true,
    };
    Person::say_hello();

    let student = Student {
        name: "Alice".to_string(),
        age: 20,
```

```
        alive: true,
        major: "Computer Science".to_string(),
    };
    Student::say_hello();
}
```

Execution result:

```
Hello, Rustacean!
Hello, Rustacean!
```

1.5.11. Multithreading and Asynchronous Programming

Multithreading is primarily used for CPU-intensive tasks that require significant time for complex calculations. Using multithreading allows applications to distribute workload across multiple CPU cores to improve overall processing speed.

Asynchronous programming is particularly suitable for I/O-bound tasks where applications must wait for external resources like network requests or disk operations. In these scenarios, using asynchronous programming allows applications to continue processing other tasks while waiting for I/O operations to complete, improving application responsiveness and performance.

As explained earlier, to use asynchronous functions, you need an async runtime within the program that manages the execution of asynchronous functions. Since Rust doesn't have a built-in async runtime, we primarily use the third-party crate tokio.

Now we're fully prepared to start backend development using Axum. In Chapter 2, we'll start by implementing the most basic API server and progressively learn how to add complex features.

1.6. Review

- Axum is a framework for developing backends with Rust that makes writing asynchronous programs easy.

- Axum provides both low-level and high-level APIs, enabling you to create everything from simple web servers to servers with complex features.

- We installed the PostgreSQL database and Insomnia as an API testing tool.

- Rust is a modern programming language that achieves performance close to C/C++ while guaranteeing both memory safety and thread safety, earning it great popularity among many companies and individual developers.

1.7. Quiz

Problem 1: Why is Rust suitable for backend development?

① Because it's interpreter-based, making it fast.

② It provides higher execution performance than scripting languages.

③ The server doesn't recognize multi-core processors.

④ It's only suitable for client applications.

Problem 2: Which of the following is NOT a characteristic of the Axum framework?

① Support for asynchronous programming based on tokio

② Uses filter-based routing

③ Compatibility with tower middleware

④ Balance between high performance and usability

References

1.   Stack Overflow Developer Survey
2.   Figma's Journey to TypeScript
3.   Visual Studio Code Download Page
4.   DBeaver Homepage

CHAPTER 2

Exploring Axum Fundamentals

In this chapter, we'll build a REST API with Axum and Postgres. You'll learn how the server routes requests to handler functions and how to exchange different types of data between clients and servers.

Learning Points

- Creating REST APIs with basic routing

- Handling path parameters, query parameters, and JSON in handlers

- Setting HTTP headers

2.1. HTTP Fundamentals

HTTP (Hypertext Transfer Protocol) is the standard protocol for API communication between clients and servers. It consists of request methods, headers, request bodies, and response codes.

Request methods tell the server what operation to perform. Common API methods include

- **GET**: Fetch data from the server (e.g., retrieving product listings)

- **POST**: Create new resources (e.g., submitting an order)

- **PUT**: Update existing resources (e.g., modifying product details)

- **DELETE**: Remove resources (e.g., deleting user accounts)

© Indo Yoon 2026
I. Yoon, *Beginning Axum*, https://doi.org/10.1007/979-8-8688-2631-3_2

Headers carry additional request information like authentication tokens and desired data formats. Servers send response headers back containing information about the data format and size.

The request body contains the actual data being sent. Both clients and servers can send bodies to each other, typically in JSON format.

JSON (JavaScript Object Notation) takes its name from JavaScript's object syntax. It's the go-to format for APIs because it's both human-readable and hierarchically structured.

JSON uses key-value pairs where values can be booleans, numbers, strings, arrays, or nested JSON objects.

```
{
  "name": "John Doe",
  "age": 30,
  "occupation": "Software Engineer",
  "address": {
    "street": "123 Main St",
    "city": "Anytown",
    "state": "CA",
    "zip": "90210"
  },
  "hobbies": ["coding", "reading", "hiking"]
}
```

Besides headers and bodies, you can pass information through the URL itself using path parameters and query parameters. For example:

http://localhost:8000/items?status=ok

Here, `items` is the path, and `status=ok` after the ? is a query parameter with value ok.

Path parameters help group related APIs. For example, putting login and logout under /user makes their purpose clear:

http://localhost:8000/user/login
http://localhost:8000/user/logout

The server uses the path to route a request to the correct handler, while query parameters provide additional options or filters for that handler's logic.

Response codes tell clients what happened with their request. Common codes include

- **200 OK**: Request successful

- **400 Bad Request**: Invalid request

- **404 Not Found**: Resource doesn't exist

- **500 Internal Server Error**: Server error

With an understanding of these fundamentals, we're ready to explore how Axum handles these incoming requests and constructs appropriate responses.

2.2. Creating an Axum Project

Open the rust_project folder from Chapter 1 in VSCode. In the terminal, create a new Rust project by running the following command to generate a project in the axum-project folder:

cargo init axum-project

Inside the folder, you'll find the auto-generated `Cargo.toml` file. This file manages project metadata and records package information. Add the following dependencies. We enable the `json` feature for Axum to handle JSON request and response bodies. While Axum depends on Tokio, we add `tokio` explicitly with the `full` feature to enable all of its functionality for our application:

```
[dependencies]
axum = { version = "0.8", features = ["json"] }
tokio = { version = "1.35.1", features = ["full"] }
```

Alternatively, use these terminal commands:

```
cargo add axum@0.8 --features "json"
```

```
cargo add tokio@1.35.1 --features "full"
```

After adding both crates, let's create a basic Axum app. Start by importing what we need in main.rs:

```rust
use axum::{
    routing::{delete, get, post, put},
    Router,
};
```

Add #[tokio::main] to run main in tokio's async runtime and make it async:

```rust
#[tokio::main]
async fn main() {
    // async main function
    let app = Router::new()
        .route("/", get(|| async move { "Welcome to Axum!" }))
        .route("/", post(|| async move { "Post Something!" }))
        .route("/", put(|| async move { "Updating..." }))
        .route("/", delete(|| async move { "Deleting..." }));
    let listener = tokio::net::TcpListener::bind("127.0.0.1:8000")
        .await
        .unwrap(); // If port 8000 is already occupied, the server
                        will crash.
    axum::serve(listener, app).await.unwrap();
}
```

Axum's Router makes it easy to implement routing—the process of directing client requests to matching paths. You create a Router instance and chain .route() methods to configure multiple routes. Each .route() method takes an address to connect and a function representing the HTTP method to use. For example, route("/", get(|| async move { "Welcome to Axum!" })) means when a GET request comes to the root address /, call the closure that returns "Welcome to Axum!".

The root path / refers to the base URL of your server. If your server runs at myserver.com, the root is myserver.com/ with the trailing slash—it's the most basic address. Each .route() method specifies POST, PUT, or DELETE using routing::{delete, get, post, put} and takes a closure to call as the second argument. These functions passed to route methods are called *handlers*, which we'll explore in detail soon.

Next, we use `tokio::net::TcpListener` to set the server's address and port. The bind method takes an address string. 127.0.0.1 means localhost—your local machine. Port 8000 is common for development and usually available unless another server is using it. If port 8000 is taken, use a different port. Finally, `axum::serve` starts the server at the specified address and port.

Reference

localhost and 0.0.0.0

Both 0.0.0.0 and localhost point to your local machine on a network, but they work differently. localhost (127.0.0.1) only accepts connections from the same computer. This is true local-only networking. In contrast, 0.0.0.0 accepts connections from any available network, allowing other computers on your network to connect. This is crucial for Docker: since containers have their own network, you need 0.0.0.0 to access a containerized server from the host.

In short:

- **localhost (127.0.0.1)**: Same computer only

- **0.0.0.0**: All network interfaces (other computers, Docker containers, etc.)

Let's run the server and test it with Insomnia. In the terminal:

cargo run

Once the code compiles and the server starts successfully, let's send a GET request to the root address. In Insomnia, click the [+] button on the left to create a new HTTP request. Add a new request, set the method to GET and the URL to http://localhost:8000. Click [Send] and the server's response appears on the right. If you see "Welcome to Axum!" with a 200 OK status code at the top right, success!

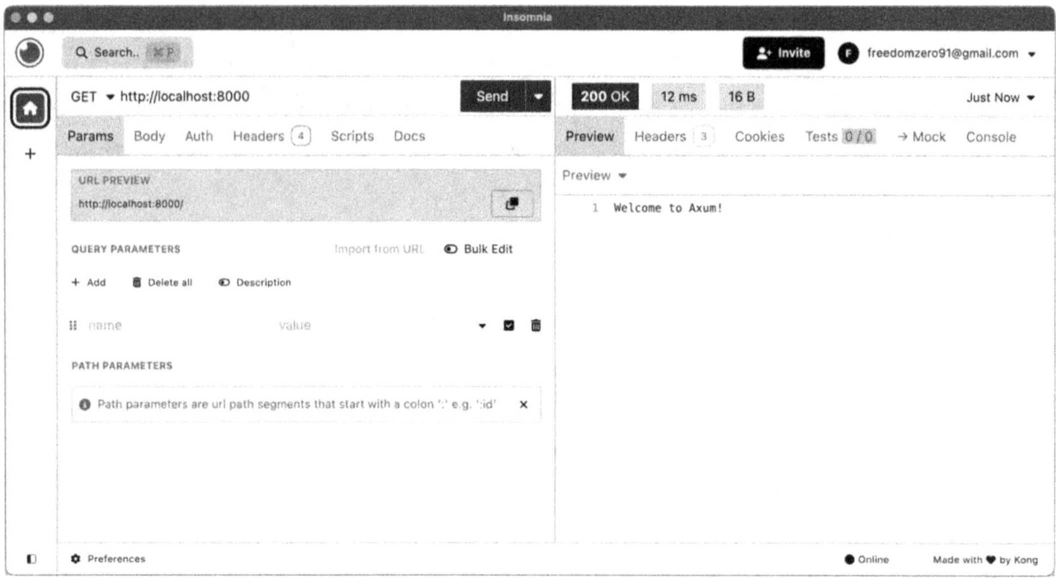

Figure 2-1. *Welcome to Axum!*

Try the same with POST, PUT, and DELETE requests in Insomnia.

Two important notes: First, instead of `cargo run`, we'll use `cargo watch` for automatic recompilation on code changes. This eliminates the need to manually stop and restart the server every time you modify code. Install it with

cargo install cargo-watch

Then run it with -x to execute a command on changes (here, `cargo run`):

cargo watch -x run

Second, the official docs suggest `bind(&"0.0.0.0:8000")`, but on macOS this triggers a connection permission popup every time (Figure 2-2).

Figure 2-2. *localhost and 0.0.0.0*

That's why we use 127.0.0.1 instead, different from the official documentation. However, for production deployments or Docker environments, you should use 0.0.0.0.

2.3. Routers and Handlers

In server programs, client requests are sent to the appropriate handler function for processing, then responses are sent back to clients. The router's job is to direct client requests to the correct handler. In this section, we'll explore how to define routers and handlers in Axum.

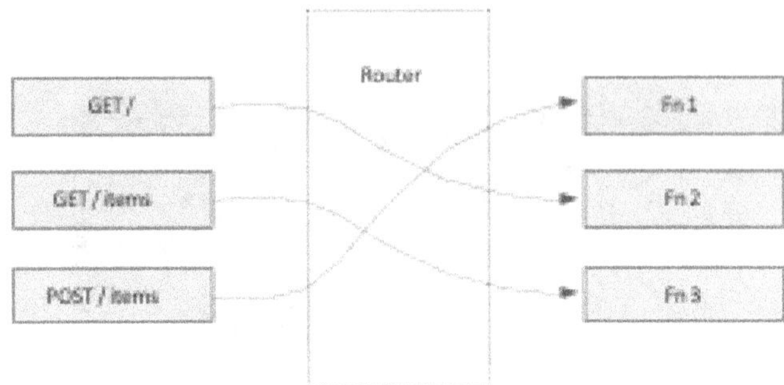

Figure 2-3. *Routers and Handlers*

2.3.1. Defining Routers

Routers determine which handler processes each request. We've already seen basic routing to / in the section "Creating an Axum Project."

Routers are created with Router::new() and various methods are chained to connect paths to handlers. The most basic approach is chaining route functions as we saw in the section "HTTP Fundamentals":

```rust
let app = Router::new()
    .route("/", get(|| async move { "Welcome to Axum!" }))
    .route("/", post(|| async move { "Post Something!" }))
    .route("/", put(|| async move { "Updating..." }))
    .route("/", delete(|| async move { "Deleting..." }));
```

However, this approach gets unwieldy as you add more paths, causing code to grow very long like this:

```rust
let app = Router::new()
    .route("/", get(|| async move { "Welcome to Axum!" }))
    .route("/", post(|| async move { "Post Something!" }))
    .route("/", put(|| async move { "Updating..." }))
    .route("/", delete(|| async move { "Deleting..." }));
    .route("/user", get(|| async move { "Welcome to Axum!" }))
    .route("/user", post(|| async move { "Post Something!" }))
    .route("/user", put(|| async move { "Updating..." }))
    .route("/user", delete(|| async move { "Deleting..." }));
```

Furthermore, changing a common path prefix becomes tedious and error-prone. Renaming /user to /my_user would require editing four separate lines, which is cumbersome and risks typos. For these reasons, repeatedly connecting route methods is not ideal when you have many paths and handlers to define in your router.

Since having many paths and handlers makes code lengthy and difficult to manage, you can solve this problem by grouping multiple handlers under one path. Chain get, post, put, and delete methods as the second parameter of the route function:

```
let app = Router::new()
    .route(
        "/",
        get(|| async move { "Welcome to Axum!" })
            .post(|| async move { "Post Something!" })
            .put(|| async move { "Updating..." })
            .delete(|| async move { "Deleting..." }),
    );
```

Now, let's consider paths like /api/users and /api/teams that share a common /api prefix.

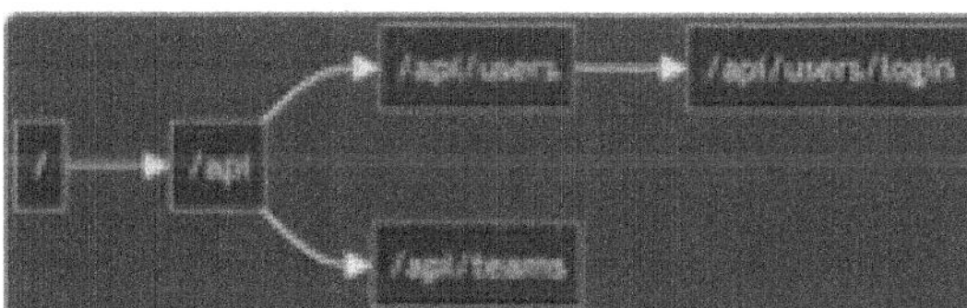

Figure 2-4. */api Path*

When you have common paths, use the .nest() method to connect sub-paths. Create separate routers user_routes for /users and team_routes for /teams. Then connect them to api_routes representing the /api path using nest. Finally, connect api_routes to the root router, also using nest:

```
let user_routes = Router::new()
    .route("/", get(|| async move { "user" }))
    .route("/login", get(|| async move { "login" }));
```

```
let team_routes = Router::new().route("/", post(|| async move { "teams" }));

let api_routes = Router::new()
    .nest("/users", user_routes)
    .nest("/teams", team_routes);
```

Router definition strategies we've learned so far:

- **Simple Paths Without Complexity**: Chain multiple route methods on the root router

- **Multiple Nested Paths**: Use the nest method

2.3.2. Defining Handlers

2.3.2.1. Handler Basics

Remember the closures we passed to methods like get() and post() when defining routers?

```
route("/", get(|| async move { "user" }))
```

These functions are called *handler functions* because they handle requests. Handler functions registered to each router path must be asynchronous functions created using the async keyword. While we've used async closures so far, regular functions work too:

```
async fn user() -> &'static str {
    "user"
}

Router::new().route("/", get(user));
```

A handler's job is to interpret various types of incoming requests to the server, process them, and return results in various formats. Axum automatically sends the handler's return value (like the string "user" returned by the user function) as an HTTP response to the client. When defining handler functions, you only need to decide what format to return.

Now let's explore defining various handler functions. We'll learn how to extract values from path parameters, query parameters, and request bodies in handlers. Struct types that extract values from paths, query parameters, and request bodies and convert them to usable Rust types are defined in the `axum::extract` module. These value-extracting types are called *extractors*. All of Axum's extractors implement the `FromRequest` or `FromRequestPart` trait, and to create custom extractors, you must implement these traits. Figure 2-5 organizes extractors by type.

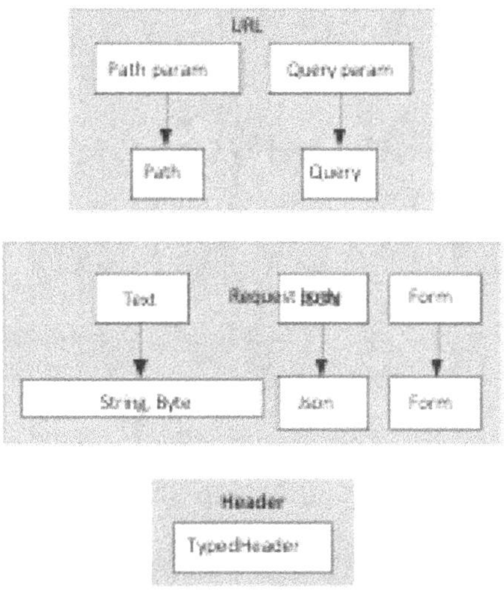

Figure 2-5. *Extractors*

2.3.2.2. Path Parameters

Path parameters let you use parts of the URL as variables. In these examples, the parts enclosed in {} are path parameters:

- /users/{userId} • /products/{productId}

- /articles/{year}/{month}

So in the URL `/users/1234`, the path parameter userId has value 1234.

Axum uses `{variable_name}` syntax for path parameters. For example, the path /{id}/{name} contains two variables: id and name.

```
let app = Router::new().route("/{id}/{name}", get(hello));
```

In the hello handler function, use `extract::Path` to convert path parameters to specified types. In the following code, we use `Path((id, name))` as the hello function's parameter. Note that id and name are wrapped in a tuple. Matching the tuple type, we declare the parameter type as `Path<(i32, String)>`. The hello function converts the two received path parameters into a string and returns it:

```rust
use axum::{
    extract::Path,
    Router,
};

async fn hello(Path((id, name)): Path<(i32, String)>) -> String {
    format!("{id} : {name}")
}

let app = Router::new()
    .route("/{id}/{name}", get(hello));
```

Now send a GET request to http://localhost:8000/1/indo to receive this response:

```
1 : indo
```

When using path parameters, you need to specify the correct type for each parameter. If types don't match, a compilation error occurs. For example, sending a request like http://localhost:8000/a/indo will give you the following response. An error occurs because the variable id corresponding to the first path parameter is of type i32, so the string "a" cannot be converted to an integer:

```
Invalid URL: Cannot parse value at index 0 with value `"a"` to a `i32`
```

If there's only one path parameter, you can omit the tuple in the type and specify just one variable. The following code example defines a handler that takes only the path parameter id as input:

```rust
async fn hello(Path(id): Path<i32>) -> String {
    id.to_string()
}

let app = Router::new().route("/{id}", get(hello));
```

2.3.2.3. Query Parameters

Query parameters are a way to provide additional information by adding key-value pairs to a URL. You can add a ? after the URL path and insert variables in the form `variable_name=value`. You can include various options such as sorting criteria, limiting the number of results, filtering, etc. For example, query parameters appear in URLs like this:

```
/users?role=admin
```

This sets `role` to `admin`. Chain multiple parameters with &. This URL has `onSale=true` and `category=toys`:

```
/products?onSale=true&category=toys
```

`extract::Query` is used to convert query parameter values to specific types like `i32`, `String`, etc. You can create handler parameters and types in the form `Query(variable): Query<Type>`. In this case, use a `HashMap` to represent key-value pairs:

```rust
use axum::{extract::Query, Router};
use std::collections::HashMap;

async fn hello(Query(user): Query<HashMap<String, String>>) -> String {
    format!("{} : {}", user["id"], user["name"])
}

let app = Router::new().route("/", get(hello));
```

For example, sending a request to `http://localhost:8000/?id=1&name=indo` returns

```
1 : indo
```

Using a `HashMap` for query parameters presents two challenges. First, you cannot handle non-string types and string types simultaneously. Here, the id parameter should actually be an integer, but it's treated as a string just like name. To use id as a number, you must manually convert it to i32 inside the function body:

```rust
async fn hello(Query(user): Query<HashMap<String, String>>) -> String {
    format!(
        "{} : {}",
        user["id"].parse::<i32>().unwrap(),
```

```
            user["name"],
        )
}
```

Second, if even one query parameter is missing a value, an error will occur. For example, if you send a GET request to the address `http://localhost:8000/?id=1`, the following error occurs because the name variable is missing:

```
Failed to deserialize query string: missing field `name`
```

Due to these problems, it's more convenient to declare a separate struct type rather than using a HashMap. The newly declared struct must implement the `serde::Deserialize` trait to extract query parameters from the URL. Therefore, add the serde crate, which defines this trait, to Cargo.toml dependencies:

```
serde = { version = "1.0.193", features = ["derive"] }
```

In the following code, we declare a User struct with integer id and string name fields, and the hello function receives query parameters as that type:

```
use axum::{
    extract::Query,
    Router,
};

#[derive(serde::Deserialize)]
struct User {
    id: i32,
    name: String,
}

async fn hello(Query(user): Query<User>) -> String {
    format!("{} : {}", user.id, user.name)
}

let app = Router::new().route("/", get(hello));
```

Now sending a GET request to http://localhost:8000/?id=1&name=indo returns the same response as when using a HashMap. The first problem from using a HashMap has been resolved:

```
1 : indo
```

If you want to prevent errors even when certain query parameters are missing, you can use Option for the field type. However, be careful that handling of each parameter specified as Option must be done directly within the handler function. In the following code, when the name parameter is missing, it's handled as the string "No name":

```rust
#[derive(serde::Deserialize)]
struct User {
    id: i32,
    name: Option<String>,
}

async fn hello(Query(user): Query<User>) -> String {
    format!(
        "{} : {}",
        user.id,
        user.name.as_ref().unwrap_or(&"No name".to_string())
    )
}
```

Now sending a GET request to http://localhost:8000/?id=1 won't cause an error:

```
1 : No name
```

2.3.2.4. Request Body

Request bodies carry data from clients to servers. Common formats for request bodies in HTTP APIs include text, JSON, and forms.

Let's start with a text data example. Since the hello function's parameter name has type String, the request body is converted to a string for use.

Note there's no Query or Path wrapper for the parameter type.

Unlike path or query parameters, basic types like String don't need to be wrapped in extractors. You can use them directly in the handler. Here's how to receive a request body as a String type:

```
async fn hello(name: String) -> String {
    format!("Hello, {name}!")
}

let app = Router::new().route("/", post(hello));
```

Now let's send a POST request to http://localhost:8000 with the text indo as the request body. In Insomnia, select [Body] as [Plain] to send plain text as the request body. You can see the server successfully echoes back the text from the request body in the response.

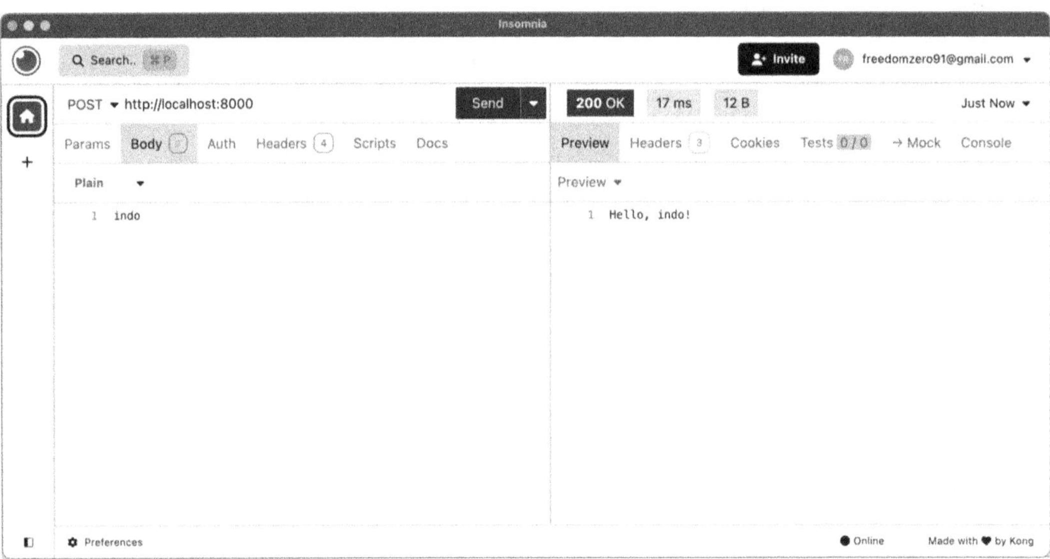

Figure 2-6. *Text Response*

Next, let's look at receiving the request body as an axum::body::Bytes type. The handler converts the byte input to String type and returns it. The `String::from_utf8_lossy` function is used to convert Vec (here, Bytes) encoded in UTF-8 to a string. Note that data loss may occur when encountering invalid UTF-8 byte sequences:

Computers express information using two basic values: 0 and 1. These basic values are called bits, and 8 bits make 1 byte. Since bytes are the most basic form of data storage in computers, they can represent various information like text, images, and files. For text, an encoding method called UTF-8 is widely used—an efficient way to represent various characters as bytes.

Axum provides the Bytes type to work with bytes. However, directly handling raw data is very complex and error-prone, so in most cases it's better to use other pre-implemented extractors.

```rust
use axum::body::Bytes;

async fn hello(age: Bytes) -> String {
    format!("Hello, {}!", String::from_utf8_lossy(&age))
}

let app = Router::new().route("/", post(hello));
```

Send the same request again to see:

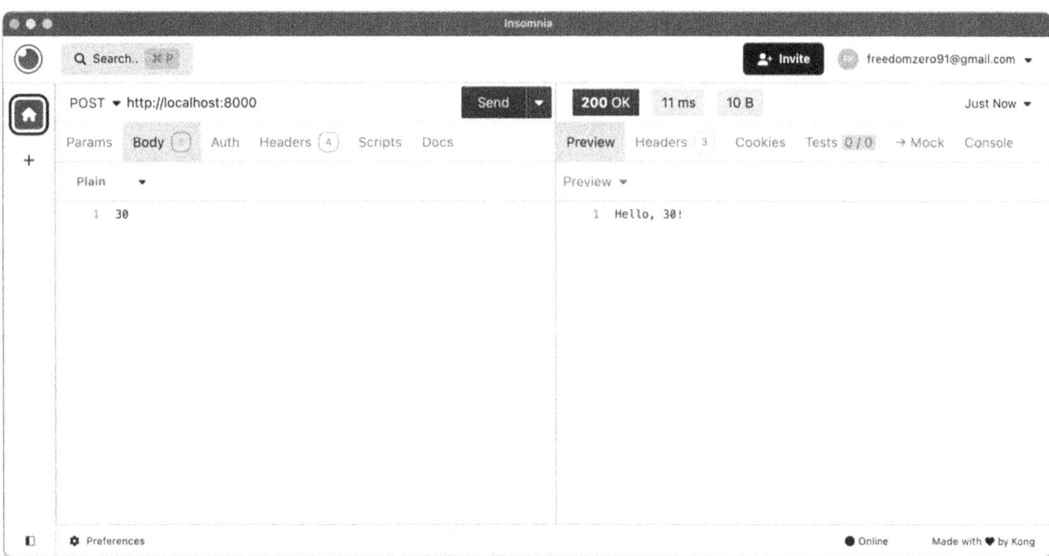

Figure 2-7. *Byte Type*

The Bytes type can be used not only for request bodies but also for responses. This type is mainly used when you cannot use regular strings, such as when you need to directly handle byte streams to receive very large files or text. If you want to create and return an entire file as a string, you need memory space equal to the file size, making it difficult to handle when the file size is large.

The Bytes type has Stream and AsyncRead traits implemented internally that can deliver data asynchronously, allowing you to write or read values to/from disk without storing values in memory. For example, you can provide a video stored on disk to the client as a byte stream as follows. Here, the code that actually reads the file from disk has been omitted for convenience:

```rust
use axum::{body::Body, response::IntoResponse};
use tokio_util::io::ReaderStream;

async fn get_video() -> impl IntoResponse {
    let file = tokio::fs::File::open("video.mp4").await.unwrap();
    let metadata = file.metadata().await.unwrap();

    let stream = ReaderStream::new(file);
    let body = Body::from_stream(stream);

    (
        [
            ("content-type", "video/mp4"),
            ("content-length", &metadata.len().to_string()),
        ],
        body,
    )
}
```

In modern REST APIs, the most common request body format is JSON. Its hierarchical structure is both machine-parsable and human-readable, making it popular for data exchange. You can also extract JSON-formatted values using extract::Json. Just like we declared a struct with each parameter as a field for query parameters, you need to define a struct that matches the format of the JSON you want to receive in the request. Here, we defined a User struct with a name field of string type. Since the name field is of string type, the value that the name field has in JSON format must also be a string. Don't forget to add the Deserialize trait as an attribute here:

```rust
use axum::Json;

#[derive(serde::Deserialize)]
struct User {
    name: String,
}

async fn hello(Json(user): Json<User>) -> String {
    format!("Hello, {}!", user.name)
}
```

Send this JSON via POST to http://localhost:8000:

```json
{
    "name": "indo"
}
```

In Insomnia, select POST method, and change the [Body] to [JSON].

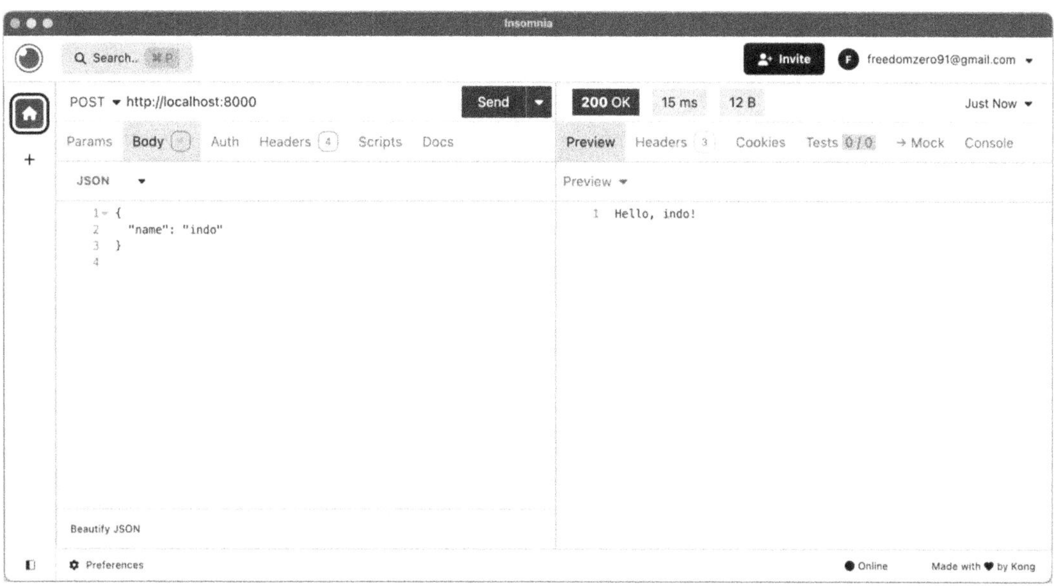

Figure 2-8. *Json Type*

Through the API response, you can see that the `Json` extractor properly parsed the name field as a string.

Serialization and Deserialization

Serialization is the process of converting objects to byte streams. It means converting objects into a form computers can understand—binary (0s and 1s). These converted byte streams can be transmitted to other computers over networks. The computer that receives the data deserializes the byte stream to convert it back into files. In summary, serialization converts data to byte streams, and deserialization converts byte streams back to the desired data format.

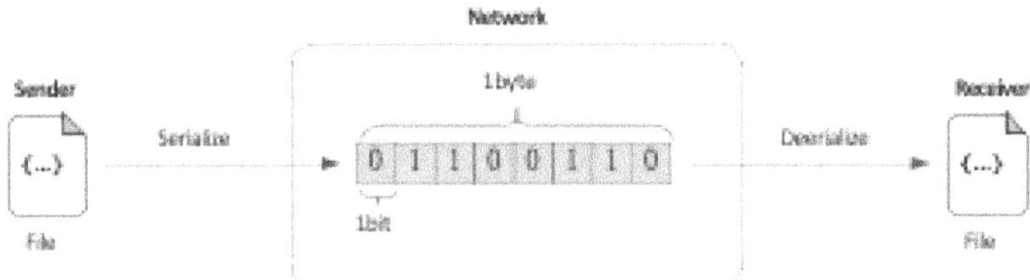

Figure 2-9. *Serialization and Deserialization*

Next is forms. Forms are the standard way to send predefined formatted data to web servers. They're commonly used to collect user input and are utilized for various purposes such as login forms, search forms, and order forms. You've probably seen screens like Figure 2-10 when signing up for or logging into a site. Here, when you enter your ID and password and click the [Login] button, the data you entered is transmitted to the API server in form format.

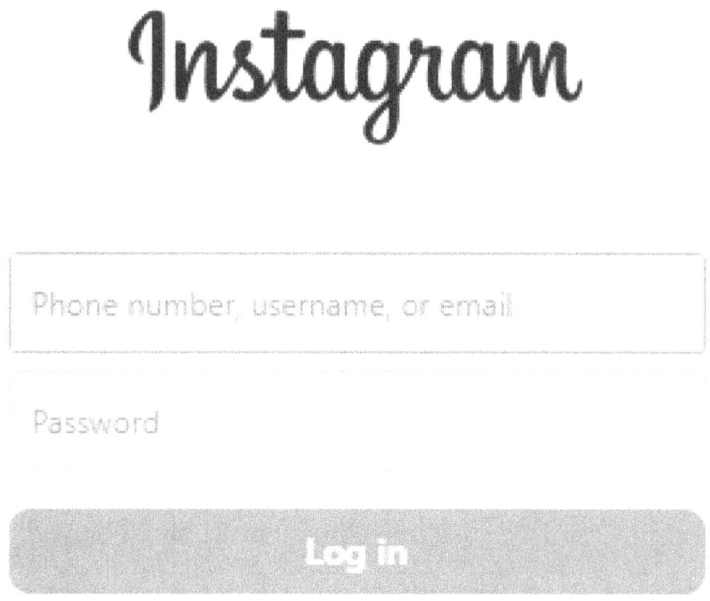

Instagram

Phone number, username, or email

Password

Log in

Figure 2-10. *Form Example*

If the request body is in form format, you can use extract::Form to retrieve it. Just like handling Json requests above, define what data to receive from the form with the User struct. Don't forget to add the Deserialize trait as an attribute:

```rust
use axum::extract::Form;

#[derive(serde::Deserialize)]
struct User {
    name: String,
}

async fn hello(Form(user): Form<User>) -> String {
    format!("Hello, {}!", user.name)
}
```

To send a request to the hello function, POST to http://localhost:8000 with key "name" and value "indo" as form data. You must set the header type to application/x-www-form-urlencoded so that keys and values are formatted like query parameters as http://localhost:8000?name=indo to properly transmit form data. In Insomnia, setting the body to Form automatically changes the header as shown in Figure 2-10, so no separate modification is needed.

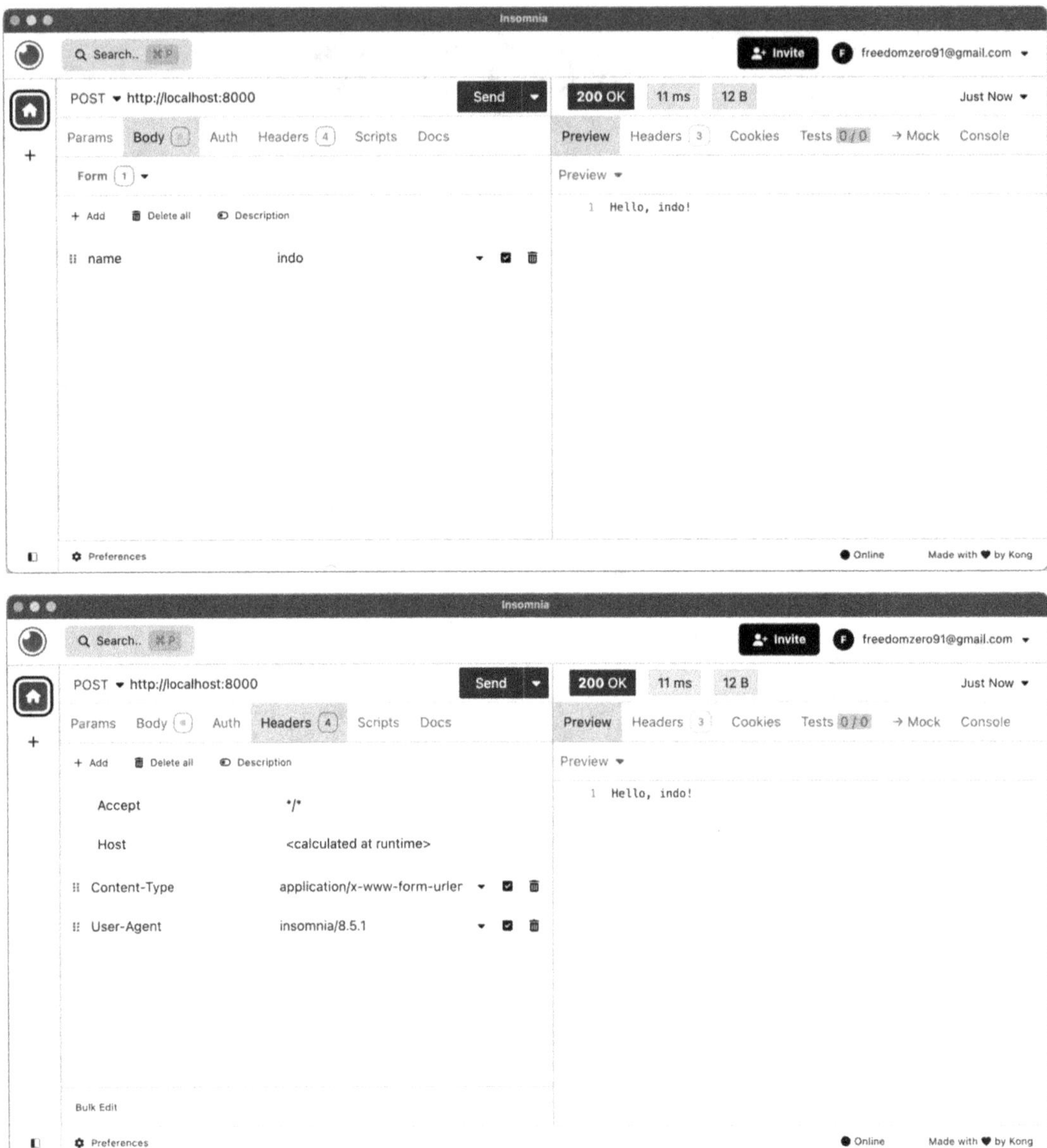

Figure 2-11. Form Request and Response

From the API response, you can see the form data was processed correctly.

Finally, let's look at implementing file uploads, one of the frequently developed features in backend services. Axum already implements `extract::Multipart` for file uploads. Since this functionality is implemented in the multipart feature, add multipart to the axum features in Cargo.toml:

axum = { version = "0.8", features = ["json", "multipart"] }

Let's create an upload function that receives files from clients in multipart format and returns the file size. Multipart is a format used to transmit various file types like documents, images, and videos. Multipart data basically has a form structure, so form field names and values are included together. Note here that the upload function's body parameter is declared as mutable (mut keyword). The reason is that the Multipart trait's next_field method returns an iterator that uses the current field's value and creates the next field. In other words, body's value changes each time next_field is called, so mutable ownership is needed:

```rust
use axum::extract::Multipart;
use axum::{routing::post, Router};

async fn upload(mut body: Multipart) -> String {
    if let Ok(Some(field)) = body.next_field().await {
        let name = field.name().unwrap().to_string();
        let data = field.bytes().await.unwrap();
        format!("{} : {} bytes", name, data.len())
    } else {
        "No fields found in multipart data".to_string()
    }
}

#[tokio::main]
async fn main() {
    let app = Router::new().route("/", post(upload));
    let listener = tokio::net::TcpListener::bind("127.0.0.1:8000")
        .await
        .unwrap();
    axum::serve(listener, app).await.unwrap();
}
```

Now in Insomnia, change the [Body] type to [Multipart] and enter image for name. Then click the triangle icon to the right of value to select the value type, and choose [File].

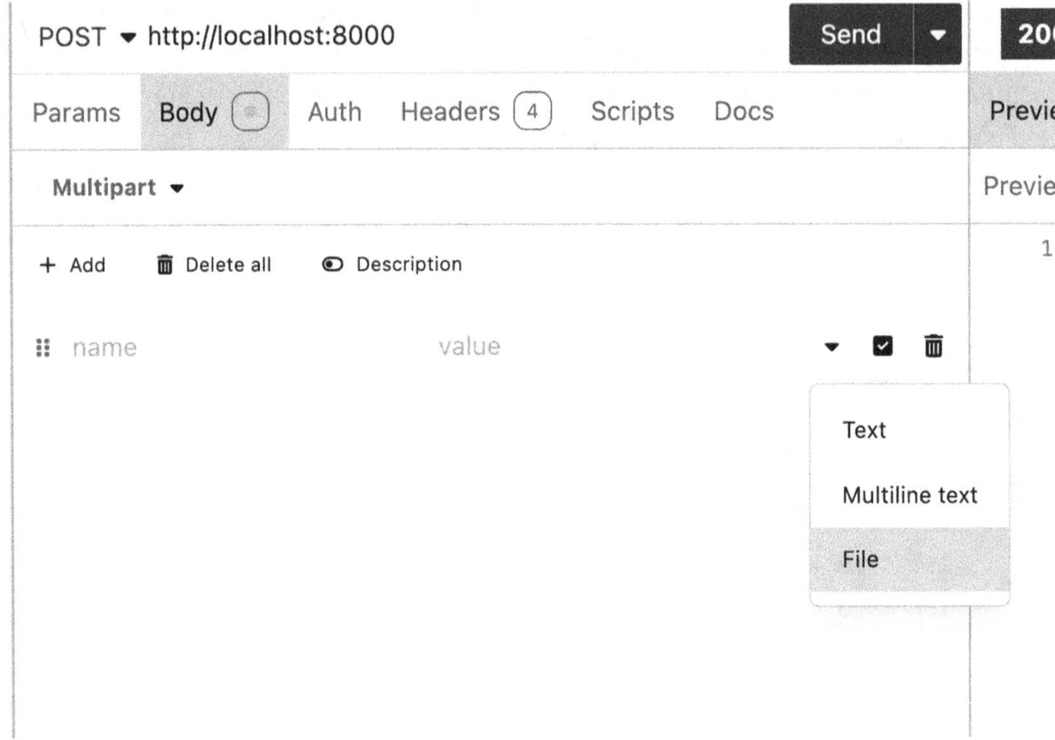

Figure 2-12. *Multipart File Transmission*

Then a [Choose File] button appears as shown in Figure 2-13, and clicking this button lets you select a file to transmit.

Figure 2-13. *Select File to Transmit*

Select a file smaller than 2MB. Then send a POST request and you'll see the file size converted to bytes and returned.

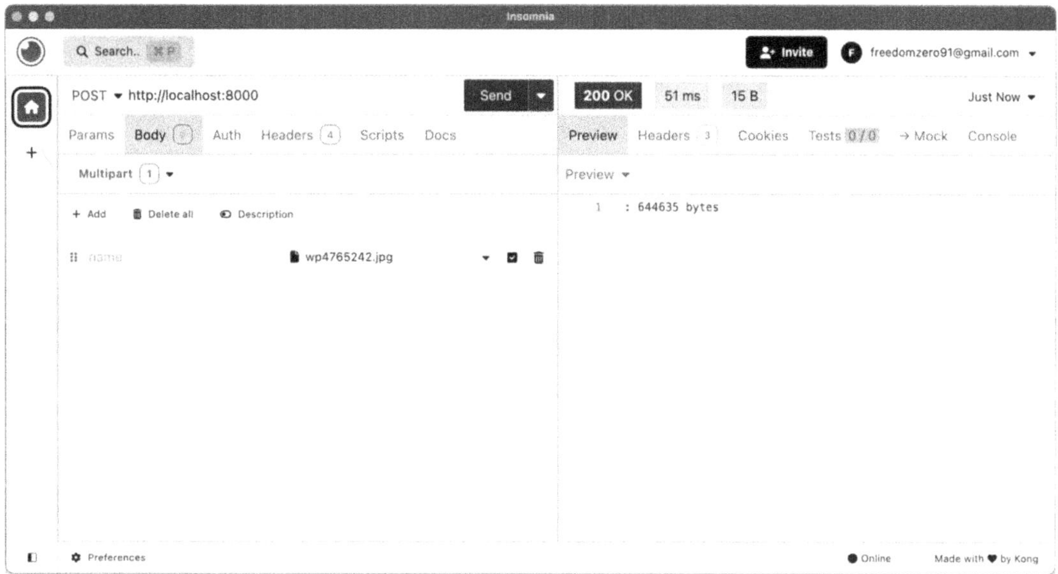

Figure 2-14. *File Transmission Result*

Request Body Length Limits

If you try to upload a file over 2MB to the Multipart we just examined, the following error occurs:

```
called `Result::unwrap()` on an `Err` value: MultipartError { source:
failed to read stream }
```

This is because, for security reasons, large data cannot be sent to the server. Malicious users can attempt Denial of Service (DoS) attacks by sending very large byte data to the server to overload it and interfere with other users' request processing.

Therefore, for security reasons, the Bytes type cannot receive values larger than 2MB by default. This limitation also applies to String, Json, Form, and Multipart, which internally use the Bytes type. To disable this, you can use the layer middleware and DefaultBodyLimit we'll learn later:

```
.layer(DefaultBodyLimit::max(4096)) // unit is usize
```

However, even in this case, it's important to accurately determine the necessary size and not set it too large.

2.3.2.5. Headers

In HTTP, headers contain metadata about requests, authentication information, and other supplementary information. To extract headers from requests in Axum, use http::header::HeaderMap. HeaderMap stores values as key-value pairs similar to HashMap, so you can extract desired values using the get method.

Header values are defined as HeaderName types under http::header. Let's write code to extract values from headers. We'll extract User-Agent and Content-Type headers and send the extracted values as strings in the response:

```
use axum::http::header::{HeaderMap, CONTENT_TYPE, USER_AGENT};

async fn hello(headers: HeaderMap) -> String {
    let user_agent = headers
        .get(USER_AGENT)
        .map(|v| v.to_str().unwrap().to_string());
    let content_type = headers
        .get(CONTENT_TYPE)
        .map(|v| v.to_str().unwrap().to_string());
    format!(
        "User-Agent: {}, Content-Type: {}",
        user_agent.unwrap_or_default(),
        content_type.unwrap_or_default(),
    )
}
```

Register this function as a handler for get requests in app:

```
#[tokio::main]
async fn main() {
    let app = Router::new().route("/", get(hello));
    let listener = tokio::net::TcpListener::bind("127.0.0.1:8000")
        .await
        .unwrap();
    axum::serve(listener, app).await.unwrap();
}
```

Now let's add User-Agent and Content-Type to the headers when sending requests. In Insomnia, User-Agent is already set, so just add the Content-Type header. For reference, values that can be set in the Content-Type header are predefined, so we used plain/text, which is one of them.

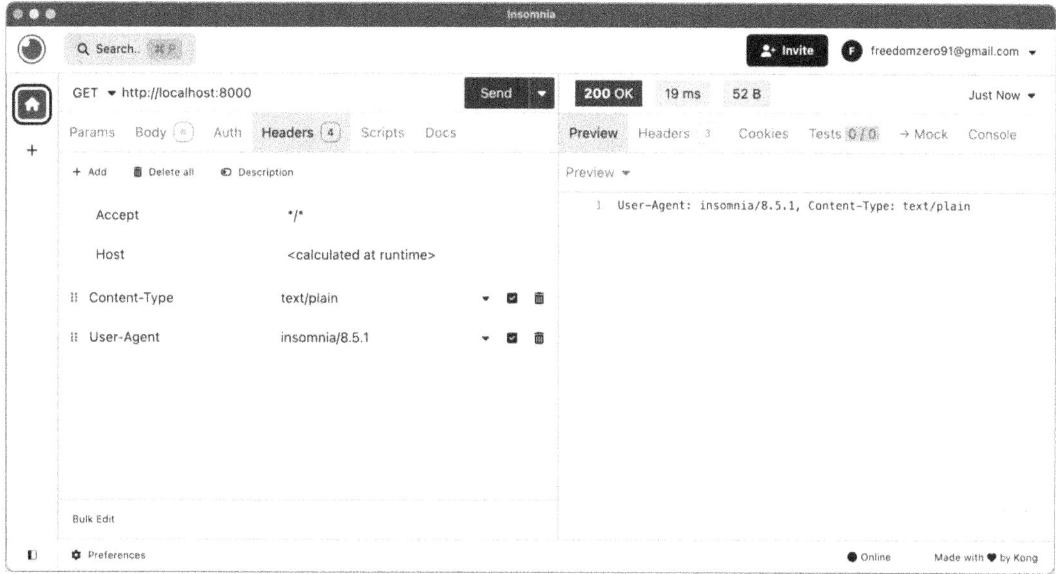

Figure 2-15. *plain/text Transmission Result*

Learn More: TypedHeader

With the HeaderMap we examined above, any type of header is allowed without pre-determining what types of headers the handler will receive. Therefore, you must check the function body to see which headers are used.

If you want to use only predefined headers for more explicit type notation, you can use TypedHeader. This type requires adding the typed-header feature from the axum_ extra crate. Add the following line to Cargo.toml:

```
axum-extra = { version = "0.12", features = ["typed-header"] }
```

The types of headers that can be extracted are defined in axum_extra::headers. For example, use TypedHeader to extract the User-Agent header. In this case, the extracted values go into user_agent and content_type, unlike HeaderMap where we extracted values with the get method:

```rust
use axum_extra::{
    extract::TypedHeader,
    headers::{ContentType, UserAgent},
};

async fn hello(
    TypedHeader(user_agent): TypedHeader<UserAgent>,
    TypedHeader(content_type): TypedHeader<ContentType>,
) -> String {
    format!(
        "User-Agent : {}, Content-Type : {}",
        user_agent, content_type
    )
}
```

2.3.3. Sending Responses from Handlers

Remember how we said handlers just need to return values and Axum automatically sends them to the client? Actually, not all types can be returned from handlers. Handlers can only return types that implement the IntoResponse trait. Axum has implemented IntoResponse for Rust's basic types, so you can return these types directly from functions. For example, types like String, &str, and Vec can be returned directly from handlers without special handling:

```rust
async fn hello() -> &'static str {
    "Hello, World!"
}

async fn hello2() -> String {
    "Hello, World!".to_string()
}
```

```rust
async fn hello3() -> Vec<u8> {
    "Hello, World!".as_bytes().to_vec()
}
```

For non-basic types like user-defined structs, you must implement IntoResponse yourself. There are too many types that have IntoResponse implemented, so check the official documentation for the complete list.

Using structs like we did for JSON request bodies, you can send JSON responses in a predefined format. In the following code, the handler's return type is specified as Json. This means using the Json extractor to convert the Message struct to JSON format and send the response. Note that the User struct's attribute is serde::Serialize, not serde::Deserialize. This is because we need to serialize the struct to create JSON format:

```rust
use axum::Json;

#[derive(serde::Serialize)]
struct Message {
    message: &'static str,
}

async fn hello() -> Json<Message> {
    Json(Message {
        message: "Hello, World!",
    })
}
```

The advantage of JSON is that data can be easily structured. But what if you want to return data like this?

```json
{
  "items": [
    { "name": "apple",
      "details": { "color": "red", "origin": "South Korea" } },
    {
      "name": "banana",
      "details": { "color": "yellow", "origin": "South America" }
    }
  ]
}
```

Creating equivalent Rust structs looks like this:

```rust
use serde::{Deserialize, Serialize};

#[derive(Serialize, Deserialize)]
pub struct Inventory {
    pub items: Vec<Item>,
}

#[derive(Serialize, Deserialize)]
pub struct Item {
    pub name: String,
    pub details: ItemDetails,
}

#[derive(Serialize, Deserialize)]
pub struct ItemDetails {
    pub color: String,
    pub origin: String,
}
```

The JSON looked relatively simple, but expressing it as structs created three structs! As shown in the example, if the JSON format to send as a response is too complex to express as structs, you can also use the json! macro from the serde_json crate. Add the following line to Cargo.toml:

```
serde_json = "1.0.108"
```

The json! macro is a way to simply create serializable strings with JSON-like syntax. The type returned by the macro is Value. For example, you can declare it as follows. It internally has keys and values in pairs like JSON, and values can be strings, numbers, arrays, etc.:

```rust
let data = json!({
    "name": "John Doe",
    "age": 43,
    "addresses": [
        {"city": "Saintsville", "state": "WV"},
```

```
            {"city": "Old Town", "state": "ME"}
    ]
});
```

Now you can create JSON responses without specifying a separate format by wrapping the json! macro with Json() as follows. Specify the return type as Json:

```
use axum::Json;
use serde_json::Value;

async fn hello() -> Json<Value> {
    Json(serde_json::json!(
        {
            "items": [
                { "name": "apple",
                  "details": { "color": "red", "origin": "South Korea" } },
                {
                  "name": "banana",
                  "details": { "color": "yellow", "origin": "South
                  America" }
                }
            ]
        }
    ))
}
```

This method is convenient but has disadvantages: types aren't determined at compile time so you can't use Rust's powerful type system, and performance can be slower because values are created dynamically every time. Therefore, it's better to use structs or HashMaps to define JSON format when possible.

2.3.4. Status Codes and Headers

We learned that status codes are a way for servers to transmit the success or failure of responses when sending responses to clients. For example, if a client sends an incorrect request to the server, the server returns status code 400.

Axum uses the StatusCode enum for status codes. When requests are performed normally, Axum uses StatusCode::OK by default, which means status code 200. If you want to use different status codes based on the situation, you can create them using axum::http::StatusCode. Here are some representative status codes and their corresponding enums:

- 200 OK StatusCode::OK

- 201 Created StatusCode::CREATED

- 204 No Content StatusCode::NO_CONTENT

- 400 Bad Request StatusCode::BAD_REQUEST

- 401 Unauthorized StatusCode::UNAUTHORIZED

- 403 Forbidden StatusCode::FORBIDDEN

- 404 Not Found StatusCode::NOT_FOUND

- 500 Internal Server Error StatusCode::INTERNAL_SERVER_ERROR

The simplest way to use status codes in handlers is using tuples. Construct a tuple with the status code and the value to send as a response. Note that you can return the tuple as is. As observant readers may have noticed, StatusCode also implements IntoResponse, and (IntoResponse, IntoResponse) is also IntoResponse:

```
use axum::http::StatusCode;
use serde_json::Value;

async fn hello() -> (StatusCode, Json<Value>) {
    (
        StatusCode::CREATED,
        Json(serde_json::json!({
            "message": "Hello, World!"
        })),
    )
}
```

If you send a request in Insomnia, you'll see that the response body is still in JSON format, but now the status code is recorded as 201.

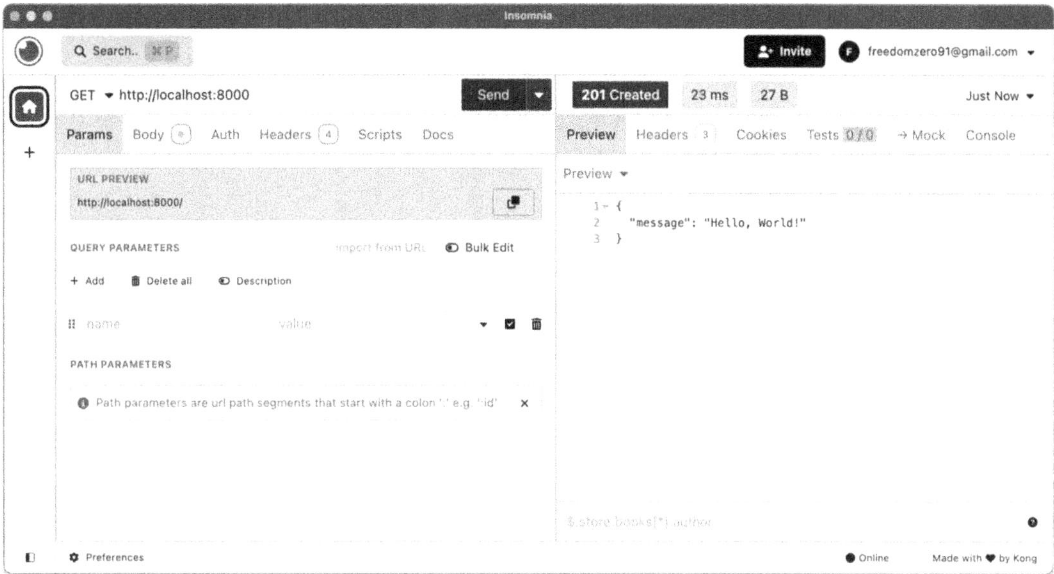

Figure 2-16. *Status Code 201*

Error handling plays a crucial role in building stable and resilient applications in software development. You must anticipate and handle potential problems that can occur during program execution to prevent the program from terminating due to unexpected errors. Similarly in server development, problems can occur while processing API requests. There are various cases: unexpected input values, problems with authentication servers, database connection issues, etc.

When problems occur in handlers, you must inform clients through status codes that a problem has occurred. Otherwise, you can't tell if requests aren't being processed because the client sent a bad request or because the server has a problem. If a function performs normally, send StatusCode::OK, and if an error occurs midway requiring you to send StatusCode::INTERNAL_SERVER_ERROR (status code 500), you can do it as follows:

```rust
async fn hello() -> (StatusCode, &'static str) {
    if true {
        (StatusCode::OK, "Hello, World!")
    } else {
        (StatusCode::INTERNAL_SERVER_ERROR, "Something went wrong")
    }
}
```

For tuple types, you can express return types simply by using IntoResponse instead of explicitly specifying types like (StatusCode, &'static str):

```rust
async fn hello() -> impl IntoResponse {
    (StatusCode::OK, "Hello, World!")
}
```

However, this doesn't clearly show what format the handler returns data in, making it inconvenient for code readers who must read through the code one by one. Therefore, in most situations except simple cases, using tuples is a clearer and more explicit way to express things.

Along with status codes, useful information you can provide to clients is headers. Just as we extracted headers from requests using TypedHeader earlier, you can also set headers in responses using TypedHeader:

```rust
use axum_extra::{headers::ContentType, TypedHeader};

async fn hello() -> (TypedHeader<ContentType>, &'static str) {
    (TypedHeader(ContentType::text_utf8()), "Hello, World!")
}
```

However, in REST APIs, the most common case is sending headers, status codes, and data together. If you want to return three pieces of information from a handler, how do you do it? In this case, create nested tuples in the form (header, (code, value)). Let's look at the following code:

```rust
async fn hello() -> (TypedHeader<ContentType>, (StatusCode,
&'static str)) {
    (
        TypedHeader(ContentType::text()),
        (StatusCode::CREATED, "Hello, World!"),
    )
}
```

The reason for grouping status code and text in a tuple is, as explained before, because that tuple's type implements IntoResponse. Then the above code can be written like this:

```rust
use axum::response::IntoResponse;

async fn hello() -> (TypedHeader<ContentType>, impl IntoResponse) {
    (
        TypedHeader(ContentType::text()),
        (StatusCode::CREATED, "Hello, World!"), // impl IntoResponse
    )
}
```

The return type becomes (TypedHeader, impl IntoResponse), and since this tuple type also implements IntoResponse, the final type ultimately becomes impl IntoResponse. Therefore, the above code can be modified as follows:

```rust
use axum::response::IntoResponse;

async fn hello() -> impl IntoResponse {
    (
        TypedHeader(ContentType::text()),
        (StatusCode::CREATED, "Hello, World!"), // impl IntoResponse
    )
}
```

However, as we've continually emphasized, it's best to fully write out the type by nesting tuples rather than simplifying the type representation like this.

Finally, here's a handler example using multiple headers with status codes and body. The branches split by match indicate the text length of the response body in the second header. When using multiple headers like this, you simply list the headers in the return type without needing to group them in a tuple:

```rust
use axum_extra::{
    headers::{ContentLength, ContentType},
    TypedHeader,
};
use serde_json::{json, Value};

async fn hello(
    Path(num): Path<i32>,
) -> (
    TypedHeader<ContentType>,
```

```rust
    TypedHeader<ContentLength>,
    (StatusCode, Json<Value>),
) {
    match num {
        0 => (
            TypedHeader(ContentType::json()),
            TypedHeader(ContentLength(12)),
            (
                StatusCode::CREATED,
                Json(json!({"message" : "Hello, World!".to_string()})),
            ),
        ),
        _ => (
            TypedHeader(ContentType::json()),
            TypedHeader(ContentLength(20)),
            (
                StatusCode::INTERNAL_SERVER_ERROR,
                Json(json!({"message" : "Error during creation".to_
                string()})),
            ),
        ),
    }
}
```

However, in general, using builder pattern of Response is a much more idiomatic and nicer pattern to use.

```rust
use axum::{
    Json,
    response::{IntoResponse, Response},
    body::Body,
    http::StatusCode,
};

async fn response() -> Response {
    Response::builder()
        .status(StatusCode::NOT_FOUND)
```

```
    .header("x-foo", "custom header")
    .body(Body::from("not found"))
    .unwrap()
}
```

2.4. State Management

Consider the case where each handler needs to read and use values from configuration files:

```
async fn func1() -> String {
    let data = read_data_from_file().await;
    // Perform function content
    ...
}

async fn func2() -> String {
    let data = read_data_from_file().await;
    // Perform function content
    ...
}
```

The problem with designing handlers this way is that each handler must repeatedly read information from the same file multiple times, and multiple handlers duplicate reading the same information. So if we could read the file just once, reuse it in handlers, and share it among each handler, couldn't we solve this problem?

The solution to this problem is state management—creating and managing state shared across the entire application. Situations where you might want to share state across the entire app include

- **Database Connections**: Generally, when connecting to databases and executing queries, you don't create new connections each time you execute a query—you reuse one or more existing connections. The reason is that creating new connections takes a long time, and closing connections also takes a long time. Therefore, if you create database connections in advance and share them across the entire app, you can execute queries much faster whenever needed. Most database drivers manage connections in a Pool manner—creating multiple connections in advance and retrieving connections to use whenever needed. By sharing this connection pool via State, you can efficiently execute queries.

- **Internal State**: Besides database connections, state worth sharing across the entire app includes logged-in user information, caches, and settings. For example, consider the case where you need to serve deep learning models in the backend. Deep learning models are usually created independently of backend code, so depending on circumstances, you may need to download and serve new models without restarting the backend app. In this case, if you share the model as State throughout the app, you can efficiently serve the deep learning model.

2.4.1. State

In Axum, you can use State to manage state shared across the entire app. Here, let's look at an example of sharing a vector of length 3 inside the app. Declare the data vector in the main function and use the with_state function to share data among multiple handlers. Axum's with_state function works by taking values and wrapping them in Arc. Once data is secured, with_state creates a new router instance. Handlers registered to this new router can access shared data using the State extractor.

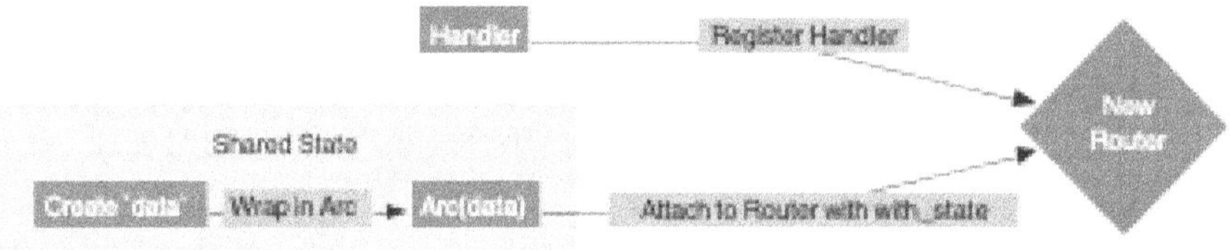

Figure 2-17. *Shared State*

```
use axum::{extract::State, routing::get, Router};

#[tokio::main]
async fn main() {
    let data = vec![0; 3];
    let app = Router::new().route("/", get(hello)).with_state(data);
    let listener = tokio::net::TcpListener::bind("127.0.0.1:8000")
        .await
        .unwrap();
    axum::serve(listener, app).await.unwrap();
}
```

Now let's use data in the hello handler function. Use the State extractor when defining the function's parameters. If you declare internal variables as mutable, modifying values is also possible. The following code increments data's first value by 1 each time it's called:

```
async fn hello(State(mut data): State<Vec<u8>>) -> String {
    data[0] += 1;
    format!("Hello, world! {data:?}")
}
```

However, even if you send multiple requests to http://localhost:8000, the value always arrives as "Hello, world! [1, 0, 0]" and the value doesn't increase further. The reason is that values shareable through State must implement the Clone trait, and when shared through State, cloned values are always passed. If you want to "truly" modify values, you must use Arc for thread safety.

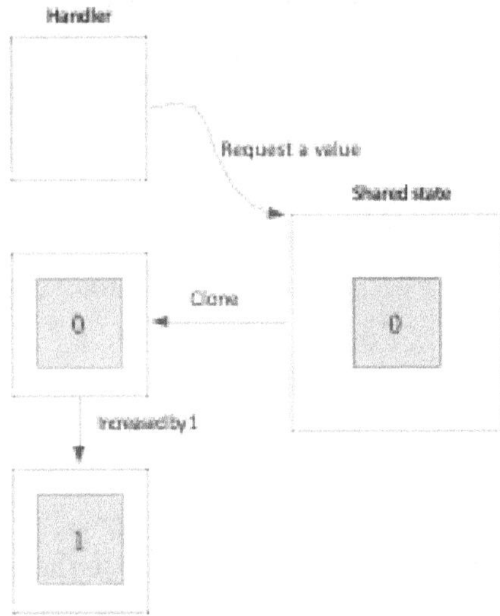

Figure 2-18. *Value Changes Using State*

Learn More: Arc<Mutex>

Let's understand Arc and Mutex separately, then see how Arc combines them.

Arc (atomic reference counting) is the thread-safe version of Rc (reference counting). It's a way to create safe shared ownership that multiple threads can share when you want to use values across threads. Each time a thread references Arc, it internally increments the current reference count. When Arc is deleted from memory in a thread, the reference count decreases by one. When all references go out of scope—when all threads no longer use Arc and the reference count becomes 0—Arc is automatically deleted.

Arc is created with Arc::new as follows, and new references are made through the clone method. Each time clone is performed, the reference count increases, and when a cloned reference is deleted, the reference count decreases:

```
use std::sync::Arc;

let my_arc = Arc::new("hello".to_string());
let cloned_arc = my_arc.clone();
```

Mutex is a data structure meaning mutual exclusion. It prevents two or more threads from accessing the same value simultaneously by granting access to values through locks. Only one thread can modify values at a time, so values can be safely modified in threads. To access mutex data, the thread must first request to acquire the mutex lock, signaling it wants access. If another thread has acquired the lock, it waits until the lock is released:

```rust
use std::sync::Mutex;

let my_mutex = Mutex::new(5);

// Automatic lock, change, unlock at deletion point
let mut data = my_mutex.lock().unwrap();
*data = 10;
```

Combining the two types as Arc<Mutex> creates a type that's shareable and modifiable across multiple threads. Arc ensures all threads have a reference to the data, and Mutex ensures only one thread can modify data at a time. In other words, Arc shares Mutex among threads, and when you need to modify values, you can safely modify them through the shared Mutex's lock:

```rust
use std::sync::{Arc, Mutex};

let counter = Arc::new(Mutex::new(0));

// Clone only Arc, which increases reference count
let cloned = counter.clone();

// Explicitly lock mutex to access data
let mut wrap = counter.lock().unwrap();
*wrap += 1;
```

Arc creates multiple readers for the same value. Mutex enables safe mutations. Together, safe shared mutable data. The following full code example using Arc creates 10 threads and then increments the counter in each thread. This process occurs safely without thread contention, so counter will ultimately be 10. To extract values from Arc, first use the Arc::into_inner function to extract the internal Mutex. Note that you can only extract values when only the original single Arc reference exists. Then use into_inner on Mutex to extract the internal value:

```rust
use std::sync::{Arc, Mutex};
use std::thread;

fn main() {
```

```rust
    let counter = Arc::new(Mutex::new(0));
    let mut handles = vec![];

    for _ in 0..10 {
        let counter = Arc::clone(&counter);
        let handle = thread::spawn(move || {
            let mut num = counter.lock().unwrap();
            *num += 1;
        });
        handles.push(handle);
    }

    for handle in handles {
        handle.join().unwrap();
    }

    println!(
        "{}",
        Arc::into_inner(counter).unwrap().into_inner().unwrap()
    );
}
```

Now let's modify the code to share Arc<Mutex<Vec>> using State:

```rust
use axum::{extract::State, routing::get, Router};
use std::sync::{Arc, Mutex};

#[tokio::main]
async fn main() {
    let data = Arc::new(Mutex::new(vec![0; 3]));
    let app = Router::new().route("/", get(hello)).with_state(data);
    let listener = tokio::net::TcpListener::bind("127.0.0.1:8000")
        .await
        .unwrap();
    axum::serve(listener, app).await.unwrap();
}

async fn hello(State(data): State<Arc<Mutex<Vec<u8>>>>) -> String {
```

```rust
    let mut data = data.lock().unwrap();
    data[0] += 1;
    format!("Hello, world! {:?}", data)
}
```

Now you can see the response increments by one each time the handler is called:

```
Hello, world! [1, 0, 0]
Hello, world! [2, 0, 0]
Hello, world! [3, 0, 0]
```

As you write applications, the amount of information shared in State increases. For example, suppose you store authentication tokens and current user information in the AppState struct and share them:

```rust
#[derive(Clone)]
struct AppState {
    auth_token: String,
    current_users: i32,
}
```

However, as in the following token function, some handlers may not need all State information and only need specific fields:

```rust
use axum::{extract::State, routing::get, Router};

async fn token(State(state): State<AppState>) -> String {
    format!("Token: {}", state.auth_token)
}

#[tokio::main]
async fn main() {
    let state = AppState {
        auth_token: "auth_token".to_string(),
        current_users: 3,
    };
    let app = Router::new().route("/token", get(token)).with_state(state);
```

```rust
    let listener = tokio::net::TcpListener::bind("127.0.0.1:8000")
        .await
        .unwrap();
    axum::serve(listener, app).await.unwrap();
}
```

Instead of repeatedly finding and extracting needed fields, you can use the extract::FromRef trait to extract each field inside State declared as a struct. This makes code more concise than extracting the entire struct. Since this trait is defined in Axum's macros feature, add the new macros feature to Cargo.toml by running the following command:

```
cargo add axum --features "macros"
```

The following code shows how to extract only the data each handler needs. The token function extracts the auth_token field from the AppState struct, and the users function extracts only the current_users field:

```rust
use axum::{
    extract::{FromRef, State},
    routing::get,
    Router,
};

#[derive(FromRef, Clone)] // Add FromRef
struct AppState {
    auth_token: String,
    current_users: i32,
}

async fn token(State(auth_token): State<String>) -> String {
    format!("Token: {}", auth_token)
}

async fn users(State(current_users): State<i32>) -> String {
    format!("Current user: {}", current_users)
}

#[tokio::main]
```

```rust
async fn main() {
    let state = AppState {
        auth_token: "auth_token".to_string(),
        current_users: 3,
    };
    let app = Router::new()
        .route("/token", get(token))
        .route("/users", get(users))
        .with_state(state);
    let listener = tokio::net::TcpListener::bind("127.0.0.1:8000")
        .await
        .unwrap();
    axum::serve(listener, app).await.unwrap();
}
```

However, this method has limitations: you can't use FromRef when declaring fields of the same type. Let's change the current_users field above to a string username field:

```rust
#[derive(FromRef, Clone)]
struct AppState {
    auth_token: String,
    username: String,
}

async fn users(State(username): State<String>) -> String {
    format!("Current user: {username}")
}

let state = AppState {
    auth_token: "auth_token".to_string(),
    username: "admin".to_string(),
};
Execution result:
error[E0119]: conflicting implementations of trait `FromRef<AppState>` for
type `String`
  --> src/main.rs:10:15
   |
9  | auth_token: String,
```

```
   | ------ first implementation here
10 | username: String,
   | ^^^^^^ conflicting implementation for `String`
```

The compile error means the same type field appears duplicate, so when extracting values from State, it can't determine which field to select. Therefore, when using State, it's better to design how to arrange values first, then implement handlers to reduce duplicate work.

2.4.1.1. Note: Choosing Between std and tokio Mutexes

In an asynchronous Rust environment, choosing the correct Mutex implementation is critical for both performance and correctness. The decision primarily hinges on whether the lock needs to be held across an .await point.

Feature	std::sync::Mutex	tokio::sync::Mutex
Behavior	Blocks the entire OS thread.	Yields the current task to the executor.
.await Compatibility	**Must not** be held across .await.	**Safe** to hold across .await.
Performance	Extremely low overhead (Synchronous).	Higher overhead (Asynchronous scheduling).
Primary Risk	Executor starvation / Deadlocks.	Contention overhead in high-throughput apps.

- **Use std::sync::Mutex** for protecting simple data structures where the critical section is short and does not involve any asynchronous operations. It is significantly faster because it avoids the overhead of task switching and async state machine management.

- **Use tokio::sync::Mutex** only when you must hold the lock while performing I/O or other asynchronous tasks (i.e., you need to call .await while the lock is active).

Holding a std::sync::MutexGuard across an .await point is a common pitfall. Since the guard does not implement Send in most cases, it will lead to compilation errors. Even if it compiles, it risks blocking the entire worker thread, preventing other independent tasks on the same thread from making progress, which can lead to a complete system hang under load.

2.4.2. Extension

Extension, like State, is a way to share one state across multiple handlers. However, Extension doesn't guarantee type safety for shared values. Let's look at the following example. You can share AppState using Extension as the handler's parameter type:

```rust
use axum::{routing::get, Extension, Router};

#[derive(Clone)]
struct AppState {}

async fn handler(Extension(state): Extension<AppState>) {}

#[tokio::main]
async fn main() {
    let state = AppState {};
    let app = Router::new().route("/", get(handler));
    let listener = tokio::net::TcpListener::bind("127.0.0.1:8000")
        .await
        .unwrap();
    axum::serve(listener, app).await.unwrap();
}
```

However, if you send a request to this handler, you'll see a runtime error with status code 500 as follows. Looking at the error content, it says there's no Extension of AppState. What does this mean?

```
Missing request extension: Extension of type `axum::AppState` was not found. Perhaps you forgot to add it? See `axum::Extension`.
```

The correct code actually needs to explicitly add Extension to the router as follows. After modifying the code and sending the request again, you'll see it works normally:

```
let app = Router::new()
    .route("/", get(handler))
    .layer(Extension(state));
```

For these reasons, it's better to use State, which was added in Axum version 0.6.0, instead of Extension for sharing application state.

WARNING

The extractors we learned about in the section "Defining Handlers" have an important declaration order. Request bodies are one-time-use async streams. Therefore, only one extractor that consumes the request body is allowed. Consequently, Axum enforces that such extractors must be the last parameter the handler takes.

The following handler compiles

```
async fn handler(headers: HeaderMap, State(state): State<AppState>, body:
String) {}
```

But if you swap the order of State and String as follows, a compile error occurs:

```
async fn handler(headers: HeaderMap, body: String, State(state):
State<AppState>) {}
```

If you're unsure what's causing a compile error, first check if the extractor order is correct.

2.5. Handler Debugging

While writing handler code, you may encounter errors that are difficult to understand. For example, let's try compiling the following code:

```
use axum::{routing::get, Router};

#[tokio::main]
async fn main() {
```

```rust
    let app = Router::new().route("/", get(handler));
    let listener = tokio::net::TcpListener::bind("127.0.0.1:8000")
        .await
        .unwrap();
    axum::serve(listener, app).await.unwrap();
}

fn handler() -> &'static str {
    "Hello, world"
}
```

Execution result:

```
error[E0277]: the trait bound `fn() -> &'static str {handler}: Handler<_,
_>` is not satisfied
  --> src/main.rs:5:44
   |
5  | let app = Router::new().route("/", get(handler));
   |                                        --- ^^^^^^^ the trait `Handler<_,
_>` is not implemented for fn item `fn() -> &'static str {handler}`
   |                                            |
   |                                            required by a bound introduced by
   |                                            this call
   |
= help: the following other types implement trait `Handler<T, S>`:
          <Layered<L, H, T, S> as Handler<T, S>>
          <MethodRouter<S> as Handler<(), S>>
```

The handler says the Handler<, > trait isn't defined for the fn() -> &'static str {handler} type function. Even reading the error content carefully, it's difficult to understand how it relates to the code you wrote. In fact, the error content has little to do with the actual problem in your code. In such cases, you can use the #[debug_handler] attribute provided by Axum's macros feature to understand the error's detailed cause. Add the macros feature to dependencies as follows:

If other features like multipart are already added, just add macros at the end.

```
axum = { version = "0.8", features = ["json", "macros"] }
```

Then add the attribute to the handler as follows and compile again:

```
use axum::debug_handler;

#[debug_handler]
fn handler() -> &'static str {
    "Hello, world"
}
```

Execution result:

```
error[E0277]: `&str` is not a future
  --> src/main.rs:16:17
   |
16 | fn handler() -> &'static str {
   |    ----------- ^ `&str` is not a future
   |    |
   |    this call returns `&str`
   |
   = help: the trait `Future` is not implemented for `&str`
   = note: &str must be a future or must implement `IntoFuture` to be awaited
   = note: required for `&str` to implement `IntoFuture`
help: remove the `.await`
   |
16 | fn handler() -> &'static str {
   |
help: alternatively, consider making `fn __axum_macros_check_handler_into_
response_make_value` asynchronous
   |
16 | fn handler() -> async &'static str {
   |                 +++++
```

Interpreting the error content, it says the returned &str type is not a Future. This means the handler is not an async function. Adding the async keyword to the function definition as the compiler recommended makes the code compile normally. When unexpected compile errors occur in handlers, you can easily identify the cause using debug_handler.

If you want to learn more about how Future and async functions work, refer to the tokio official documentation.

2.6. Example: Creating a Proxy Server

Let's build a proxy server that fetches data from external APIs and sends it to clients. Most web browsers have CORS (Cross-Origin Resource Sharing) enabled, which blocks frontend requests to domains different from the one in use. For example, if the frontend domain is service.rs, requests can only be sent to addresses ending with the same service.rs, like api.service.rs. If you try to send requests to addresses with different domains like another.rs, CORS blocks the request. Therefore, when frontends need to access external APIs with different domains, using a proxy server is the common approach.

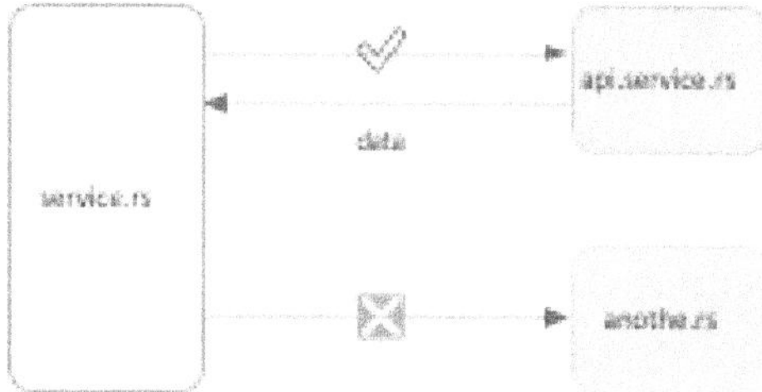

Figure 2-19. *CORS Problem*

Proxy servers are backend servers configured to run on the same domain, acting as intermediaries that call external APIs needed by the frontend and then deliver the results to the frontend.

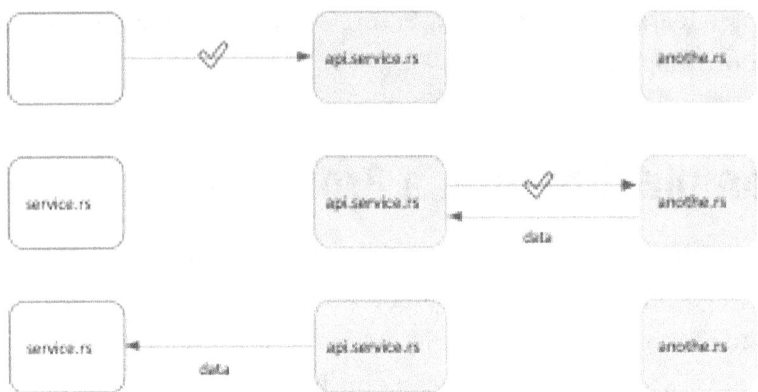

Figure 2-20. *Proxy Server Operation Principle*

Beyond simply relaying data from other sources to the original requester, proxy servers also handle additional authentication needed to use external APIs, send cached data instead for identical requests, and provide rate-limiting functionality to prevent excessive API calls.

We'll now develop a proxy server that calls dog.ceo—an API that provides random dog photos—on behalf of clients. We'll also add caching functionality to send previously stored data when clients request the same dog breed. To send API requests to other servers in Rust, we'll add the reqwest crate to dependencies. The json feature is needed to parse JSON responses. Here's the complete Cargo.toml including this:

```toml
[package]
name = "proxy"
version = "0.1.0"
edition = "2021"

[dependencies]
axum = { version = "0.8", features = ["json", "tokio", "multipart"] }
reqwest = { version = "0.11.24", features = ["json"] }
tokio = { version = "1.15.0", features = ["full"] }
serde = { version = "1.0.130", features = ["derive"] }
serde_json = "1.0.68"
```

First, let's define the format of JSON data the handler will receive. We defined breed and num_pics fields to receive the dog breed and number of photos. Also add the Deserialize trait so we can deserialize JSON data into the struct. Add the following code to main.rs:

```rust
use serde::Deserialize;

#[derive(Deserialize)]
struct Data {
    // Breed
    breed: String,
    // Number of photos option
    num_pics: Option<i32>,
}
```

Next, let's define a handler that calls the API. Receive the desired dog breed and number of photos through the JSON request body, and construct the complete URL to send the request. Then return the status code from the server along with the byte format body as a tuple. The reason for returning bytes is that deserializing JSON data from bytes to structs or serde_json::Value, etc., for cache storage occupies a lot of memory space. If this part is difficult to understand, think of byte format as the closest form to computers and JSON format as a form easy for humans to understand—naturally the human-readable form would require more memory. Therefore, unless you need to access cached JSON data structurally, storing bytes directly is efficient:

```rust
use axum::{body::Bytes, http::StatusCode, Json};
use reqwest::Client;
use serde::Deserialize;

async fn proxy_handler(Json(data): Json<Data>) -> (StatusCode, Bytes) {
    let mut url = format!("https://dog.ceo/api/breed/{}/images/random",
    &data.breed);
    if let Some(num_pics) = data.num_pics {
        url.push_str(&format!("/{}", num_pics));
    }
```

```rust
    // Request to backend server
    let client = Client::new();
    let res = client.get(url).send().await.unwrap();

    // Return proxy response
    let code = res.status().as_u16();
    let body = res.bytes().await.unwrap();
    (StatusCode::from_u16(code).unwrap(), body)
}
```

Now declare the Cache type to store the cache using Arc:

```rust
type Cache = Arc<Mutex<HashMap<String, Bytes>>>;
```

```
<note>
You can use slotmap or dashmap for easier cache management.
</note>
```

Based on this, modify the handler function to receive the State to actually share in handlers. Store dog breeds as keys in the HashMap, so when requests come for the same breed, send cached data as the response to clients, and for first-time breeds, store new data in the HashMap. The complete modified code is as follows:

```rust
use axum::{body::Bytes, extract::State, http::StatusCode, routing::post,
Json, Router};
use reqwest::Client;
use serde::Deserialize;
use std::collections::HashMap;
use std::sync::{Arc, Mutex};

// HashMap for cache
type Cache = Arc<Mutex<HashMap<String, Bytes>>>;

#[derive(Deserialize)]
struct Data {
    // Breed
    breed: String,
    // Number of photos option
    num_pics: Option<i32>,
}
```

```rust
async fn proxy_handler(State(state): State<Cache>, Json(data): Json<Data>)
-> (StatusCode, Bytes) {
    // Check cache
    if let Some(body) = state.lock().unwrap().get(&data.breed).cloned() {
        println!("{} cache hit", &data.breed);
        return (StatusCode::OK, body);
    }

    println!("{} cache miss", &data.breed);
    let mut url = format!("https://dog.ceo/api/breed/{}/images/random",
    &data.breed);
    if let Some(num_pics) = data.num_pics {
        url.push_str(&format!("/{}", num_pics));
    }

    // Request to backend server
    let client = Client::new();
    let res = client.get(url).send().await.unwrap();

    // Cache response
    let code = res.status().as_u16();
    let body = res.bytes().await.unwrap();
    let mut cache = state.lock().unwrap();
    cache.insert(data.breed, body.clone());

    // Return proxy response
    (StatusCode::from_u16(code).unwrap(), body)
}

#[tokio::main]
async fn main() {
    let state: Cache = Arc::new(Mutex::new(HashMap::new()));
    let app = Router::new()
        .route("/", post(proxy_handler))
        .with_state(state);
```

```rust
let listener = tokio::net::TcpListener::bind("127.0.0.1:8000")
    .await
    .unwrap();
axum::serve(listener, app).await.unwrap();
}
```

Let's send a request in Insomnia to see the response. Change the method to POST, Body type to JSON, and enter the following JSON data:

```json
{

    "breed": "chihuahua",
    "num_pics": 3
}
```

Click the [Send] button to send the request and receive the response as follows. It takes about 1.1 seconds for the response to arrive.

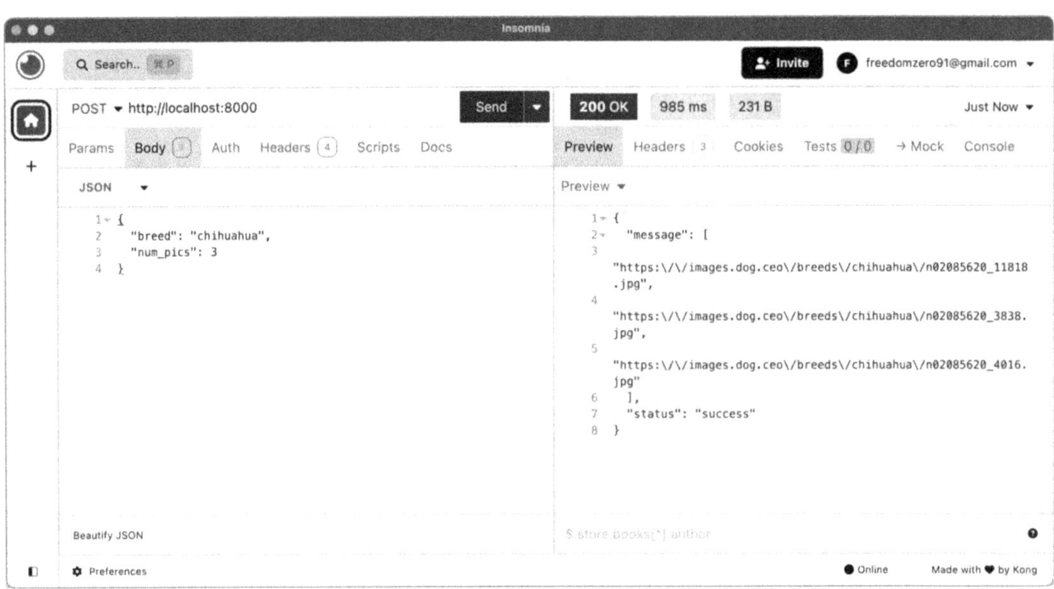

Figure 2-21. *Proxy Server Execution Result*

If you send the same request once more, thanks to caching, it retrieves previously stored data, and the response time only takes 15ms.

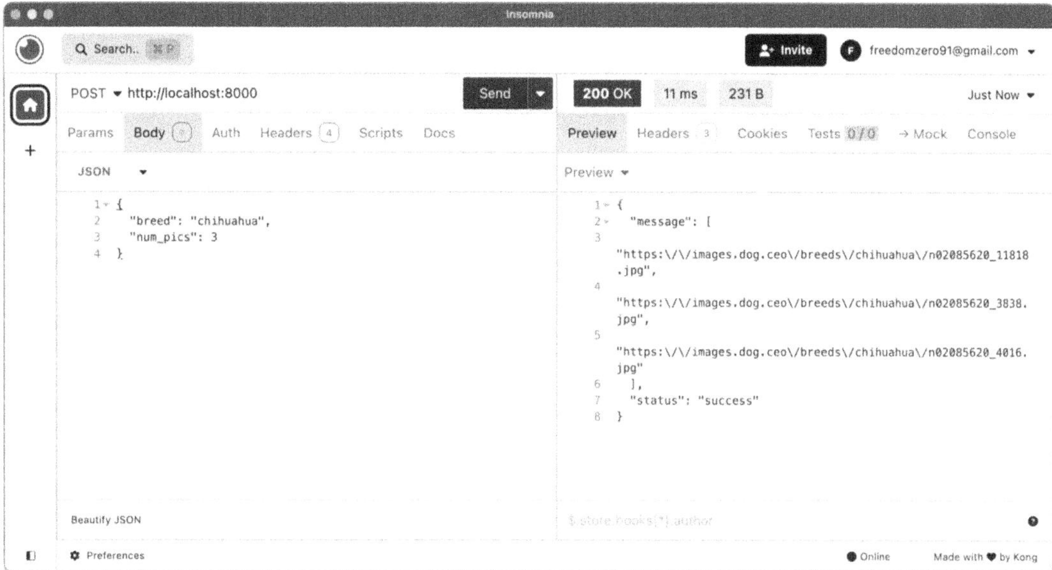

Figure 2-22. *Performance Improvement from Caching*

However, this code has one problem: caching is determined only by dog breed regardless of the number of photos. You should modify it to randomly select from stored images and send them to the client based on the number of photos the user requested, or fetch and send additional photos if there aren't enough. We'll leave this part for you to work on.

2.7. Review

- You can connect paths to handlers using Router.

- You can extract path parameters, query parameters, request bodies, headers, etc. using extractors defined in extract::Extractor.

- You can send status codes, headers, and data in responses grouped as tuples, or use impl IntoResponse to express types simply.

- You can use State to manage data shared across the entire app.

- Using debug_handler makes it easy to identify the causes of compile errors occurring in handler code.

CHAPTER 3

Database Integration with SeaORM

This chapter explains how to integrate databases using SeaORM. SeaORM (sea query and object relational mapper) is a popular ORM (object-relational mapping) library for Rust that lets you define and manage database schemas directly in your code. This keeps your code and database in sync and allows database interaction without writing raw SQL.

Key advantages of SeaORM include compile-time query safety checks and a command-line interface (CLI) for managing schema migrations. It also supports async processing, making it suitable for use with Axum. In this chapter, we'll learn how to use SeaORM to define Users, Category, and Product tables and manage them through database migrations.

Learning Points

- Understanding ORM concepts

- Defining schemas with SeaORM

- Replacing SQL with SeaQuery builder

3.1. What Is ORM?

When developing backends, you'll often need to change database table schemas. This includes modifying column types or constraints, adding or removing columns. However, changes to your application's data structures do not automatically propagate to the database schema. Developers must manually keep the two in sync, and any oversight can lead to runtime errors.

© Indo Yoon 2026
I. Yoon, *Beginning Axum*, https://doi.org/10.1007/979-8-8688-2631-3_3

ORM solves these sync issues between code and databases. By defining and managing database schemas directly in your code, you eliminate inconsistencies. Because an ORM allows you to define your schema in your application's native language, it can automate the process of generating and applying the necessary SQL to keep the database synchronized.

Note that some ORMs still require SQL for certain operations. When ORMs don't support specific database features, you'll need to write raw SQL in your code.

3.1.1. What Is SeaORM?

Figure 3-1. *SeaORM Logo*

While several ORMs exist for Rust, the two most prominent are Diesel (12.2k stars) and SeaORM (6.6k stars). We'll use SeaORM in this book, primarily for its first-class `async` support, which integrates seamlessly with Axum. Unlike Diesel, which requires third-party crates and a more complex setup for asynchronous operations, SeaORM is async-native. It also offers an intuitive API, compile-time query checks, a powerful migration system, and excellent performance, making it an ideal choice for modern web backends.

While Diesel requires detailed customization for advanced features, SeaORM provides most features by default, making it more convenient to use.

SeaORM connects to databases through sqlx, a query engine crate. It officially supports MySQL (including MariaDB and MySQL Server), PostgreSQL, and SQLite. You can also connect to other databases like SurrealDB or CockroachDB, though they're not officially supported. GraphQL support is available through the seaography crate.

Figure 3-2. *SeaORM Ecosystem (Logo source:* `https://www.sea-ql.org/`*)*

3.2. Creating Schemas and Models

3.2.1. Defining Database Schema

Database schemas define table structures and relationships. To learn SeaORM, we'll work with three tables: Users, Category, and Product.

The Users table has an auto-generated integer id as primary key, plus username and password columns (varchar). The Category table has just a name column, which the Product table references as a foreign key. The Product table includes an id primary key, plus title and price columns.

Here's the ER (entity-relationship) diagram showing these tables:

Users		Category		Product	
id 🔑	integer	name	varchar(255)	id 🔑	integer
username	varchar(255)			title	varchar
password	varchar(255)			price	integer
				category	varchar

Figure 3-3. *ER Diagram*

An ER diagram graphically represents database design and real-world data relationships. Tools like dbdiagram.io make creating these diagrams easy.

3.2.2. Installing Dependencies

To use SeaORM in your project, add these dependencies. We're enabling two features for sea-orm: sqlx-postgres connects to PostgreSQL through sqlx (choose a different feature for other databases). runtime-tokio-native-tls enables TLS encryption for database connections using the tokio runtime.

```
[dependencies]

...

sea-orm = { version = "1.0.0", features = [ "sqlx-postgres", "runtime-
tokio-native-tls", "macros" ] }
```

SeaORM's CLI tool handles database migrations and entity generation. Install it with

```
cargo install sea-orm-cli
```

3.2.3. Migration

In the context of application development, *database migration* is the process of managing incremental and reversible changes to your database schema. Instead of writing raw SQL to create our tables, we'll use SeaORM's migration system. This allows us to define our database structure in Rust code, track changes over time, and easily apply or roll back those changes, which is invaluable for debugging and maintaining a project long term.

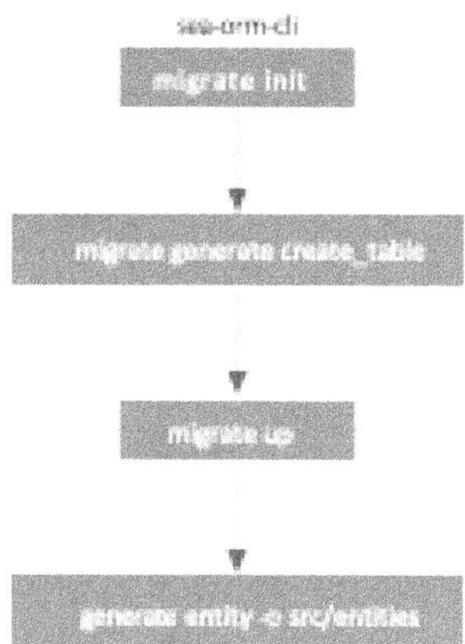

Figure 3-4. *Migration Execution Order*

Initialize migration with

```
sea-orm-cli migrate init
```

This creates a sample migration file. Use `sea-orm-cli migrate generate` to create additional migration files later.

After initialization, you'll find these files in the migration/src folder. The Migrator API handles database connections and schema management, while the Migrator CLI provides user commands for migrations.

```
migration
├── Cargo.toml
├── README.md
└── src
    ├── lib.rs # File where Migrator API is defined
    ├── m20220101_000001_create_table.rs # Sample migration file
    └── main.rs # File where Migrator CLI is defined
```

Before continuing, add these dependencies to the migration folder's Cargo.toml to enable CLI migrations:

```
[package]
name = "migration"
version = "0.1.0"
edition = "2021"
publish = false
```

...

```
[dependencies.sea-orm-migration]
version = "1.0.0"
features = [
    # Enable at least one `ASYNC_RUNTIME` and `DATABASE_DRIVER` feature if
      you want to run migration via CLI.
    # View the list of supported features at https://www.sea-ql.org/SeaORM/
      docs/install-andconfig/database-and-async-runtime.
    # e.g.
    "runtime-tokio-rustls", # `ASYNC_RUNTIME` feature
    "sqlx-postgres", # `DATABASE_DRIVER` feature
]
```

Delete the sample file m20220101_000001_create_table.rs and generate a new migration file. Replace NAME_OF_MIGRATION with create_table:

```
sea-orm-cli migrate generate create_table
```

This generates a timestamped migration file like

```
m20240211_163337_create_table.rs
```

Now let's define the table creation migration. Migrations require two functions: up (runs the migration) and down (rolls back the migration). The down function lets you quickly revert if something goes wrong.

First, the Users table. Here's the equivalent SQL:

```
CREATE TABLE IF NOT EXISTS Users ( id INT NOT NULL AUTO_INCREMENT PRIMARY
KEY, username VARCHAR(255) NOT NULL, password VARCHAR(255) NOT NULL );
```

Here's the migration code for this SQL. The up function signature:

```
async fn up(&self, manager: &SchemaManager) -> Result<(), DbErr> {
    ...
}
```

Use the manager object to create tables and define columns. Here's the Users table creation code with SQL equivalents in comments:

```
manager
```

```
.create_table( // CREATE TABLE
    Table::create()
        .table(Users::Table) // `Users`
        .if_not_exists() // IF NOT EXISTS
        .col(
            ColumnDef::new(Users::Id) // `Id`
                .integer() // INT
                .not_null() // NOT NULL
                .auto_increment() // AUTO_INCREMENT
                .primary_key(), // PRIMARY KEY
        )
        // `Username` VARCHAR(255) NOT NULL
        .col(ColumnDef::new(Users::Username).string().not_null())
        // `Password` VARCHAR(255) NOT NULL
        .col(ColumnDef::new(Users::Password).string().not_null())
        .to_owned(), // Returns `Table` object that created `Users`
        table and defined columns
)
.await?;
```

Now for the Category and Product tables. Each uses manager.create_table and mirrors the SQL table declarations:

manager.create_table(Table::create().table(Category::Table). if_not_exists().col(ColumnDef::new(Category::Name). string().unique_key().not_null()	CREATE TABLE IF NOT EXISTS Category (name VARCHAR(255) NOT NULL UNIQUE PRIMARY KEY);
.primary_key(),).to_owned(),).await?;	
manager	
.create_table(	
Table::create()	
.table(Product::Table)	
.if_not_exists()	
.col(	

(*continued*)

```
ColumnDef::new(Product::Id)          CREATE TABLE IF NOT
.integer()                           EXISTS Product (
.not_null()                          id INT NOT NULL AUTO_INCREMENT
.auto_increment()                    PRIMARY KEY,
.primary_key(),                      title VARCHAR(255) NOT NULL,
)                                    price INT NOT NULL,
.col(ColumnDef::new(Product::Title).string().not_null())     category VARCHAR(255)
.col(ColumnDef::new(Product::Price).integer().not_null())    NOT NULL,
.col(ColumnDef::new(Product::Category).string().not_null())  FOREIGN KEY (category)
.foreign_key(                        REFERENCES
ForeignKey::create()                 Category(name)
.name("fk_product_category")         );
.from(Product::Table, Product::Category)
.to(Category::Table, Category::Name),
)
.to_owned(),
)
.await?;
```

The crate used to write Rust code identical to SQL queries is SeaQuery. Besides DDL (data definition language) that defines tables or columns, DML (data manipulation language) that queries and modifies data is also included in SeaQuery. How to write queries using SeaQuery is covered in detail in the "SeaQuery" section below.

The complete code of the up function combining all the above code is as follows:

```
async fn up(&self, manager: &SchemaManager) -> Result<(), DbErr> {
    manager
        .create_table(
            Table::create()
                .table(Users::Table)
                .if_not_exists()
```

```
                .col(
                    ColumnDef::new(Users::Id)
                        .integer()
                        .not_null()
                        .auto_increment()
                        .primary_key(),
                )
                .col(ColumnDef::new(Users::Username).string().not_null())
                .col(ColumnDef::new(Users::Password).string().not_null())
                .to_owned(),
        )
        .await?;
manager
    .create_table(
        Table::create()
            .table(Category::Table)
            .if_not_exists()
            .col(
                ColumnDef::new(Category::Name)
                    .string()
                    .unique_key()
                    .not_null()
                    .primary_key(),
            )
            .to_owned(),
    )
    .await?;
manager
    .create_table(
        Table::create()
            .table(Product::Table)
            .if_not_exists()
            .col(
                ColumnDef::new(Product::Id)
                    .integer()
```

```
                            .not_null()
                            .auto_increment()
                            .primary_key(),
                    )
                    .col(ColumnDef::new(Product::Title).string().not_null())
                    .col(ColumnDef::new(Product::Price).integer().not_null())
                    .col(ColumnDef::new(Product::Category).string().not_null())
                    .foreign_key(
                        ForeignKey::create()
                            .name("fk_product_category")
                            .from(Product::Table, Product::Category)
                            .to(Category::Table, Category::Name),
                    )
                    .to_owned(),
            )
        .await?;
    Ok(())
}
```

To roll back migrations, you need to reverse the changes. Since we're creating tables, rollback means dropping them. The SQL:

```
DROP TABLE IF EXISTS `Users`;
DROP TABLE IF EXISTS `Category`;
DROP TABLE IF EXISTS `Product`;
```

The corresponding down function, which reverses the migration by dropping the tables, is as follows:

```
async fn down(&self, manager: &SchemaManager) -> Result<(), DbErr> {
    manager
        .drop_table(Table::drop().table(Users::Table).if_exists().to_
        owned())
        .await?;
    manager
        .drop_table(Table::drop().table(Category::Table).if_exists().to_
        owned())
```

```
        .await?;
    manager
        .drop_table(Table::drop().table(Product::Table).if_exists().to_
        owned())
        .await?;
    Ok(())
}
```

We still need to define the Users, Category, and Product enums. The DeriveIden trait lets SeaORM use enum names as table names and identify migration targets. The Table variant represents the table itself, while other variants represent columns:

```
#[derive(DeriveIden)]
enum Users {
    Table,
    Id,
    Username,
    Password,
}

#[derive(DeriveIden)]
enum Category {
    Table,
    Name,
}

#[derive(DeriveIden)]
enum Product {
    Table,
    Id,
    Title,
    Price,
    Category,
}
```

Now let's apply the migration. First, SeaORM needs to know how to connect to your database. Create a .env file in your project root with the DATABASE_URL variable. Use the user and database from Chapter 1:

```
DATABASE_URL=postgres://axum:1234@localhost/axum
```

Run the migration:

```
sea-orm-cli migrate up
```

Execution result:

```
Running `cargo run --manifest-path ./migration/Cargo.toml -- up -u
postgres://axum:1234@localhost/axum`
Compiling migration v0.1.0 (/temp/migration)
Finished dev [unoptimized + debuginfo] target(s) in 4.66s
Running `migration/target/debug/migration up -u 'postgres://axum:1234@
localhost/axum'`
Applying all pending migrations

Applying migration 'm20240211_163337_create_table'

Migration 'm20240211_163337_create_table' has been applied
```

To roll back, use `sea-orm-cli migrate down`.

Next, generate Rust query models from your database schema. These models let you easily work with table columns and types through the SeaQuery builder. Generate them in src/entities:

```
sea-orm-cli generate entity -o src/entities
```

Execution result:

```
Connecting to Postgres ...
Discovering schema ...
... discovered.
Generating category.rs
> Column `name`: String, not_null
Generating product.rs
> Column `id`: i32, auto_increment, not_null
> Column `title`: String, not_null
```

```
> Column `price`: i32, not_null
> Column `category`: String, not_null
Generating user.rs
> Column `id`: i32, auto_increment, not_null
> Column `username`: Option<String>
> Column `password`: Option<String>
Generating users.rs
> Column `id`: i32, auto_increment, not_null
> Column `username`: String, not_null, unique
> Column `password`: String, not_null
Writing src/entities/category.rs
Writing src/entities/product.rs
Writing src/entities/user.rs
Writing src/entities/users.rs
Writing src/entities/mod.rs
Writing src/entities/prelude.rs
... Done.
```

Note   Both user.rs and users.rs may be generated. In this book, we use users.rs which corresponds to the Users table we created.

3.3. SeaQuery

Let's explore writing SQL queries in Rust using SeaQuery.

3.3.1. Query Builder

To understand SeaORM's SQL capabilities, we need to explore SeaQuery, its query builder. SeaQuery lets you compose complex SQL queries expressively with type safety guaranteed by your schema definitions. Its high-level SQL abstraction makes backend queries easy to write and maintain.

SeaQuery powers all SQL operations in SeaORM. Even the migrations we just wrote use SeaQuery under the hood. It's included with SeaORM, so no extra installation needed. Let's see how to express various SQL operations with SeaQuery.

3.3.2. Identifiers and Iden

SQL identifiers name database objects like tables, columns, views, indexes, triggers, procedures, and constraints. There are two types:

Figure 3-5. *Identifiers*

Ordinary identifiers start with letters and contain only letters, numbers, and underscores (like EmployeeID or order_date). Delimited identifiers, enclosed in quotes or brackets, are used for names that contain spaces, special characters, start with a number, or conflict with an SQL keyword (e.g., "Employee ID" or "order").

Why does this matter for SeaORM? SQL identifiers are case-sensitive. EmployeeID, employeeid, and EMPLOYEEID are all different. But Rust enums require PascalCase:

```
#[derive(DeriveIden)]
enum Employee {
    Table,
    Id,
    EmployeeID,
    Department,
}
```

PascalCase capitalizes the first letter of each word.

But our SQL uses snake_case field names like id, employee_id, department.

```
CREATE TABLE Employee (
    id,
    employee_id,
    department
) ...
```

The DeriveIden macro handles this conversion automatically, translating PascalCase enum variants like EmployeeID into snake_case SQL identifiers like employee_id.

DeriveIden simplifies the Iden trait implementation. Adding #[derive(DeriveIden)] automatically implements sea_orm::sea_query::Iden. Without it, you'd need complex manual implementation:

```rust
use sea_orm::sea_query::Iden;
use std::fmt::Write;

pub enum Employee {
    Id,
    EmployeeID,
    Department,
}

impl Iden for Employee {
    fn unquoted(&self, s: &mut dyn Write) {
        match self {
            Self::Id => write!(s, "id").unwrap(),
            Self::EmployeeID => write!(s, "employee_id").unwrap(),
            Self::Department => write!(s, "department").unwrap(),
        }
    }
}
```

DeriveIden handles all this complexity for you.

You can also explicitly set SQL identifiers with DeriveIden:

```rust
use sea_orm::DeriveIden;

#[derive(DeriveIden)]
pub enum Employee {
    Id,
    #[sea_orm(iden = "employee_id")]
    MyColumn,
    #[sea_orm(iden = "department")]
    YourColumn,
}
```

Here, MyColumn maps to employee_id and YourColumn to department. This helps when your Rust names differ from SQL column names.

3.3.3. Database Connection

Create a database connection by passing DATABASE_URL to Database::connect. We'll cover details later in this chapter. For now, just know that this conn lets you query the database:

```
use sea_orm::Database;

let conn = Database::connect(DATABASE_URL).await.unwrap();
```

3.3.4. SELECT

Before querying, you need a database connection. We'll assume you have one ready as conn, which you'll reference as &conn when needed.

For SELECT queries, import the table entities from src/entities. Here's the Users entity import. Also import Model since query results use this type:

```
use crate::entities::users::{Entity, Model};
```

Import EntityTrait to connect entities with database tables:

```
use sea_orm::EntityTrait;
```

The EntityTrait provides the link between a generated Entity and its corresponding database table, exposing the methods needed to perform CRUD operations.

Let's work with this sample Users table data:

id	username	Password
1	Indo	Dev
2	Buzzi	Prod
3	mellon	Test
4	cameron	Admin
5	james	Rust

To get all records: find() acts as SELECT, all(&conn) fetches all rows. This returns all five records:

let users: Vec =	SELECT * FROM
Entity::find().all(&conn).await.unwrap();	Users

For LIMIT 1, use one() instead of all(). This returns Option instead of Vec:

let user: Model = Entity::find().one(&conn).await.unwrap().unwrap();	SELECT * FROM Users LIMIT 1
Id	username
1	indo

To add WHERE filters, import ColumnTrait for column comparisons and QueryFilter for filtering:

```rust
use sea_orm::{ColumnTrait, QueryFilter};
```

Use filter() for WHERE clauses. For example, username = 'indo' becomes Users::Column::Username.eq("indo"):

let users: Vec = Entity::find().filter(Users::Column::Username.	SELECT * FROM Users WHERE
eq("indo")).all(&conn).await.unwrap();	username = indo
id	username
1	indo

For ORDER BY, import QueryOrder and Order:

```rust
use sea_orm::{Order, QueryOrder};
```

To sort usernames ascending for users with id > 1, chain order_by() after filter():

let users: Vec = Entity::find().filter(Users::Column::Id.gt(1)).order_by(Users::Column::Username, Order::Asc).all(&conn).await.unwrap();	SELECT * FROM Users WHERE id > 1 ORDER BY username
Id	username
2	buzzi
4	cameron
5	james
3	mellon

3.3.5. INSERT

Before exploring INSERT queries, let's understand ActiveValue and ActiveModel.

Figure 3-6. *Entity and ActiveModel*

Entity represents static database records from queries. ActiveModel represents records you can modify or create, with fields of type ActiveValue.

ActiveValue has three states:

- **Set**: Value to be saved

- **NotSet**: No value provided

- **Unchanged**: Value hasn't changed

You'll mainly use Set and NotSet; Unchanged is rarely needed.

Entity uses EntityTrait for table records; ActiveModel uses ActiveModelTrait for modifiable records. This trait provides insert() and update() functions to save changes to the database.

Import these for working with ActiveModel:

```rust
use crate::entities::users::ActiveModel;
use sea_orm::{ActiveModelTrait, ActiveValue};
```

The simplest INSERT: create an ActiveModel and call insert(). This returns Result<Model, DbErr>. We're using unwrap() for simplicity, but you should handle errors properly:

```
let new_user: Model = ActiveModel {

id: NotSet,

username: Set("sam".to_owned()),

password: Set("code456".to_owned())        INSERT INTO Users (username, password)

}                                          VALUES ("sam", "code456");

.insert(&conn)

.await

.unwrap();
```

Alternatively, call insert() directly on Entity like with SELECT. This returns InsertResult:

```
let result: InsertResult = Entity::insert(ActiveModel {

id: NotSet,

username: Set("sam".to_owned()),           INSERT INTO Users (username,

password: Set("code456".to_owned()),        password)

})                                          VALUES ("sam", "code456");

.exec(&conn)

.await

.unwrap();
```

Get the inserted record's id from InsertResult:

```
let last_id = result.last_insert_id;
```

Note   last_insert_id only works with auto-increment ids, not manually specified ones.

For bulk inserts, use insert_many() with a vector of ActiveModels. You get the last inserted id and can calculate others if you know the count:

```
let result = Entity::insert_many(vec![
ActiveModel {
id: NotSet,
username: Set("mary".to_owned()),
password: Set("456xyz".to_owned()),
},
ActiveModel {                                    INSERT INTO Users (username, password)
id: NotSet,                                      VALUES ("mary", "456xyz"),
username: Set("pete".to_owned()),                ("pete", "login123");
password: Set("login123".to_owned()),
},
])
.exec(&conn)
.await
.unwrap();
```

3.3.6. UPDATE

For UPDATE, find the record with find_by_id(), convert to ActiveModel with into(), set new values, then call update():

```
let mut user: ActiveModel = Entity::find_by_
id(1)
.one(&conn)
.await
.unwrap()
.unwrap()                              UPDATE Users
.into();                               SET username = "john", password = "new_pass"
user.username = ActiveValue::Set("john".   WHERE id = 1;
to_owned());
user.password = ActiveValue::Set("pass".
to_owned());
let updated_user = user.update(&conn).await.
unwrap();
```

3.3.7. DELETE

DELETE directly uses entities. Delete by id:

```
Entity::delete_by_id(1)
.exec(&conn)                           DELETE FROM Users WHERE id = 1;
.await.unwrap();
```

For conditional deletes, use delete_many() with filters like in find():

Entity::delete_many()	
.filter(Users::Column::Username.contains("indo")). exec(&conn).await?;	DELETE FROM Users WHERE username LIKE indo;

Figure 3-7 summarizes CRUD operations. Understanding when to use Entity vs. ActiveModel is crucial.

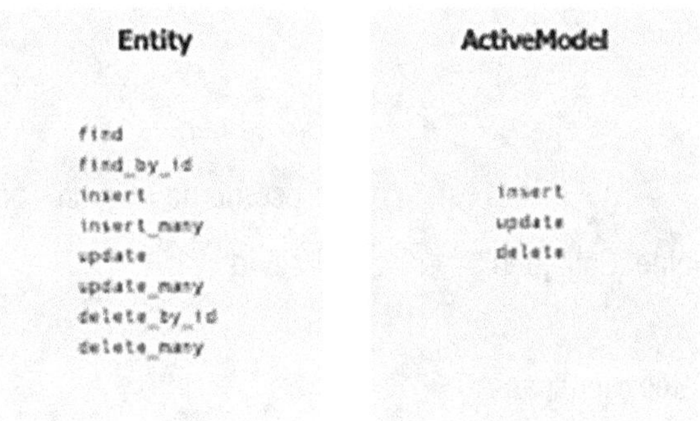

Figure 3-7. *Methods of Entity and ActiveModel*

3.3.8. Error Handling

Since a database is an external system, operations can fail for reasons outside of your application's control. Proper error handling is therefore crucial for server stability. Let's examine how to handle both general SQL errors and database-specific error codes.

Use DbErr to handle SQL errors like unique constraint or foreign key violations:

```rust
use sea_orm::{DbErr, SqlErr};

let new_user: Result<Model, DbErr> = ActiveModel {
    id: NotSet,
    username: Set("sam".to_owned()),
    password: Set("code456".to_owned())
}
.insert(&conn)
.await;

match new_user {
```

```
    Ok(user) => {
        ...
    }
    Err(err) => match err {
        DbErr::Query(SqlErr::UniqueConstraintViolation(details)) => {
            ...
        }
        DbErr::Query(SqlErr::ForeignKeyConstraintViolation(details)) => {
            ...
        }
        _ => {
            ...
        }
    },
}
```

Different databases return different error codes. For example, PostgreSQL uses error code 23505 for unique violations and 23503 for foreign key violations. RuntimeErr helps handle these database-specific codes:

This code handles insertion errors using DbErr::Exec with RuntimeErr. Internal covers SeaORM errors, while SqlxError handles database execution errors with specific error codes:

```
use sea_orm::RuntimeErr;

let new_user_result - ActiveModel {
    id: NotSet,
    username: Set("sam".to_owned()),
    password: Set("code456".to_owned())
}
.insert(&conn)
.await;

match new_user_result {
    Ok(user) => {
        ...
    }
```

```rust
Err(err) => match err {
    DbErr::Exec(RuntimeErr::Internal(details)) => {
        println!("Internal runtime error: {}", details);
    }
    DbErr::Exec(RuntimeErr::SqlxError(error)) => {
        match error {
            sqlx::Error::Database(db_error) => {
                if let Some(code) = db_error.code() {
                    match code.as_ref() {
                        "23505" => println!("Unique constraint
                        violation"),
                        "23503" => println!("Foreign key constraint
                        violation"),
                        _ => println!("Other database error:
                        {}", code),
                    }
                }
            }
            _ => println!("Other SQLx error: {}", error),
        }
    }
},
}
```

3.4. Connecting Users Table to HTTP Requests

Let's connect Axum handlers to the database for queries. We'll use JSON for requests and responses. First, we need to modify the auto-generated Users model in entities/users.rs. Add Deserialize and Serialize traits to enable JSON serialization (Rust to JSON) and deserialization (JSON to Rust).

> **Tip**   Serialization converts in-memory objects to byte streams for storage or network transmission. Deserialization reverses this, reconstructing objects from byte streams.

```rust
use sea_orm::entity::prelude::*;
use serde::{Deserialize, Serialize};

#[derive(Clone, Debug, PartialEq, DeriveEntityModel, Eq, Serialize,
Deserialize)]
#[sea_orm(table_name = "users")]
pub struct Model {
    #[sea_orm(primary_key)]
    pub id: i32,
    #[sea_orm(unique)]
    pub username: String,
    pub password: String,
}
```

Let's write a handler in main.rs for GET requests to /users. The get_user function takes id and username query parameters and returns matching users.

Database queries use Entity's find() function. Here's how to get the first result, with equivalent SQL:

let user = Entity::find().one(&db)	SELECT *
.await	FROM users
.unwrap().unwrap();	LIMIT 1;

We use two structs for the Users table:

- **Entity**: performs queries via EntityTrait

- **Model**: converts to/from JSON via Serialize and Deserialize

Here's the complete get_user function:

```rust
async fn get_user(Query(params): Query<HashMap<String, String>>) ->
Json<Model> {
    let conn = Database::connect(DATABASE_URL).await.unwrap();

    let mut condition = Condition::any();

    if let Some(id) = params.get("id") {
        condition = condition.add(Column::Id.eq(id.parse::<i32>().
        unwrap()));
    }
    if let Some(username) = params.get("username") {
        condition = condition.add(Column::Username.contains(username));
    }

    let user = Entity::find()
        .filter(condition)
        .one(&conn)
        .await
        .unwrap()
        .unwrap();

    Json(user)
}
```

Add the GET handler to main:

```rust
 mod entities;
use std::collections::HashMap;
use axum::{extract::Query, routing::get, Json, Router};
use sea_orm::{ColumnTrait, Condition, Database, EntityTrait, QueryFilter};
use entities::users::{Column, Entity, Model};

const DATABASE_URL: &str = "postgres://axum:1234@localhost/axum";

async fn get_user( ... ) { .. }
```

```
#[tokio::main]
async fn main() {
    let listener = tokio::net::TcpListener::bind("127.0.0.1:8000")
        .await
        .unwrap();
    axum::serve(listener, app).await.unwrap();
}
```

Now, go back to pgsql console and add a user to Users table for a test. Execute the following query.

```
INSERT INTO Users (username, password) VALUES ('test', 'test');
```

Now, run the Axum server and send a request to /users endpoint with GET method. Set the url as http://localhost:8000/users?id=1. Then you will get the response like this.

```
{"id":1,"username":"test","password":"test"}
```

3.5. Database Connection

Figure 3-8. *Database Connection vs. Pool Connection*

3.5.1. Connection Pool

When connecting to a database with DatabaseConnection, sqlx::Pool is used internally. A Pool is a data structure designed to pre-create multiple connections and provide them on demand. The main reason for using a connection pool instead of a single connection is that server applications receive multiple requests simultaneously, and each request needs to execute database queries. If there were only one connection, each request would have to wait in line until the connection becomes available.

While you could create a new database connection for each request in the handler, establishing new connections takes time, which degrades API response speeds. Additionally, databases have a maximum connection limit, so creating unlimited new connections is not a good approach.

Therefore, by creating a pool of multiple connections that requests can share, you can process multiple queries simultaneously. For more details on database connection pools, refer to the "Pool in sqlx" documentation: `https://docs.rs/sqlx/latest/sqlx/struct.Pool.html`

Since Pool implements the Send, Sync, and Clone traits, it's best to create a DatabaseConnection when the program starts and share it across handlers. We'll look at how to share this connection state later. As you might have guessed, we'll use State.

3.5.2. Connection Options

When creating a DatabaseConnection, you can specify detailed additional options. Create a ConnectOptions object using ConnectOptions::new, then use various methods to add options. Each option is explained in the comments:

```rust
use sea_orm::{Database, DatabaseConnection, ConnectOptions};

let mut opt = ConnectOptions::new("protocol://username:password@host/database");

opt.max_connections(100)          // Set maximum connections in the
                                  // connection pool
    .min_connections(5)           // Set minimum connections in the
                                  // connection pool
    .connect_timeout(Duration::from_secs(8))   // Set connection
                                               // attempt timeout
```

```
.acquire_timeout(Duration::from_secs(8))      // Set timeout for acquiring
                                              //    an idle connection
.idle_timeout(Duration::from_secs(8))         // Set idle
                                              //    connection timeout
.max_lifetime(Duration::from_secs(8))         // Set connection
                                              //    lifetime timeout
.sqlx_logging(true)                           // Enable SQLx logging
.sqlx_logging_level(log::LevelFilter::Info)   // Set SQLx log level
.set_schema_search_path("my_schema");         // Set Postgres schema
                                              //    search path

let conn: DatabaseConnection = Database::connect(opt).await?;
```

The schema_search_path specifies which schema to search when looking for tables. PostgreSQL's default setting uses the username (in this case, axum) and the public schema.

3.6. Modularization

The code we examined in the section "Connecting Users Table to HTTP Requests" has handlers, routers, and database connections all written in main.rs. As we add more handlers and refine our routers, it's better to separate each component into its own module. Similarly, database-related code should be separated into its own module for logical organization.

You can modularize by creating api and db folders with the following structure. In this process, we'll complete all remaining endpoints for the Users table:

```
.
├── api
│   ├── mod.rs
│   └── users.rs
├── db
│   ├── db.rs
│   └── mod.rs
├── entities
└── main.rs
```

3.6.1. Separating the DB Module

Let's separate the DB module first. We'll define an `init_db` function in db/db.rs that can be called from main.rs to establish the database connection. However, there's one issue: the database connection information is hardcoded.

Generally, sensitive information like database connection details and passwords, or values that may change depending on the environment, are declared as environment variables. Environment variables provide values appropriate for the environment in which the application runs.

For example, if an application runs in three environments—production, development, and test—each environment uses a different database, so connection information must be provided accordingly. However, if connection information is stored as strings in the code, you'd need to develop separate source code for each environment, which is inconvenient.

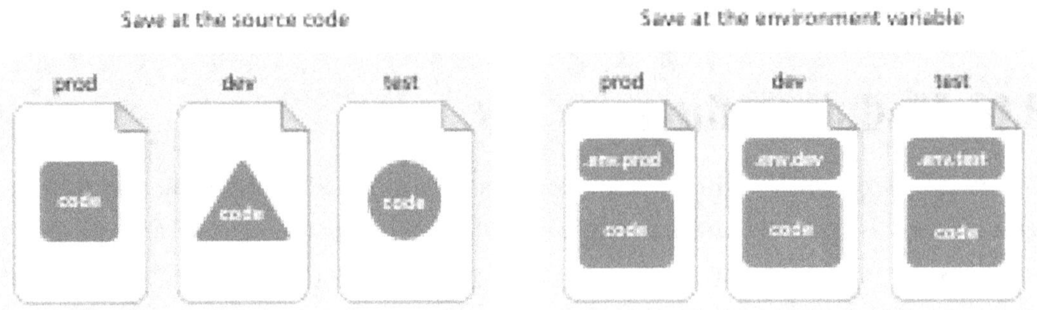

Figure 3-9. *Hardcoding vs. Environment Variables*

Therefore, we'll use an approach where environment variables are stored in a file and read by the application. Environment variables are typically stored in a .env file.

.env Files and .gitignore for Junior Developers

The .env file stores various configuration values used in a project. This can include sensitive information such as API keys, database connection details, and passwords. Since exposing this sensitive information on public repositories like GitHub can create security risks, you need to be careful.

The .gitignore file is used to exclude specific files or directories from Git version control. By adding the .env file to .gitignore, the .env file won't be uploaded to Git and will remain only in your local environment. This keeps sensitive information safe.

Here's how to add the .env file to .gitignore:

1. If there's no .gitignore file in your project's root directory, create one.

2. Open .gitignore and add `.env` on a new line.

3. Add the .gitignore file to Git and commit.

```
git add .gitignore
git commit -m "Add .env to .gitignore"
```

To enable Rust to read database connection information from the .env file, add the dotenvy crate to Cargo.toml:

```
dotenvy = "0.15.7"
```

Enter the database connection information in the .env file as follows. We're replacing the connection information that was previously hardcoded as constants with environment variables. Note that environment variables treat whitespace as part of the string, so you must specify the variable and value without spaces around the equals sign:

```
DATABASE_URL=postgres://axum:1234@localhost/axum
```

To read values from the .env file, add the following at the very top of the main function in main.rs:

```
dotenvy::dotenv().ok();
```

If you want to read environment variables from a different file, you can use `dotenvy::from_filename("custom.env")?;`

Let's return to the `init_db` function in db.rs. `init_db` connects to the database based on connection information read from environment variables. If the environment variable `DATABASE_URL` doesn't exist in the .env file, it causes a panic with an error message. If the environment variable exists and the connection succeeds, it returns that connection; if it fails, it panics to terminate the program since proceeding is impossible:

```rust
use std::env;
use sea_orm::{Database, DatabaseConnection};

pub async fn init_db() -> DatabaseConnection {
    match Database::connect(
```

```
        env::var("DATABASE_URL").expect("DATABASE_URL is not set in
        .env file")
    )
    .await
    {
        Ok(db) => db,
        Err(e) => panic!("Error connecting to database: {}", e),
    }
}
```

In db/mod.rs, enter the following to declare the `init_db` function as public:

```
pub mod db;
pub use db::init_db;
```

Returning to main.rs, instead of creating database connections in each handler, declare the connection pool returned from init_db as State so that all handlers share the connection created initially:

```
dotenvy::dotenv().ok();
let conn: DatabaseConnection = init_db().await;

let app = Router::new()
    .route(
        "/users",
        // ...
    )
    .with_state(conn); // Declare as State
```

Now handlers can share and use the database connection via State:

```
pub async fn get_user(
    State(conn): State<DatabaseConnection>,
    Query(params): Query<HashMap<String, String>>,
) -> Json<Vec<Model>>
```

3.6.2. API Module Separation

Let's move the handler from main.rs to api/users.rs and add filtering. To filter by id, use Id.eq:

```rust
let condition = Condition::all(Column::Id.eq(id.parse::<i32>().unwrap()));
Entity::find().filter(condition).all(&conn).await.unwrap()
```

But what if the id parameter isn't provided? We need to build our query dynamically: filter by id if it's present, or return all users if it's not.

Use Condition to build filters dynamically. Conditions combine with all() (AND logic) or any() (OR logic).

Condition's add() method chains AND conditions. Start with all() to match everything, then add specific filters. When you AND "all records" with "id equals X", you get just "id equals X":

```rust
let mut condition = Condition::all();

if let Some(id) = params.get("id") {
    condition = condition.add(Column::Id.eq(id.parse::<i32>().unwrap()));
}
Entity::find().filter(condition).all(&conn).await.unwrap()
```

Think of it as set intersection (Figure 3-10). The intersection of "all records" and "specific records" is always the specific records.

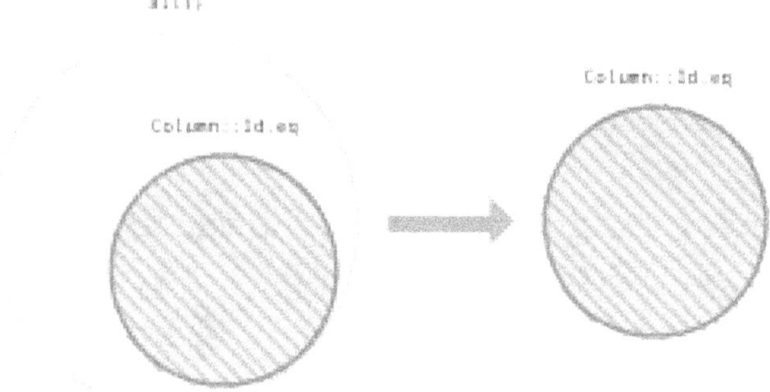

Figure 3-10. *all() and Id.eq*

Here's the response:

Add username filtering the same way:

```rust
if let Some(username) = params.get("username") {
    condition = condition.add(Column::Username.contains(username));
}
```

Here's the complete get_user in users.rs. It accepts multiple filters via Query and returns Vec since results can be multiple. The code uses three filters: all(), Id.eq, and Username.contains:

```rust
use crate::entities::users::{ActiveModel, Column, Entity, Model};
use axum::{
    extract::{Query, State},
    Json,
};
use sea_orm::{
    ActiveModelTrait, ActiveValue, ColumnTrait, Condition,
DatabaseConnection, EntityTrait,
    ModelTrait, QueryFilter,
};
use std::collections::HashMap;

pub async fn get_user(
    State(conn): State<DatabaseConnection>,
    Query(params): Query<HashMap<String, String>>,
) -> Json<Vec<Model>> {
    let mut condition = Condition::all();
    if let Some(id) = params.get("id") {
        condition = condition.add(Column::Id.eq(id.parse::<i32>().
        unwrap()));
    }
    if let Some(username) = params.get("username") {
        condition = condition.add(Column::Username.contains(username));
    }
    Json(Entity::find().filter(condition).all(&conn).await.unwrap())
}
```

What if someone sends a non-integer id, or the database query fails? The parse::(). unwrap() panics on non-integer strings. While Axum recovers from handler panics and keeps serving other requests, a panic results in a generic server error, leaving the user with no useful information. They cannot tell if the error was their fault (a bad request) or a server-side problem, leading to a poor user experience. Sending GET /users?id=a in Insomnia shows the screen in Figure 3-11.

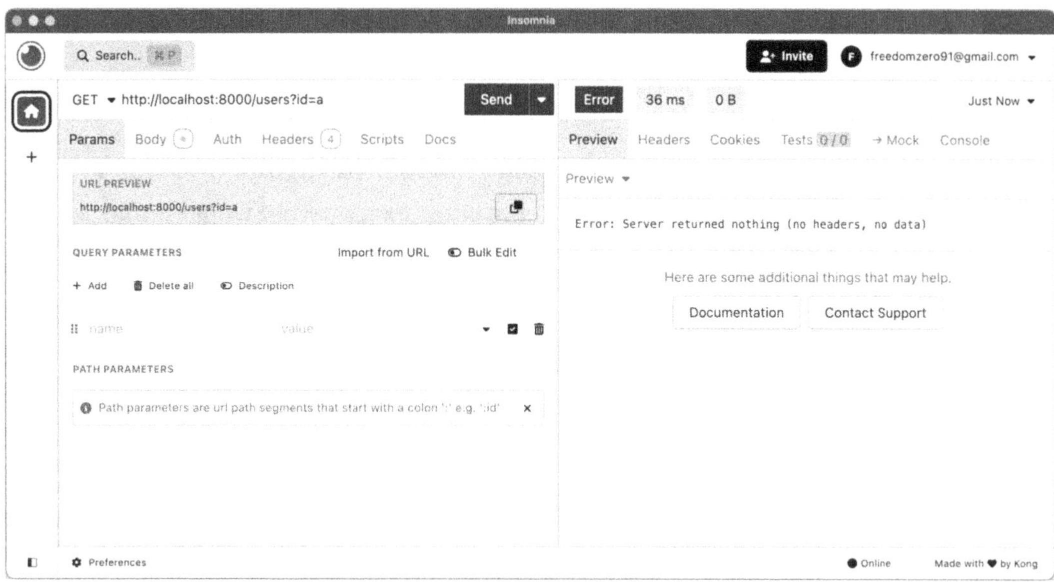

Figure 3-11. *When Specific Server Error Cannot Be Known*

Let's handle errors properly instead of using unwrap. Define AppError in utils/app_ error.rs with a status code and message. Implement IntoResponse so handlers can return it. The get_users handler will return Result<Json<Vec>, AppError>:

```rust
use axum::{http::StatusCode, response::IntoResponse, Json};

pub struct AppError {
    code: StatusCode,
    message: String,
}

impl AppError {
    pub fn new(code: StatusCode, message: impl Into<String>) -> Self {
        Self {
            code,
```

```
            message: message.into(),
        }
    }
}

impl IntoResponse for AppError {
    fn into_response(self) -> axum::response::Response {
        (self.code, Json(self.message.clone())).into_response()
    }
}
```

Here's the error handling with match. Each error returns an AppError with appropriate status code and message, so clients know exactly what went wrong:

```
pub async fn get_users(
    State(conn): State<DatabaseConnection>,
    Query(params): Query<HashMap<String, String>>,
) -> Result<Json<Vec<Model>>, AppError> {
    let mut condition = Condition::all();

    if let Some(id) = params.get("id") {
        match id.parse::<i32>() {
            Ok(parsed_id) => condition = condition.add(Column::Id.
            eq(parsed_id)),
            // id parsing error handling
            Err(_) => {
                return Err(AppError::new(
                    StatusCode::BAD_REQUEST,
                    "ID must be an integer",
                ))
            }
        }
    }
    if let Some(username) = params.get("username") {
        condition = condition.add(Column::Username.contains(username));
    }
```

```
match Entity::find()
    .filter(condition)
    .order_by(Column::Username, Order::Asc)
    .all(&conn)
    .await
{
    Ok(users) => Ok(Json(users)),
    // DB query error handling
    Err(_) => Err(AppError::new(
        StatusCode::INTERNAL_SERVER_ERROR,
        "Database error",
    )),
}
}
```

Now GET /users?id=a returns a clear error message (Figure 3-12).

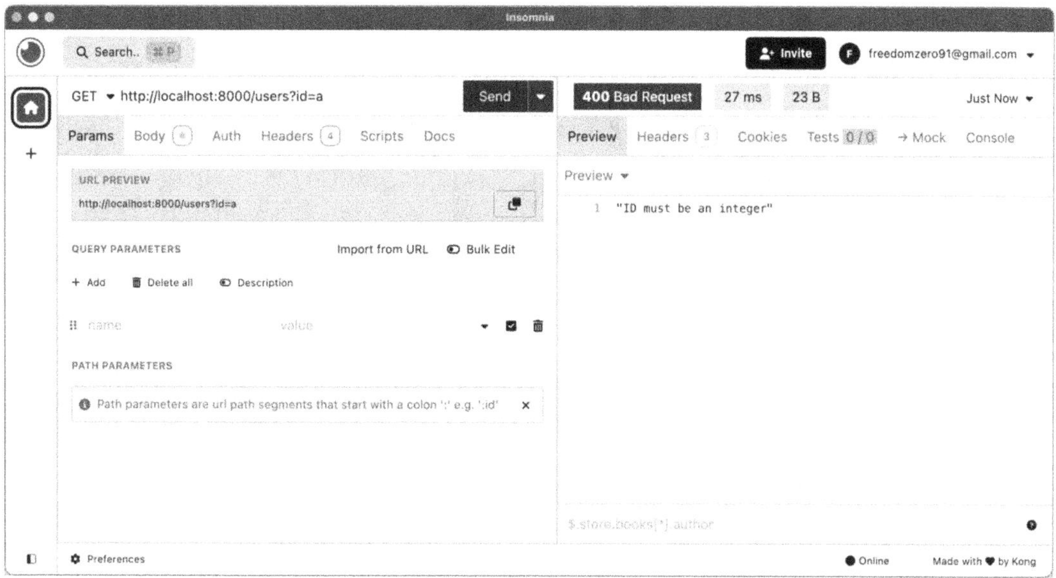

Figure 3-12. *Server Error Message*

The post_user and put_user handlers use UpsertModel with Optional fields. Without this, clients would need to send all fields every time, even auto-generated ones like id. With Option, clients send only what they need:

```rust
#[derive(serde::Deserialize)]
pub struct UpsertModel {
    id: Option<i32>,
    username: Option<String>,
    password: Option<String>,
}
```

post_user receives UpsertModel and creates ActiveModel without id (using NotSet for auto-generation). Username and password are required, so we return an error if they're None. On success, we return the created Model:

UpsertModel only needs Deserialize since handlers return Model, not UpsertModel.

```rust
pub async fn post_user(
    State(conn): State<DatabaseConnection>,
    Json(user): Json<UpsertModel>,
) -> Result<Json<Model>, AppError> {
    if user.username.is_none() || user.password.is_none() {
        return Err(AppError::new(
            StatusCode::BAD_REQUEST,
            "Username or password not provided",
        ));
    }

    let new_user = ActiveModel {
        id: ActiveValue::NotSet,
        username: ActiveValue::Set(user.username.unwrap()),
        password: ActiveValue::Set(user.password.unwrap()),
    };

    match new_user.insert(&conn).await {
        Ok(result) => Ok(Json(result)),
        Err(_) => Err(AppError::new(
            StatusCode::INTERNAL_SERVER_ERROR,
            "Database error",
```

```
        )),
    }
}
```

Let's break down put_user. It uses UpsertModel for selective field updates but requires id to identify the update target:

```
pub async fn put_user(
    State(conn): State<DatabaseConnection>,
    Json(user): Json<UpsertModel>,
) -> Result<Json<Model>, AppError> {
    let id = match user.id {
        Some(id) => id,
        None => {
            return Err(AppError::new(
                StatusCode::BAD_REQUEST,
                "User ID not provided",
            ))
        }
    };
```

Check if the record exists. Handle both query errors (Err) and missing records (Ok(None)):

```
    let found_user = match Entity::find_by_id(id).one(&conn).await {
        Ok(user) => user.ok_or(AppError::new(StatusCode::NOT_FOUND, "User
        not found"))?,
        Err(_) => {
            return Err(AppError::new(
                StatusCode::INTERNAL_SERVER_ERROR,
                "Database error",
            ))
        }
    };
```

Convert the found Model to ActiveModel with into(). Now you can update fields and save changes:

```rust
let mut active_user: ActiveModel = found_user.into();
```

Check which fields the client wants to update. Map provided values to ActiveValue::Set, keeping original values for unspecified fields:

```rust
active_user.username = user
    .username
    .map(ActiveValue::Set)
    .unwrap_or(active_user.username);

active_user.password = user
    .password
    .map(ActiveValue::Set)
    .unwrap_or(active_user.password);
```

Save the updates and return the result with proper error handling:

```rust
match active_user.update(&conn).await {
    Ok(result) => Ok(Json(result)),
    Err(_) => Err(AppError::new(
        StatusCode::INTERNAL_SERVER_ERROR,
        "Database error",
    )),
}
}
```

delete_user takes an id query parameter:

```rust
pub async fn delete_user(
    State(conn): State<DatabaseConnection>,
    Query(params): Query<HashMap<String, String>>,
) -> Result<Json<&'static str>, AppError> {
    let id = match params.get("id") {
        Some(id) => id,
        None => {
            return Err(AppError::new(
                StatusCode::BAD_REQUEST,
```

```
                "User ID not provided",
            ))
        }
    };
```

Parse the id and delete. Return "User deleted" on success:

```
    match Entity::delete_by_id(
        id.parse::<i32>()
            .map_err(|_| AppError::new(StatusCode::BAD_REQUEST, "ID must be
            an integer"))?,
    )
    .exec(&conn)
    .await
    {
        Ok(_) => Ok(Json("User deleted")),
        Err(_) => Err(AppError::new(
            StatusCode::INTERNAL_SERVER_ERROR,
            "Database error",
        )),
    }
}
```

Add the module to api/mod.rs:

```
pub mod users;
```

In main.rs, chain the handlers to /users. Clients use different HTTP methods on the same path:

```
let app = Router::new()
    .route(
        "/users",
        get(get_users)
            .post(post_user)
            .put(put_user)
            .delete(delete_user),
    )
    .with_state(conn);
```

3.7. Completing Remaining Endpoints

We've built CRUD handlers for Users. Let's add similar endpoints for Category and Product tables. Create category.rs and product.rs in the api folder, then update mod.rs:

```rust
pub mod category;
pub mod product;
```

3.7.1. Category

Category uses its name as a primary key, so updates aren't supported. Only create, read, and delete. The handlers are similar to Users but simpler:

```rust
use crate::{
    entities::category::{ActiveModel, Column, Entity, Model},
    utils::app_error::AppError,
};
use axum::{
    extract::{Query, State},
    http::StatusCode,
    Json,
};
use sea_orm::{
    ActiveModelTrait, ActiveValue, ColumnTrait, Condition,
DatabaseConnection, EntityTrait,
    ModelTrait, QueryFilter,
};
use std::collections::HashMap;

pub async fn get_category(
    State(conn): State<DatabaseConnection>,
    Query(params): Query<HashMap<String, String>>,
) -> Result<Json<Vec<Model>>, AppError> {
    let mut condition = Condition::all();
```

```rust
    if let Some(name) = params.get("name") {
        condition = condition.add(Column::Name.contains(name));
    }

    match Entity::find().filter(condition).all(&conn).await {
        Ok(categories) => Ok(Json(categories)),
        Err(_) => Err(AppError::new(
            StatusCode::INTERNAL_SERVER_ERROR,
            "Database error",
        )),
    }
}

pub async fn post_category(
    State(conn): State<DatabaseConnection>,
    Json(category): Json<Model>,
) -> Result<Json<Model>, AppError> {
    let new_category = ActiveModel {
        name: ActiveValue::Set(category.name),
    };

    match new_category.insert(&conn).await {
        Ok(result) => Ok(Json(result)),
        Err(_) => Err(AppError::new(
            StatusCode::INTERNAL_SERVER_ERROR,
            "Database error",
        )),
    }
}
```

delete_category validates the name, checks if the category exists, then deletes it. The match handles three cases: found, not found, and database errors:

```rust
pub async fn delete_category(
    State(conn): State<DatabaseConnection>,
    Query(params): Query<HashMap<String, String>>,
) -> Result<Json<&'static str>, AppError> {
    if params.get("name").is_none() {
```

```rust
        return Err(AppError::new(StatusCode::BAD_REQUEST, "Name is
        required"));
    }

    let category = match Entity::find()
        .filter(Condition::any().add(Column::Name.contains(params.
        get("name").unwrap())))
        .one(&conn)
        .await
    {
        Ok(Some(category)) => category,
        Ok(None) => return Err(AppError::new(StatusCode::NOT_FOUND,
        "Category not found")),
        Err(_) => {
            return Err(AppError::new(
                StatusCode::INTERNAL_SERVER_ERROR,
                "Database error",
            ))
        }
    };

    match category.delete(&conn).await {
        Ok(_) => Ok(Json("Deleted")),
        Err(_) => Err(AppError::new(
            StatusCode::INTERNAL_SERVER_ERROR,
            "Database error",
        )),
    }
}
```

3.7.2. Product

Product handlers mirror Users but with a key difference: get_product uses UpsertModel for query parameters instead of HashMap<String, String>. This automatically handles type conversion for id and price integers, avoiding manual parsing and type checking:

```rust
use crate::{
    entities::product::{ActiveModel, Column, Entity, Model},
    utils::app_error::AppError,
};
use axum::{
    extract::{Query, State},
    http::StatusCode,
    Json,
};
use sea_orm::{
    ActiveModelTrait, ActiveValue, ColumnTrait, Condition,
DatabaseConnection, EntityTrait,
    ModelTrait, QueryFilter,
};

#[derive(serde::Deserialize)]
pub struct UpsertModel {
    id: Option<i32>,
    title: Option<String>,
    price: Option<i32>,
    category: Option<String>,
}

pub async fn get_product(
    State(conn): State<DatabaseConnection>,
    Query(params): Query<UpsertModel>,
) -> Result<Json<Vec<Model>>, AppError> {
    let mut condition = Condition::all();
    if let Some(id) = params.id {
        condition = condition.add(Column::Id.eq(id))
    }
    if let Some(title) = params.title {
        condition = condition.add(Column::Title.contains(title));
    }
    if let Some(price) = params.price {
        condition = condition.add(Column::Price.eq(price));
    }
```

```
    if let Some(category) = params.category {
        condition = condition.add(Column::Category.contains(category));
    }
    match Entity::find().filter(condition).all(&conn).await {
        Ok(products) => Ok(Json(products)),
        Err(_) => Err(AppError::new(
            StatusCode::INTERNAL_SERVER_ERROR,
            "Database error",
        )),
    }
}
```

post_product and put_product follow the same pattern. post_product creates an ActiveModel, inserts it, and returns the result as JSON:

```
pub async fn post_product(
    State(conn): State<DatabaseConnection>,
    Json(product): Json<UpsertModel>,
) -> Result<Json<Model>, AppError> {
    let new_product = ActiveModel {
        id: ActiveValue::NotSet,
        title: ActiveValue::Set(product.title.unwrap()),
        price: ActiveValue::Set(product.price.unwrap()),
        category: ActiveValue::Set(product.category.unwrap()),
    };

    match new_product.insert(&conn).await {
        Ok(inserted_product) => Ok(Json(inserted_product)),
        Err(_) => Err(AppError::new(
            StatusCode::INTERNAL_SERVER_ERROR,
            "Database error",
        )),
    }
}
```

put_product finds the record by ID, then creates an ActiveModel using new values from the request or keeping existing values for unmodified fields:

```rust
pub async fn put_product(
    State(conn): State<DatabaseConnection>,
    Json(product): Json<UpsertModel>,
) -> Result<Json<Model>, AppError> {
    let result = match Entity::find_by_id(product.id.unwrap()).
    one(&conn).await {
        Ok(result) => result.ok_or(AppError::new(StatusCode::NOT_FOUND,
        "Product not found"))?,
        Err(_) => {
            return Err(AppError::new(
                StatusCode::INTERNAL_SERVER_ERROR,
                "Database error",
            ))
        }
    };

    let new_product = ActiveModel {
        id: ActiveValue::Set(result.id),
        title: ActiveValue::Set(product.title.unwrap_or(result.title)),
        price: ActiveValue::Set(product.price.unwrap_or(result.price)),
        category: ActiveValue::Set(product.category.unwrap_or(result.
        category)),
    };

    match new_product.update(&conn).await {
        Ok(updated_product) => Ok(Json(updated_product)),
        Err(_) => Err(AppError::new(
            StatusCode::INTERNAL_SERVER_ERROR,
            "Database error",
        )),
    }
}
```

delete_product also uses UpsertModel for automatic type conversion. It finds records using complex filters before deletion:

```rust
pub async fn delete_product(
    State(conn): State<DatabaseConnection>,
    Query(params): Query<UpsertModel>,
) -> Result<Json<&'static str>, AppError> {
    let mut condition = Condition::any();

    if let Some(id) = params.id {
        condition = condition.add(Column::Id.eq(id));
    }
    if let Some(title) = params.title {
        condition = condition.add(Column::Title.contains(title));
    }
    if let Some(price) = params.price {
        condition = condition.add(Column::Price.eq(price));
    }
    if let Some(category) = params.category {
        condition = condition.add(Column::Category.contains(category));
    }

    let product = match Entity::find().filter(condition).one(&conn).await {
        Ok(product) => product.ok_or(AppError::new(StatusCode::NOT_FOUND,
        "Product not found"))?,
        Err(_) => {
            return Err(AppError::new(
                StatusCode::INTERNAL_SERVER_ERROR,
                "Database error",
            ))
        }
    };

    match product.delete(&conn).await {
        Ok(_) => Ok(Json("Deleted")),
        Err(_) => Err(AppError::new(
            StatusCode::INTERNAL_SERVER_ERROR,
```

```
            "Database error",
        )),
    }
}
```

3.7.3. Routing

Connect all handlers in main.rs by chaining them to their routes. All handlers share the database connection pool through State, providing CRUD operations at /users, /category, and /product:

```
let app = Router::new()
    .route(
        "/users",
        get(get_user)
            .post(post_user)
            .put(put_user)
            .delete(delete_user),
    )
    .route(
        "/category",
        get(get_category)
            .post(post_category)
            .delete(delete_category),
    )
    .route(
        "/product",
        get(get_product)
            .post(post_product)
            .put(put_product)
            .delete(delete_product),
    )
    .with_state(conn);
```

3.8. Trying DBeaver

Let's connect to PostgreSQL using DBeaver from Chapter 1. Launch DBeaver to see the screen in Figure 3-13.

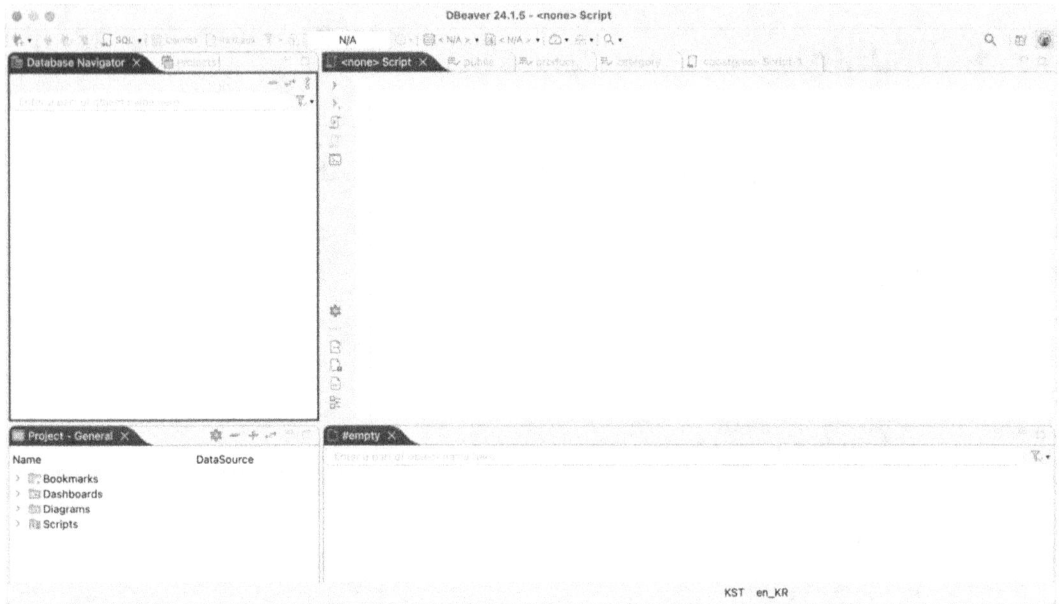

Figure 3-13. *DBeaver Main Screen*

Click the plug icon (top-left) to create a new connection.

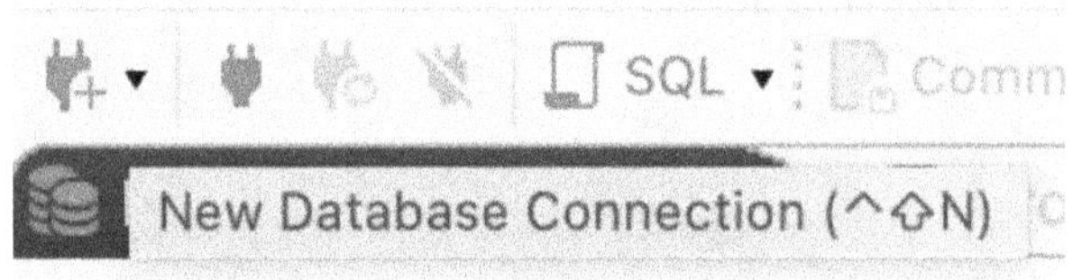

Figure 3-14. *Creating New Database Connection*

DBeaver supports many databases. Select PostgreSQL and click [Next].

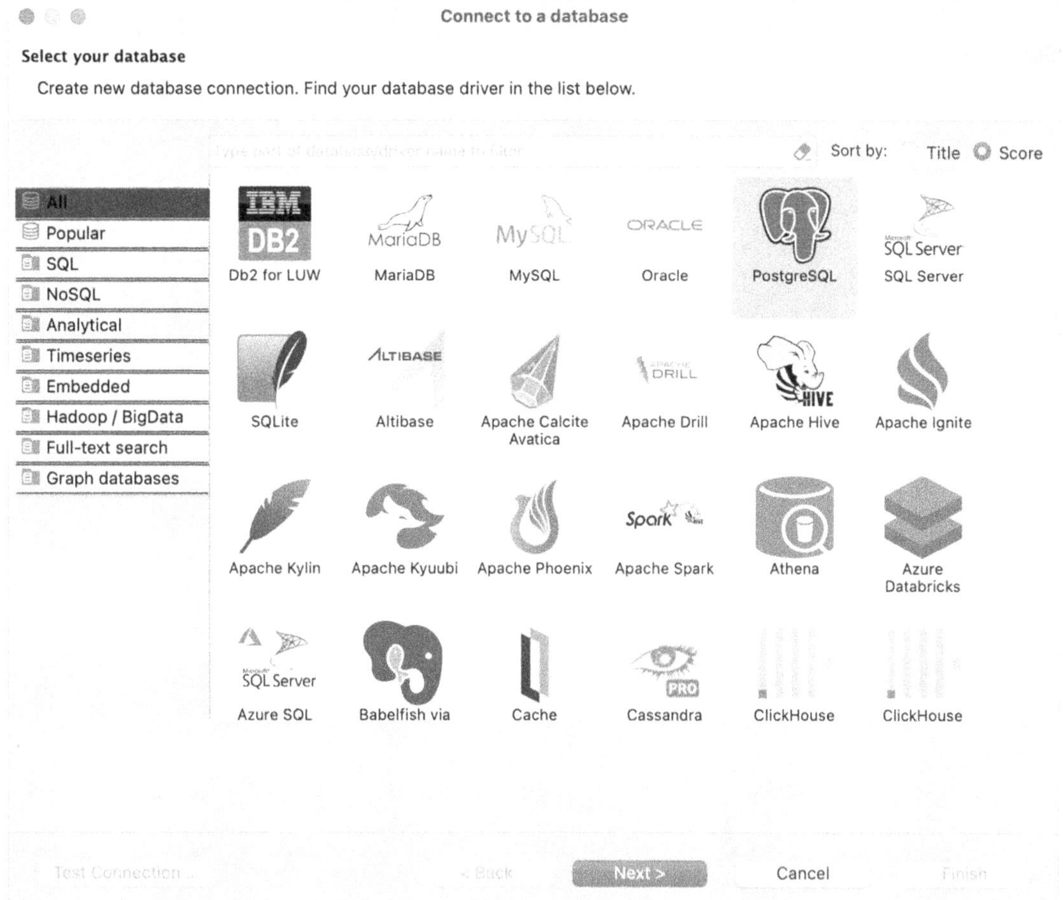

Figure 3-15. *Creating New Postgres Connection*

Use the same connection info from SeaORM:

```
postgres://axum:1234@localhost/axum
```

The server defaults to localhost:5432, so just enter

- Database: axum

- Username: axum

- Password: 1234

Figure 3-16. *Entering Postgres Axum Database Information*

Click Test Connection (bottom-left). If prompted, install the PostgreSQL driver.

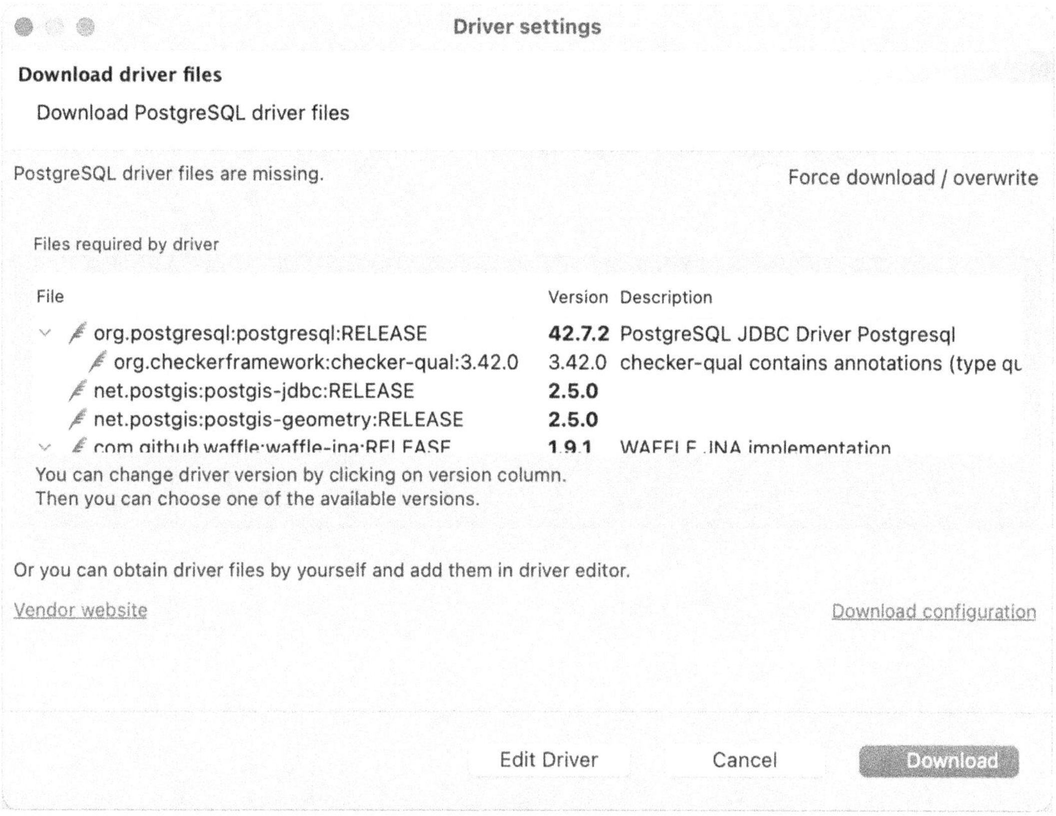

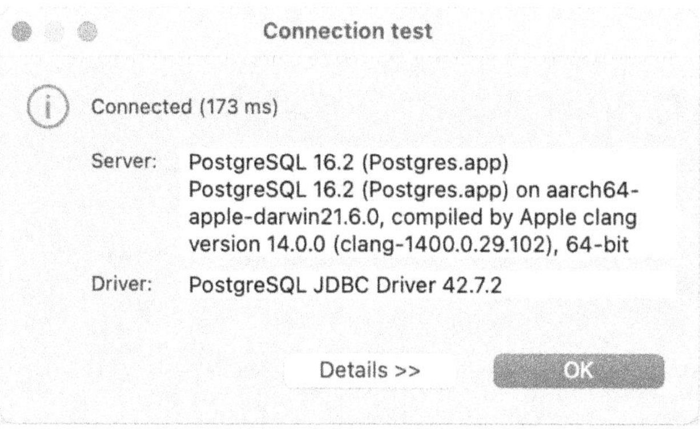

Figure 3-17. *Installing Postgres Connection Driver*

A success popup confirms the connection works.

Figure 3-18. *Connection Test Success Screen*

Click OK, then Finish. In the left panel, navigate to Databases ➤ axum ➤ Schemas ➤ public ➤ Tables. Double-click Tables to view your database tables.

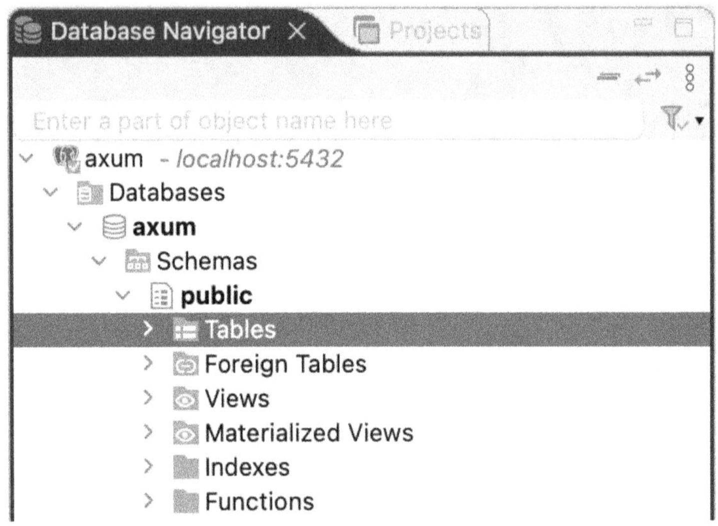

Figure 3-19. *Database Schema and Tables*

This displays table names and metadata.

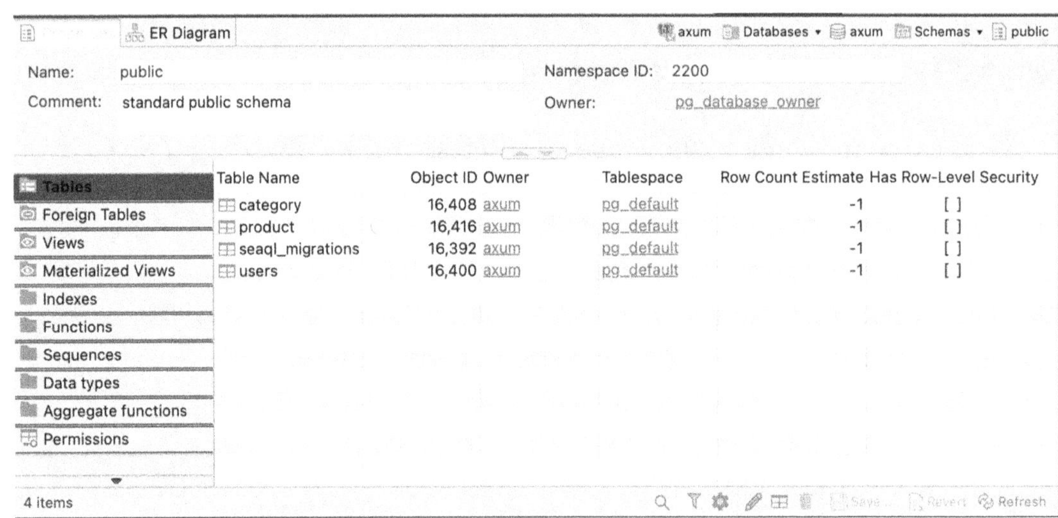

Figure 3-20. *Database Table Information*

Double-click users to see column details. This shows the same info as

```
SELECT * FROM information_schema.columns
WHERE table_name = 'users';
```

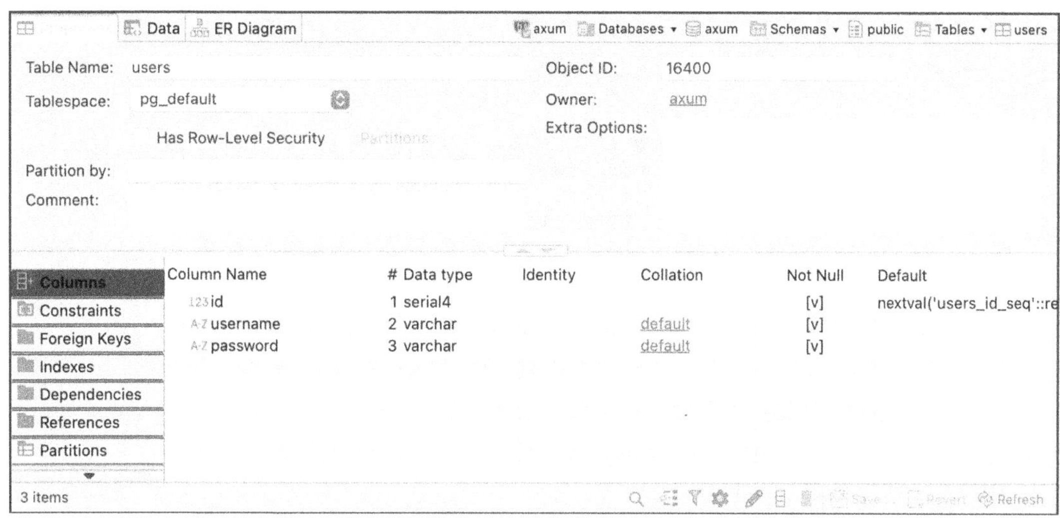

Figure 3-21. *Users Table Information*

Click the Data tab to view table records with id, username, and password columns.

Figure 3-22. *Table Data*

To run SQL queries, click the SQL button in the top toolbar.

Figure 3-23. *Creating New SQL File*

Write your query and click the Execute button (triangle icon):

```
SELECT * FROM users;
```

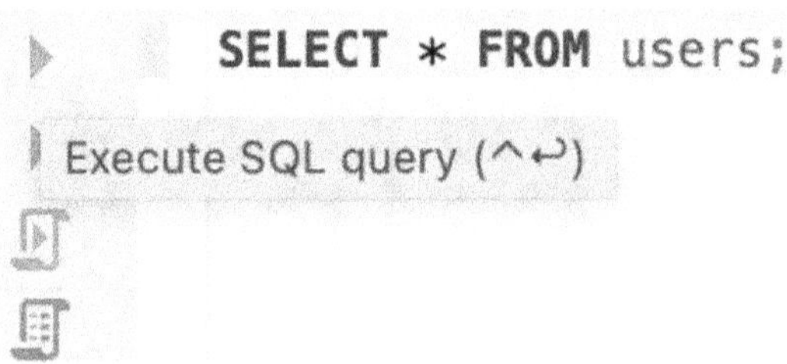

Figure 3-24. *SQL Query Execution*

Results appear below the editor, matching what you saw in the Data tab.

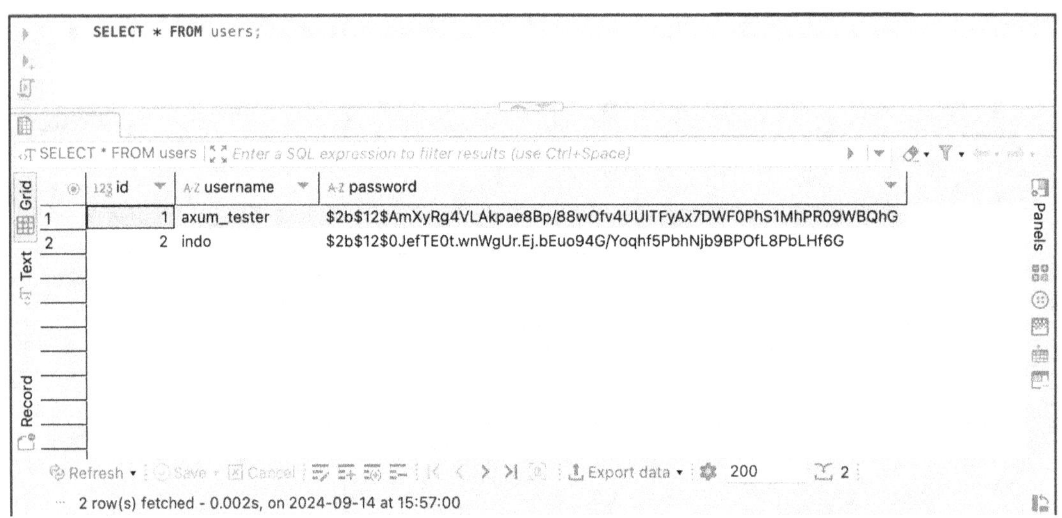

Figure 3-25. *SQL Query Execution Results*

DBeaver offers many more features for table management and user administration. Check the official documentation [1] to explore its full capabilities.

3.9. Review

- Define database schemas and run migrations with SeaORM

- Build type-safe queries using SeaQuery

- Manage connections efficiently with database pools

- Build APIs with CRUD operations by defining endpoints and connecting routing

- Query databases and execute SQL queries using DBeaver

Reference

1.   https://dbeaver.com/docs/dbeaver/

CHAPTER 4

Tower Middleware

When developing backend servers, requests from clients often require various preprocessing tasks before executing the actual logic, or responses may need post-processing. Instead of writing this common work in every function, you can use middleware that sits between the client and server to intercept and process requests and responses. In this chapter, we'll explore how to implement middleware using tower.

Learning Points

- The importance of middleware

- Using tower for fast and convenient middleware implementation

- Implementing custom middleware layers

4.1. What Is Middleware?

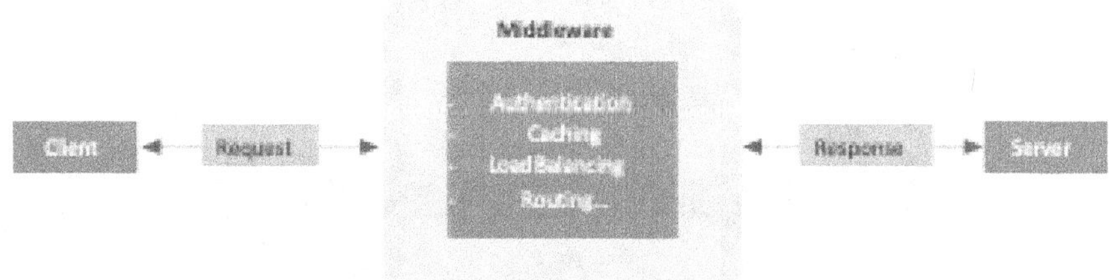

Figure 4-1. *Middleware Operating Principles*

Middleware is a layer positioned between clients and servers that performs various functions. In other words, when a client sends a request to a server, or when a server sends a response to a client, middleware can intercept requests and responses in the middle to perform various functions. Some frequently used features among the many tasks middleware can perform include

© Indo Yoon 2026
I. Yoon, *Beginning Axum*, https://doi.org/10.1007/979-8-8688-2631-3_4

- **Authentication**: Verifies whether the client is a pre-authenticated user

- **Authorization**: Verifies whether the request sent by the client is permitted, for example, restricting access so that only specific users can access certain endpoints

- **Caching**: Caches and reuses responses to requests sent by clients

- **Logging**: Records logs of requests sent by clients and responses sent by servers

Because middleware operates independently of the web server, it's largely unrelated to the web server's structure. You can add or remove middleware like inserting and removing blocks from a web server. This process of adding or removing middleware is also called manipulating the middleware stack. Therefore, rather than building middleware yourself, it's common to use pre-built functionality.

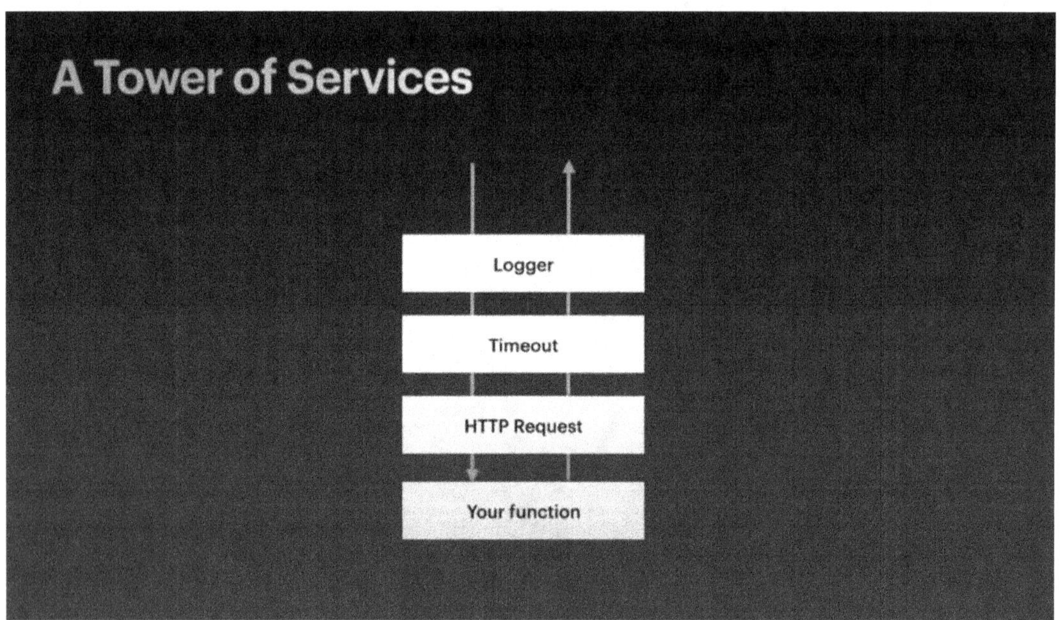

Figure 4-2. *Tower Crate*

Tower is a middleware crate that operates on the tokio runtime, just like Axum. It's named "tower" because you can stack multiple middleware like a tower. Tower is a crate that allows you to register asynchronous functions implementing the Service trait as middleware in your app. These asynchronous functions are implemented to receive requests and then return responses or errors. Each middleware is modularized like blocks, making them reusable at any time, and adding or removing middleware is very simple.

From the very beginning of Axum's development, compatibility with tower was prioritized, so you can integrate tower very smoothly within your code. Of course, tower isn't limited to Axum—it can be used with other backend frameworks as well.

4.2. Adding Middleware Layers

Tower-http is a crate that provides HTTP-specific middleware and utilities built on top of tower. tower-http includes various middleware that are generally useful when building HTTP servers and clients. Layers are used to add middleware hierarchically to Axum applications. Using layers, you can simply add new middleware to your application. The two layers we'll use in this chapter are as follows:

- **TraceLayer** adds logging for requests and responses. It supports both regular HTTP requests and gRPC.

- **TimeoutLayer** adds time limits for requests.

Other frequently used major layers include the following:

- **CompressionLayer** and **DecompressionLayer** can compress or decompress response bodies.

- **FollowRedirectLayer** automatically performs redirections.

Now add the following dependencies to your project. tracing and tracing-subscriber are crates for logging, needed when adding TraceLayer as middleware.

```
tower = { version = "0.5", features = ["full"] }
tower-http = { version = "0.6", features = ["full"] }
tracing = "0.1.40"
tracing-subscriber = { version = "0.3.18", features = ["env-filter"] }
```

4.2.1. Timeout Layer

In backend services, there are cases where you load data through database connections or receive data through third-party APIs. If there's a problem with external dependencies like databases or third-party APIs that causes data loading to take too long, it's more efficient to set a time limit and consider it a failure if data doesn't arrive within that time, rather than waiting indefinitely for data to arrive. From the client's perspective, it's also better to know that there's a time limit on the API and only need to wait until that time, rather than waiting continuously in a state where they don't know when the API call will finish. Let's add a timeout layer that terminates requests if they aren't processed within a certain time.

Add the following two lines to the beginning of main.rs.

```rust
use std::time::Duration;
use tower_http::timeout::TimeoutLayer;
```

std::time::Duration is a struct representing time spans or intervals. You can create Duration instances using methods like from_secs(), from_millis(), and new(), and perform various operations like adding, subtracting, or comparing times between instances of the same type. TimeoutLayer is the struct that can actually set time limits.

Then add the following at the end of app.

```rust
let app = Router::new()
    ...
    .layer(TimeoutLayer::new(Duration::from_millis(3000)));
```

To add a middleware layer, you simply need to use the layer method. As explained earlier, the layer method can add any struct implementing the Service trait as a layer. Duration::from_millis takes milliseconds as input, meaning we're setting the request processing time limit to 3000ms, or 3 seconds. Now any requests taking more than 3 seconds will automatically be treated as timeouts.

Let's verify that the timeout layer actually works as expected. We'll use tokio::time::sleep to intentionally make request processing take more than 5 seconds, deliberately slowing down handler execution. Add the following to the first line of delete_user in users.rs.

```
pub async fn delete_user(
    State(conn): State<DatabaseConnection>,
    Query(params): Query<HashMap<String, String>>,
) -> Json<&'static str> {
    tokio::time::sleep(tokio::time::Duration::from_secs(5)).await; // Added
    ...
}
```

When calling the DELETE method to the /users path in Insomnia, since delete_ user's execution time is 5 seconds (longer than 3 seconds), you'll receive a 408 Request Timeout response as shown below.

```
HTTP/1.1 408 Request Timeout
content-length: 0
date: Sun, 22 Oct 2023 06:34:42 GMT
```

Don't forget to delete the tokio::time::sleep line after testing.

4.2.2. Logging Layer

Rust's logging ecosystem is designed to be modular and highly flexible. Like several other modern languages, it is split into two distinct parts: **log facades** and **logging libraries**.

The facades—most notably the built-in log crate—define a common interface (or "facade") that allows developers to instrument their code with log macros without worrying about the specific output format or destination. The logging libraries, on the other hand, act as the backends that actually record and output those logs to the console, files, or external services.

While the ecosystem offers various implementations tailored to different needs, the **tracing** ecosystem has largely become the de facto standard, particularly within the asynchronous Rust landscape. Although it introduces additional layers of power and sophistication, tracing provides invaluable diagnostic capabilities for complex applications, making it the preferred choice for modern Rust development.

However, note that the tracing crate doesn't just support logging—it provides additional features like application state monitoring. Therefore, if you only want simple logging functionality, we recommend exploring other crates.

Add the following to the beginning of main.rs. Here, we use the default format and configure the log level to be read from environment variables. Add dotenvy::dotenv(). ok(); to read environment variables from the .env file.

```rust
use tower_http::trace::TraceLayer;
use tracing::info;
use tracing_subscriber::{fmt, prelude::*, EnvFilter};

#[tokio::main]
async fn main() {
    dotenvy::dotenv().ok();

    tracing_subscriber::registry()
        .with(fmt::layer())
        .with(EnvFilter::from_default_env())
        .init();
```

Set the RUST_LOG environment variable that configures the logging level in the .env file to debug level as follows:

```
RUST_LOG=debug
```

Now change all println! macros to info! macros.

```rust
#[tokio::main]
async fn main() {
    dotenvy::dotenv().ok();

    tracing_subscriber::registry()
        .with(fmt::layer())
        .with(EnvFilter::from_default_env())
        .init();

    info!("Connecting to DB...");
    let conn = init_db().await;

    info!("Starting server...");
    let app = Router::new()
        ...
}
```

You can use TraceLayer to automatically log HTTP requests and responses. Add the following at the end of app.

```
...
.layer(TraceLayer::new_for_http());
```

Now when you call GET /users, you can see logs being recorded as shown below. The reason for using logging middleware is that it's far more convenient than manually logging. When you manually log, you need to write the logging code yourself, which can make your code messy if you have a lot of logging. Additionally, logs added by developers are related to application logic, so they don't include information about HTTP requests and responses. Using logging middleware automatically logs information about HTTP requests and responses, making it very useful when debugging applications.

```
2023-10-22T06:55:14.741756Z INFO axum_project: Connecting to DB...
2023-10-22T06:55:14.758557Z INFO axum_project: Starting server...
2023-10-22T06:55:18.510396Z DEBUG hyper::proto::h1::io: parsed 3 headers
2023-10-22T06:55:18.510437Z DEBUG hyper::proto::h1::conn: incoming body
is empty
2023-10-22T06:55:18.510651Z DEBUG request{method=GET uri=/
users?id=1 version=HTTP/1.1}: tower_http::trace::on_request: started
processing request
2023-10-22T06:55:18.514643Z INFO request{method=GET uri=/users?id=1
version=HTTP/1.1}: sqlx::query: summary="SELECT \"users\".\"id\",
\"users\".\"username\", \"users\".\"password\" …" db.statement="\n\
nSELECT\n \"users\".\"id\",\n \"users\".\"username\",\n
\"users\".\"password\"\nFROM\n \"users\"\nWHERE\n \"users\".\"id\" = $1\n"
rows_affected=1 rows_returned=1 elapsed=1.692875ms
2023-10-22T06:55:18.514911Z DEBUG request{method=GET uri=/users?id=1
version=HTTP/1.1}: tower_http::trace::on_response: finished processing
request latency=4 ms status=200
2023-10-22T06:55:18.515113Z DEBUG hyper::proto::h1::io: flushed 154 bytes
```

4.2.2.1. Learn More: Log Levels

Log levels indicating the importance of logs are most commonly divided into five levels as follows. Error is the highest level. Trace is the lowest level.

- **Error**: Used to record error events requiring attention. Generally events that interfere with normal program execution.

- **Warn**: Used to record warning events that could potentially be problematic. Things that don't interfere with program execution but hint at some kind of problem.

- **Info**: Used to record informational messages highlighting application progress. Records major runtime events that are useful to know.

- **Debug**: Used to record low-priority diagnostic information useful for debugging.

- **Trace**: Used to record very detailed diagnostic data. Records information like function calls.

The Trace level contains a lot of supplementary information, making the log volume very large. Therefore, it's only used in specific situations, such as when you need to identify problems in low-level code. Typically, development or test environments record up to Debug level, while production environments record up to Info level logs. If you don't want to see Debug-level logs in your Axum application, you can change the RUST_LOG environment variable to info.

```
RUST_LOG=info
```

4.2.3. Compression Layer

Some servers or clients may have features that block request or response bodies that are too large. Additionally, since text is transmitted as byte streams, processing large text can take a lot of time for computers to restore byte streams to strings or vice versa. Therefore, when exchanging large amounts of data, clients can include Accept-Encoding in request headers, and servers can indicate compression through Content-Encoding headers in response headers.

Additionally, these headers specify which compression method to use as shown below. When a compression method is specified in the client request, the response body is sent using this method. Here, we configured it to use Gzip as the compression method.

```
Accept-Encoding: gzip
```

Compression methods vary depending on the features of the tower-http crate:

- compression-br: Brotli

- compression-deflate: Deflate

- compression-gzip: Gzip

- compression-zstd: Zstd

To add a compression layer, you must first import the module.

```rust
use tower_http::compression::CompressionLayer;
```

Then simply add one line of layer at the end.

```rust
...
.layer(TimeoutLayer::new(Duration::from_millis(1000)))
.layer(TraceLayer::new_for_http())
.layer(CompressionLayer::new());
```

The reason you need to add the layer at the end is that the order of adding middleware is important. Each middleware is structured to wrap all previously added middleware. Therefore, when a request comes from a client, it moves from the outermost layer (the last added layer) to the innermost layer (the first added layer), then a response is generated in the handler, and this response moves to the innermost layer again, then goes through the final layer to be delivered to the client.

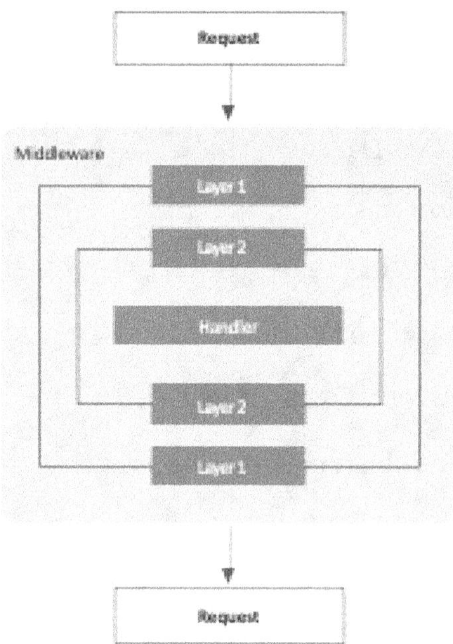

Figure 4-3. *Middleware Operating Principles*

For this reason, CompressionLayer is often added at the bottom of the middleware stack. This is because it compresses response bodies, and ideally this should be done after all other middleware have processed and modified the response. Adding CompressionLayer in the middle of the stack means all middleware added after it will receive compressed responses, potentially causing unexpected results or errors.

Now let's compare sending large amounts of text data without compression vs. with compression to see how efficiently compression works. Please access the following link to download a text file. You can also access this book's GitHub code repository, go to the alice_in_wonderland.txt file under the rest-api folder, and click the [Raw] button in the upper right to download it.

```
https://raw.githubusercontent.com/Indosaram/axum-book-code/main/rest-
api/alice_in_wonderland.txt
```

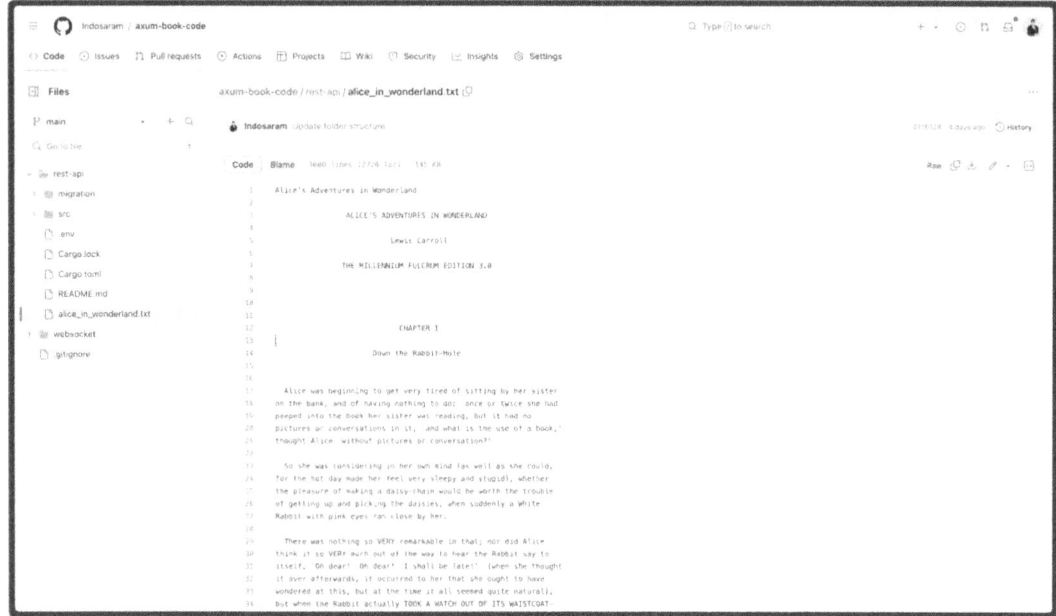

Figure 4-4. *Example File Page*

Add a text.rs file under the api folder. Enter the following content in this file. This code opens a file stream to load a text file as a string.

```rust
pub async fn text() -> String {
    tokio::fs::read_to_string("alice_in_wonderland.txt")
        .await
        .unwrap()
}
```

Add the text module to the last line of api/mod.rs.

```rust
pub mod auth;
pub mod category;
pub mod product;
pub mod users;
pub mod text; // Added
```

Finally, in main.rs, add use api::text::text; to import the text module, and add
.route("/text", get(text)) to the last line of routing.

```rust
...
use api::text::text; // Added
use db::init_db;

#[tokio::main]
async fn main() {
    dotenvy::dotenv().ok();
    tracing_subscriber::registry()
        .with(fmt::layer())
        .with(EnvFilter::from_default_env())
        .init();
    info!("Connecting to DB...");
    let conn = init_db().await;
    info!("Starting server...");
    let app = Router::new()
        .route("/users", get(get_users).put(put_user).delete(delete_user))
        ...
        .route("/auth/login", post(login))
        .route("/auth/signup", post(post_user))
        .route("/text", get(text)) // Added
        .with_state(conn)
        .layer(TimeoutLayer::new(Duration::from_millis(1000)))
        .layer(TraceLayer::new_for_http())
        .layer(CompressionLayer::new());
    let listener = tokio::net::TcpListener::bind("127.0.0.1:8000")
        .await
        .unwrap();
    axum::serve(listener, app).await.unwrap();
}
```

Now start the server and send a request using Insomnia as follows. The request address is /text. You must add Accept-Encoding: gzip to Headers to receive compressed data. The original text file size is 145.1KB, but the compressed file size is 52.5KB, reduced by about 63%. If you open the Console tab in the right panel, you can see the server sends a content-encoding: gzip header, which Insomnia reads to decompress the compressed data and display the text on screen.

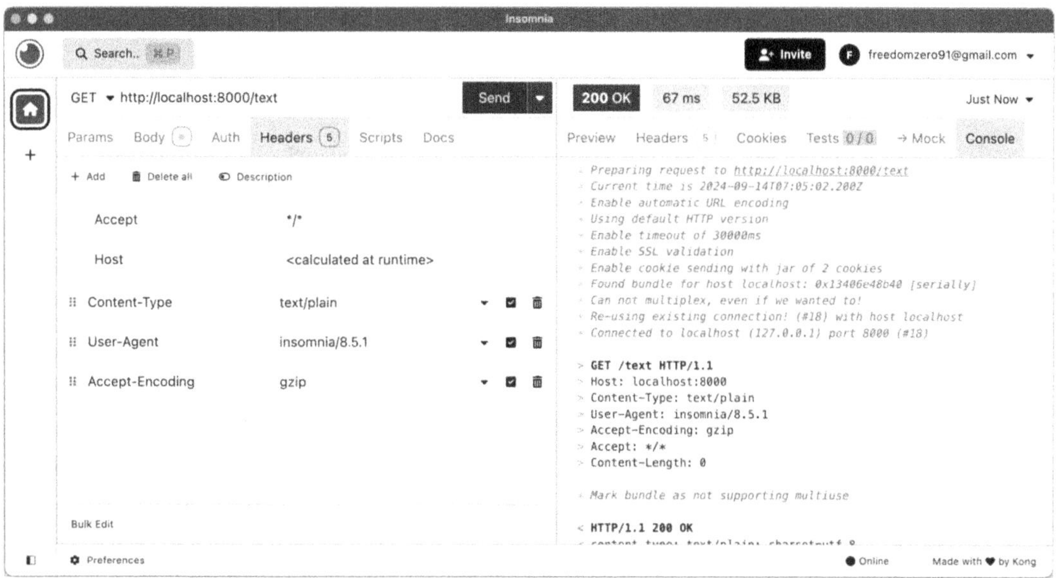

Figure 4-5. *Compressed Data Response*

If you send a request without using headers, you can see that the transmitted data size increases as shown in Figure 4-6.

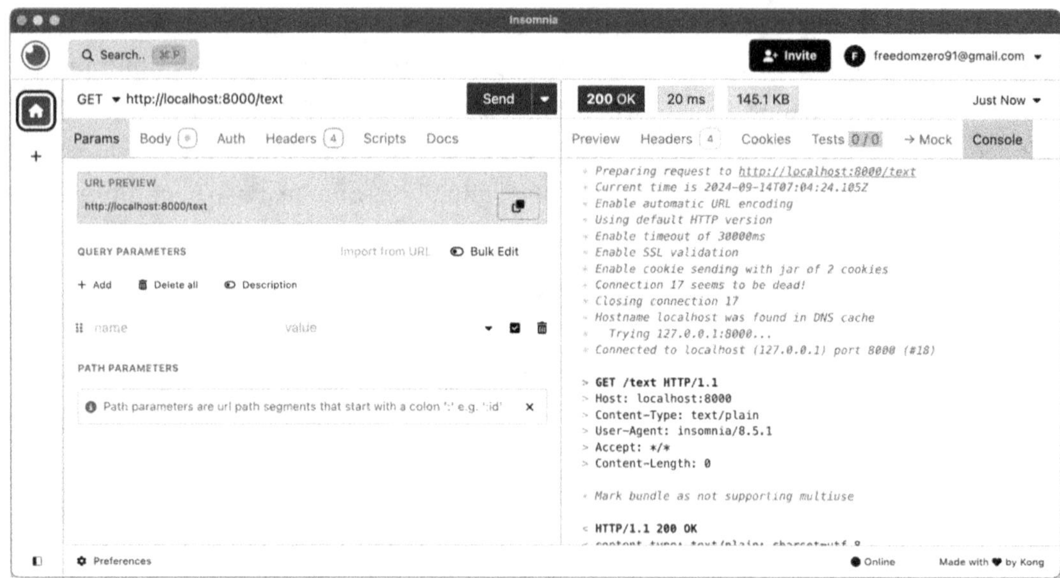

Figure 4-6. *Uncompressed Data Response*

When not compressing, the response time increases because the compression algorithm takes time to execute, but when file sizes are large or when servers and clients are physically far apart, sending compressed data of a smaller size is more efficient than the time spent compressing data, so there's no need to worry.

Note that even if you send an Accept-Encoding header with compression methods for features you haven't added, Axum won't generate errors. However, since data is transmitted uncompressed, specifying the correct compression method is important for efficient data delivery.

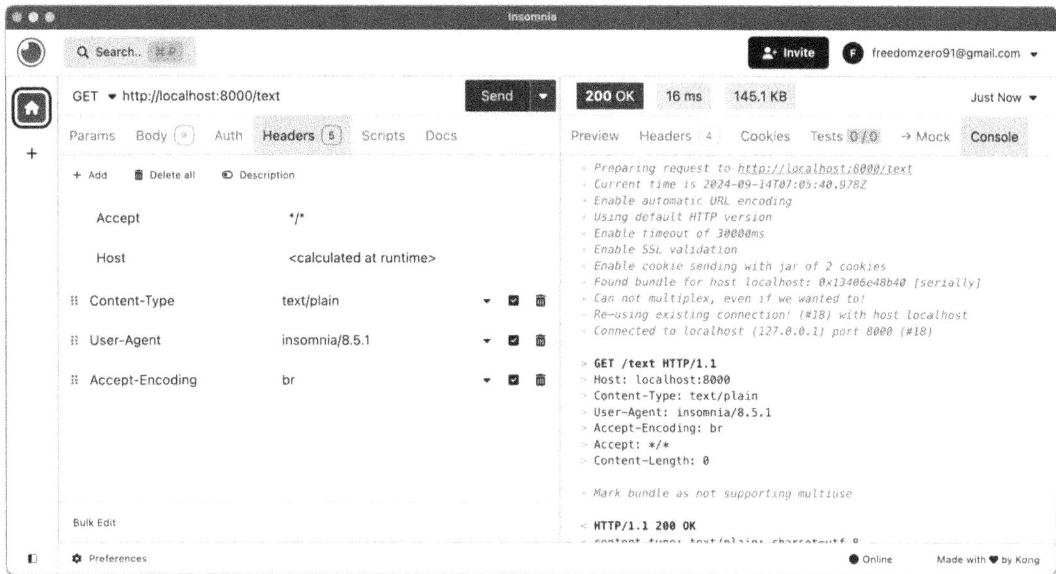

Figure 4-7. *Incorrect Compression Header Transmission*

4.3. Example: Creating a JWT Authentication Layer

Authentication is one of the critically important parts of API design. It's a method of restricting allowed users to only use allowed features and is a basic functionality for preventing indiscriminate API usage and responding to security threats. In APIs, when abbreviated to "Auth," it usually means Authorization.

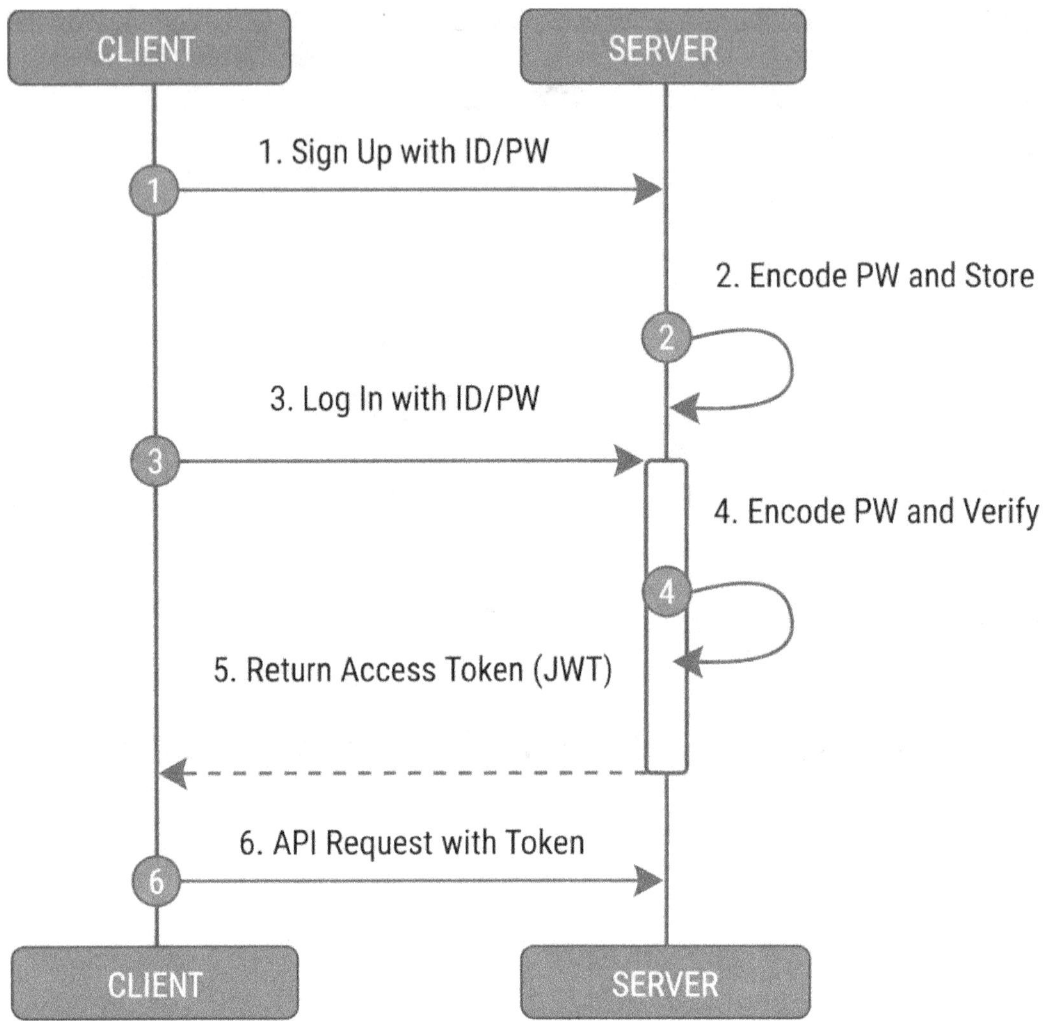

Figure 4-8. *JWT Authentication Operating Principles*

In the authentication layer, we'll implement a simplified JWT authentication method. Users sign up through the client with an ID and password. At this time, the password is encrypted and stored. When signup is complete, the client logs in using the ID and password. During login, the password entered by the user is encrypted using the same method as before, then checked to see if it matches the encrypted password stored in the database. If it matches, login succeeds, and the server issues a JWT token to the client. The client uses this token to send requests to the server. The server verifies that the user who sent the token is the owner of that token, then processes the request.

Create an auth folder to implement the authentication layer and create files as follows:

```
src/auth
├── app_error.rs
├── hash.rs
├── jwt.rs
└── mod.rs
```

Let's write app_error.rs first. Define an AppError struct to handle errors occurring in the app as follows. This struct has a code field representing the status code and a message field representing the error message. Since the AppError struct implements the IntoResponse trait, it can be converted to an axum Response and thus can be a type returned from handler functions. Also implementing From trait helps you to handle errors because ? operator will propagate the specific error types to AppError automatically.

Note   This AppError struct is similar to the one we defined in utils/app_error.rs in Chapter 3. Here, we create a separate version in the auth module to keep the authentication layer self-contained, but in a production application, you would typically share a single AppError definition across modules.

```rust
use axum::{http::StatusCode, response::IntoResponse, Json};

pub struct AppError {
    code: StatusCode,
    message: String,
}

impl AppError {
    pub fn new(code: StatusCode, message: impl Into<String>) -> Self {
        Self {
            code,
            message: message.into(),
        }
    }
}
```

```rust
impl IntoResponse for AppError {
    fn into_response(self) -> axum::response::Response {
        (self.code, Json(self.message.clone())).into_response()
    }
}

impl From<jsonwebtoken::errors::Error> for AppError {
    fn from(err: jsonwebtoken::errors::Error) -> Self {
        use jsonwebtoken::errors::ErrorKind;

        match err.kind() {
            ErrorKind::InvalidToken
            | ErrorKind::InvalidSignature
            | ErrorKind::ExpiredSignature => {
                AppError::new(StatusCode::UNAUTHORIZED, "Not
                authenticated!")
            }
            _ => {
                tracing::error!("JWT Validation Error: {:?}", err);
                AppError::new(StatusCode::INTERNAL_SERVER_ERROR, "Internal
                server error")
            }
        }
    }
}
```

Next, we'll define password encryption and password verification functions in hash.
rs. Add the following dependency:

```rust
bcrypt = "0.15.0"
```

The bcrypt crate provides encryption functionality, and using hash and verify allows
you to simply perform password encryption and verification respectively. Here, hash_
password and verify_password wrap these two functions to return AppError.

The hash_password function encrypts the input password and returns a hash
value. This function uses the bcrypt library to securely hash passwords. Hash values
are encrypted forms that cannot be decrypted from passwords. The COST constant

determines the encryption strength of the bcrypt library. Higher values provide stronger encryption but can slow down processing speed. You can choose an appropriate value to balance security and performance. Values between 10-12 are typically chosen, and 12 or higher indicates very high encryption strength.

The verify_password function compares the input password in plaintext form and the encrypted password hash to check if they match. This function uses the bcrypt library to verify the validity of hash values. It returns true if the password and hash match, otherwise returns false.

```rust
use super::app_error::AppError;
use axum::http::StatusCode;
use bcrypt::{hash, verify};
use tracing::error;

const COST: u32 = 12;

pub fn hash_password(password: &str) -> Result<String, AppError> {
    hash(password, COST).map_err(|err| {
        error!("Error hashing password: {:?}", err);
        AppError::new(StatusCode::INTERNAL_SERVER_ERROR, "Error securing
        password")
    })
}

pub fn verify_password(password: &str, hash: &str) -> Result<bool,
AppError> {
    verify(password, hash).map_err(|err| {
        error!("Error verifying password: {:?}", err);
        AppError::new(
            StatusCode::INTERNAL_SERVER_ERROR,
            "The was a problem verifying your password",
        )
    })
}
```

In jwt.rs, we'll define functions to create and verify JWTs. Add the following dependencies:

```
jsonwebtoken = "9.2.0"
chrono = "0.4.31"
lazy_static = "1.4.0"
```

The jsonwebtoken crate allows you to simply perform JWT creation and verification functions. The jsonwebtoken crate provides encode and decode functions that perform JWT creation and verification, respectively. For token information, we created a new Claims struct containing token expiration time exp and username. Since we need to serialize the token to JWT format and later deserialize from JWT back to the struct, we need to add the Serialize and Deserialize traits.

```rust
use super::app_error::AppError;
use axum::{
    http::{HeaderMap, Request, StatusCode},
    middleware::Next,
    response::Response,
    body::Body,
};
use chrono::Duration;
use jsonwebtoken::{decode, encode, DecodingKey, EncodingKey, Header,
Validation};
use serde::{Deserialize, Serialize};
use std::env;
use tracing::{debug, error};

#[derive(Serialize, Deserialize)]
pub struct Claims {
    exp: usize,
    username: String,
}
```

Here, the secret key SECRET_KEY for encryption is read from environment variables, but since environment variables can't be read at compile time, we can't create the SECRET_KEY constant in advance. Using the lazy_static! macro, you can execute code inside the macro at runtime and use the result to create the constant SECRET_KEY as a String type.

```rust
use lazy_static::lazy_static;

lazy_static! {
    static ref SECRET_KEY: String = env::var("SECRET_KEY").expect("SECRET_
    KEY must be set");
}
```

The create_token and validate_token functions wrap the encode and decode functions to return AppError. The create_token function takes a username as input and creates a JWT. This function proceeds with the following steps:

- **Set Token Expiration Time**: The value stored in the exp variable sets the expiration time to 1 hour after the current time (UTC).

- **Create Claims**: Creates a Claims struct containing username and expiration time information.

- **Set Header and Encryption Key**: Creates an encryption key object using the default header and secret key SECRET_KEY.

- **Encode Token**: Encodes the JWT using header, claims, and encryption key.

The create_token function is as follows:

```rust
pub fn create_token(username: String) -> Result<String, AppError> {
    let now = chrono::Utc::now();
    let expires_at = now + Duration::hours(1);
    let exp = expires_at.timestamp() as usize;
    let claims = Claims { exp, username };
    let token_header = Header::default();
    let key = EncodingKey::from_secret(SECRET_KEY.as_bytes());
    encode(&token_header, &claims, &key).map_err(|err| {
        error!("Error creating token: {:?}", err);
        AppError::new(
```

```
            StatusCode::INTERNAL_SERVER_ERROR,
            "There was an error, please try again later",
        )
    })
}
```

The validate_token function takes a JWT token string as input and verifies its validity. This function proceeds with the following steps:

- **Remove Token Bearer**: Removes the "Bearer" prefix from the token string

- **Set Decryption Key**: Creates a decryption key object using the secret key SECRET_KEY

- **Verify Token**: Verifies the token's validity using the token string, decryption key, and algorithm (HS256)

The following errors can occur during verification:

- **Invalid Token**: When the token format is wrong or corrupted

- **Invalid Signature**: When the token's signature doesn't match

- **Expired Token**: When the token's expiration time has passed

When such errors occur, AppError returns with HTTP status codes and appropriate error messages. If the user's token is valid and not expired, it returns the decrypted information. This claim information contains the expiration time and username from the Claims created by the create_token function.

```
pub fn validate_token(token: &str) -> Result<Claims, AppError> {
    let token_str = token.strip_prefix("Bearer ").unwrap_or(token);

    let key = DecodingKey::from_secret(SECRET_KEY.as_bytes());
    let validation = Validation::new(jsonwebtoken::Algorithm::HS256);

    let token_data = decode::<Claims>(token_str, &key, &validation)?;

    Ok(token_data.claims)
}
```

Note that how ? operator converts jsonwebtoken::Error into AppError.

Based on what we've written so far, we'll write the middleware to add to the application. The authenticate function extracts a token from headers, then verifies the token. If verification succeeds, it calls next.run(request).await to execute the next middleware. If verification fails, it returns AppError.

```rust
// `jwt.rs` continued
pub async fn authenticate(
    headers: HeaderMap,
    request: Request<Body>,
    next: Next,
) -> Result<Response, AppError> {
    if let Some(value) = headers.get("Authorization") {
        let token = value.to_str().map_err(|err| {
            error!("Error extracting token from headers: {:?}", err);
            AppError::new(StatusCode::INTERNAL_SERVER_ERROR, "Error
            reading token")
        })?;
        let claim = validate_token(token)?;
        debug!("Authenticated user: {}", claim.username);
        if claim.exp < (chrono::Utc::now().timestamp() as usize) {
            return Err(AppError::new(StatusCode::UNAUTHORIZED, "Token has
            expired"));
        }
        Ok(next.run(request).await)
    } else {
        Err(AppError::new(
            StatusCode::UNAUTHORIZED,
            "not authenticated!",
        ))
    }
}
```

Now add the auth.rs module to the api folder and enter the following content. We defined a new RequestUser struct to allow users to log in with ID and password.

```
use crate::entities::{prelude::Users, users::Column};
use crate::auth::app_error::AppError;
use crate::auth::hash::verify_password;
use crate::auth::jwt::create_token;
use axum::http::StatusCode;
use axum::{extract::State, Json};
use sea_orm::{ColumnTrait, DatabaseConnection, EntityTrait, QueryFilter};
use serde::{Deserialize, Serialize};

#[derive(Serialize, Deserialize)]
pub struct RequestUser {
    username: String,
    password: String,
}
```

In the login function, we receive RequestUser and use the username and password extracted from it to verify if the actual user information is correct. First, we use username to check if a user exists in the database's Users table. If the user exists, we use crate::auth ::hash::verify_password to verify the password's validity. At this point, we compare the password sent by the user with the password found in the database. The password stored in the database is encrypted, and the password sent by the user is plaintext, which is why the verify_password function is needed. If everything proceeds without problems up to this point, login succeeds, so we issue a JWT token.

```
pub async fn login(
    State(db): State<DatabaseConnection>,
    Json(request_user): Json<RequestUser>,
) -> Result<String, AppError> {
    let user = Users::find()
        .filter(Column::Username.eq(request_user.username))
        .one(&db)
        .await
        .map_err(|error| {
            eprintln!("Error getting user by username: {:?}", error);
```

```
                AppError::new(
                    StatusCode::INTERNAL_SERVER_ERROR,
                    "Error logging in, please try again later",
                )
            })?
            .ok_or_else(|| {
                AppError::new(
                    StatusCode::BAD_REQUEST,
                    "incorrect username and/or password",
                )
            })?;

    if !verify_password(&request_user.password, &user.password)? {
        return Err(AppError::new(
            StatusCode::UNAUTHORIZED,
            "incorrect username and/or password",
        ));
    }

    Ok(create_token(user.username.clone())?)
}
```

Now we finally return to main.rs. Add route_layer below the existing router as follows. We used middleware::from_fn to create a layer from the middleware authenticate. Then we add the login endpoint afterward. Now endpoints defined before route_layer require authentication. In other words, the login endpoint can be called without separate authentication.

```
use axum::middleware;
use api::auth::login;
use auth ::jwt::authenticate;

...
.route(
    "/product",
    get(get_product)
        .post(post_product)
```

```
        .put(put_product)
        .delete(delete_product),
)
.route_layer(middleware::from_fn(authenticate))
.route("/auth/login", post(login))
.with_state(conn)
...
```

As we proceed this far, one problem occurs. Previously when we handled user registration, that is, when adding new users to the database, we stored passwords as plaintext. Therefore, we can't issue tokens to existing users. Of course, we could manually encrypt existing user passwords, but here we'll delete all existing users. Also, to encrypt new user passwords, modify the post_user function in users.rs as follows:

```rust
pub async fn post_user(
    State(conn): State<DatabaseConnection>,
    Json(user): Json<UpsertModel>,
) -> Result<Json<Model>, AppError> {
    let hashed_password = hash_password(&user.password.unwrap())?;
    // Encrypt password
    let new_user = ActiveModel {
        id: ActiveValue::NotSet,
        username: ActiveValue::Set(user.username.unwrap()),
        password: ActiveValue::Set(hashed_password), // Store encrypted
                                                     password
    };
    let result = new_user.insert(&conn).await.unwrap();
    Ok(Json(result))
}
```

Let's create a new user, then log in with that user to get a token issued.

```
POST /auth/login HTTP/1.1
Host: localhost:8000
Content-Type: application/json
User-Agent: insomnia/8.2.0
Accept: */*
```

```
Content-Length: 44

{
    "username": "indo",
    "password": "indo"
}
```

Response

```
"eyJ0eXAiOiJKV1QiLCJhbGciOiJIUzI1NiJ9.eyJleHAiOjE2OTgyMzkONDIsInVzZXJuY
W1lIjoiaW5kbyJ9.4D1ddVMOv70CfroMV_zFOpcHAQ8m-YoSNUvm8Or9_Is"
```

By including the issued token in headers, you can send requests to
endpoints with authentication applied. If the token expires or you don't
provide a token, you'll receive a 401 Unauthorized response.

```
GET /users HTTP/1.1
Host: localhost:8000
User-Agent: insomnia/8.2.0
Authorization: Bearer eyJ0eXAiOiJKV1QiLCJhbGciOiJIUzI1NiJ9.eyJleHAiOjE2OT
gyMzkONDIsInVzZXJuYW1lIjoiaW5kbyJ9.4D1ddVMOv70CfroMV_zFOpcHAQ8m-
YoSNUvm8Or9_Is
Accept: */*
```

Response

```
[
    {
        "id": 1,
        "username": "indo",
        "password": "$2b$12$e8PmOr/MXGUetXfU9zbRoeh3RoZjxQfkJhOSx471
hmvYCuMRhOo4e"
    }
]
```

4.4. Review

- Middleware is a layer positioned between clients and servers that performs various functions.

- tower is a middleware crate that operates on the tokio runtime.

- tower-http is a crate that provides HTTP-specific middleware and utilities built on top of tower. tower-http includes various middleware that are generally useful when building HTTP servers and clients.

- Using layers, you can simply add new middleware to your application.

CHAPTER 5

WebSocket

WebSocket is a communication protocol that enables real-time, bidirectional communication between web servers and web browsers. Unlike HTTP, where clients receive responses only after sending requests, WebSocket allows continuous bidirectional communication once a connection is established. This makes it ideal for applications requiring real-time updates, such as online chat, collaborative editing, and real-time data visualization. In this chapter, we'll implement the WebSocket in Axum and explore in detail how to exchange messages between clients and servers.

Learning Points

- Understanding WebSocket

- Implementing single-connection and multi-connection WebSocket

5.1. Exploring WebSocket

© Indo Yoon 2026
I. Yoon, *Beginning Axum*, https://doi.org/10.1007/979-8-8688-2631-3_5

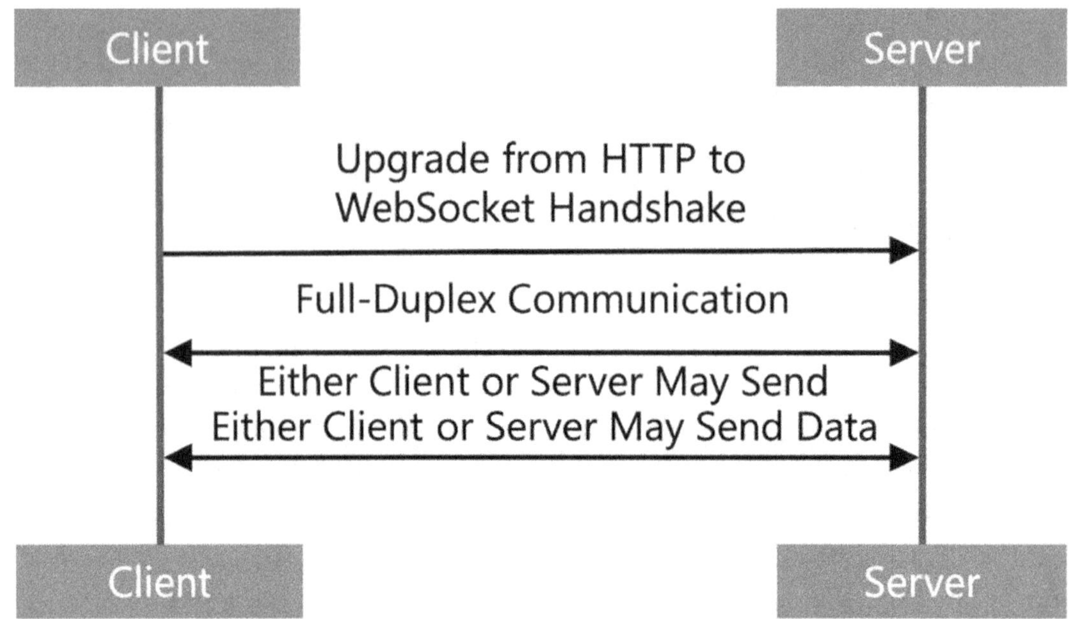

Figure 5-1. *WebSocket Operation Principles*

WebSocket operates by initiating a handshake between client and server. The handshake is a verification process that the client and server go through to establish a WebSocket connection. It's similar to confirming a connection when starting a phone call. A WebSocket connection initially starts based on the HTTP protocol, but after the connection is established, it switches to the WebSocket protocol according to the server's protocol switch request.

The handshake process proceeds as follows. First, the client sends a regular HTTP request while explicitly indicating through the Upgrade header that it's requesting a WebSocket connection. At this point, it also includes the Sec-WebSocket-Key header, transmitting a random string that the server can validate. For example, when sending an HTTP request to a socket server using Insomnia, you can see the following record in the Console:

```
> GET /ws HTTP/1.1
> user-agent: insomnia/9.3.3
> cookie: null;
> Sec-WebSocket-Version: 13
> Sec-WebSocket-Key: FNI2J4JxsCpjoEWaxIVc+Q==
> Connection: Upgrade
```

```
> Upgrade: websocket
> Sec-WebSocket-Extensions: permessage-deflate; client_max_window_bits
> Host: 127.0.0.1:3000
```

The server accepts this request and sends a response to the client. The response includes several headers. First, the Upgrade header indicates agreement to switch the protocol to WebSocket. The Connection header signals that the connection will be maintained rather than closed. Additionally, it responds with the Sec-WebSocket-Accept header containing a value calculated based on the Sec-WebSocket-Key sent by the client. Here's an example response from a socket server. The status code 101 Switching Protocols indicates that the protocol will now be changed:

```
< HTTP/1.1 101 Switching Protocols
< connection: upgrade
< upgrade: websocket
< sec-websocket-accept: 6l9K5GaV3H738zVYv/Aatw7tqYw=
< date: Fri, 06 Sep 2024 01:35:22 GMT
```

Once the handshake succeeds, the HTTP connection upgrades to a WebSocket connection, and from this point on, data is exchanged using the WebSocket protocol.

Using WebSocket allows you to avoid the inefficient polling method where clients repeatedly send requests to the server to receive new data, significantly reducing resource usage. In this way, WebSocket provides a more efficient and flexible communication method between clients and servers compared to traditional HTTP-based approaches. However, since WebSocket can introduce additional complexity and overhead, it's important to use it carefully only when truly necessary.

5.2. Using WebSocket

To use WebSocket in Axum, you need to add the following dependencies:

```
[package]
name = "websocket"
version = "0.1.0"
edition = "2021"
```

```
[dependencies]
axum = { version = "0.8", features = ["ws"] }
tokio = { version = "1.28.2", features = ["full"] }
futures-util = "0.3.28"
```

The futures-util crate is created to make asynchronous programming more convenient. It's based on the basic asynchronous programming model called futures, while providing various utility functions and types commonly used in actual development.

Expert Tip: At its core, a **Future** in Rust is a state machine representing a unit of work that may not have completed yet. Unlike "Promises" in other languages that begin executing immediately upon creation, Rust's futures are **lazy**: they do no work until they are explicitly **polled**.

The ecosystem is built on three pillars:

1. **The Standard Library (std::future::Future)**: Defines the fundamental interface. A future has a poll method that an executor calls to move the task toward completion. If the task is blocked (e.g., waiting for a network response), it returns Poll::Pending and yields control back to the executor.

2. **The Runtime (e.g., tokio)**: This is the **executor**. It manages a thread pool and is responsible for driving futures to completion by polling them. When a future is ready to make progress again, a **Waker** notifies the executor to put the future back in the queue.

3. **The Utility Crates (futures, futures-util)**: These crates provide the "glue" and convenience. While std defines what a future *is*, futures-util provides extension traits (like StreamExt) and macros (like join!) that allow you to compose multiple futures into complex asynchronous workflows.

Strictly speaking, std::future::Future is the common language everyone speaks, tokio is the engine that does the heavy lifting, and futures-util is the toolkit that makes working with those engines more ergonomic.

This time, a feature called ws has been added to the axum crate. As you can infer from the name, it's a feature that adds WebSocket functionality. This feature includes the ws extractor. Let's briefly explain a few extractors we'll be using.

Message represents data sent and received over a WebSocket connection. It can express various types of messages including text (Utf8Bytes), binary (Bytes), and connection closure (CloseFrame).

WebSocket is a bidirectional communication channel between client and server, serving as the conduit for sending and receiving Messages.

WebSocketUpgrade handles upgrading HTTP requests to WebSocket connections. When a client requests a connection, the server uses WebSocketUpgrade to create the connection. WebSocketUpgrade directly performs the handshake by inspecting HTTP headers.

Next, let's look at two traits used in futures_util. Thinking about the relationship between these two traits in terms of Figure 5-2 makes them easy to understand. When there's a pipe with an entrance and an exit, the flow of water is always created from the entrance side to the exit side. Similarly, you can think of data flowing from SinkExt to StreamExt.

Figure 5-2. *SinkExt and StreamExt*

The **SinkExt** trait extends the Sink trait to provide convenient methods for Sink operations. Sink plays the role of consuming data—receiving and processing or storing it. The **StreamExt** trait extends the Stream trait to provide convenient methods for Stream operations. You can think of Stream like a continuously flowing faucet that generates and sends out data.

Representative types of data that SinkExt and StreamExt handle include

- File reading and writing operations

- Data exchange between clients and servers through network sockets

- Inserting data into databases or reading query results

- Event streams such as user keyboard input and mouse clicks

Using these two capabilities, let's create simple socket communication code. First, in the main function, we set up the GET method for the ws endpoint. Since the client initially connects via HTTP before the protocol transitions to WebSocket, the GET method is needed:

```
use axum::{routing::get, Router};

#[tokio::main]
async fn main() {
    let app = Router::new().route("/ws", get(websocket_handler));
    let listener = tokio::net::TcpListener::bind("0.0.0.0:3000").await.
    unwrap();
    axum::serve(listener, app).await.unwrap();
}
```

Next, we define the handler to execute in this method. The websocket_handler handler function takes WebSocketUpgrade as an argument to perform the WebSocket handshake. If the handshake succeeds, the on_upgrade method registers an asynchronous callback function to execute when the connection is successfully established. If the handshake fails and the protocol doesn't transition, this handler won't execute at all:

```
use axum::{extract::WebSocketUpgrade, response::IntoResponse};

async fn websocket_handler(ws: WebSocketUpgrade) -> impl IntoResponse {
    ws.on_upgrade(handle_socket)
}
```

Finally, the handle_socket callback function receives the argument ws: WebSocket representing the WebSocket connection and performs the actual communication. ws.split() separates each from a WebSocket connection having the Sink + Stream trait to create a Sink and Stream. In other words, ws_tx serves as the Sink for sending data, and ws_rx serves as the Stream for receiving data.

Note   In reality, ws_tx is of type SplitSink<WebSocket, Message> and ws_rx is SplitStream, but we've represented them with simpler types for easier understanding.

In the while let loop, we use these two connections to continuously receive and process messages from clients, and send messages back to clients when necessary. Looking closely, you can see that ws_rx.next().await repeatedly reads the next data from the stream. If data exists, we send it to the client through ws_tx.send(). The types of data that can be sent are limited to those defined in the Message enum; here we're using the Text variant which takes a String as input to transmit data:

```rust
use axum::extract::ws::{Message, WebSocket};

async fn handle_socket(ws: WebSocket) {
    let (mut ws_tx, mut ws_rx) = ws.split();

    while let Some(Ok(msg)) = ws_rx.next().await {
        ws_tx
            .send(Message::Text(format!(
                "Message received: {}",
                msg.to_text().unwrap()
            ).into())
            .await
            .unwrap();
    }
}
```

The complete code for what we've explained so far is as follows:

```rust
use axum::{
    extract::{
        ws::{Message, WebSocket},
        WebSocketUpgrade,
    },
    response::IntoResponse,
    routing::get,
    Router,
```

```rust
};
use futures_util::{sink::SinkExt, stream::StreamExt};

#[tokio::main]
async fn main() {
    let app = Router::new().route("/ws", get(websocket_handler));
    let listener = tokio::net::TcpListener::bind("0.0.0.0:3000").await.
    unwrap();
    axum::serve(listener, app).await.unwrap();
}

async fn websocket_handler(ws: WebSocketUpgrade) -> impl IntoResponse {
    ws.on_upgrade(handle_socket)
}

async fn handle_socket(ws: WebSocket) {
    let (mut ws_tx, mut ws_rx) = ws.split();

    while let Some(Ok(msg)) = ws_rx.next().await {
        ws_tx
            .send(Message::Text(format!(
                "Message received: {}",
                msg.to_text().unwrap()
            ).into()))
            .await
            .unwrap();
    }
}
```

Now start the server with cargo run or cargo watch -x run, then connect to the WebSocket with Insomnia. Note that unlike before, when creating a new request, you need to create it as a WebSocket Request rather than an HTTP Request.

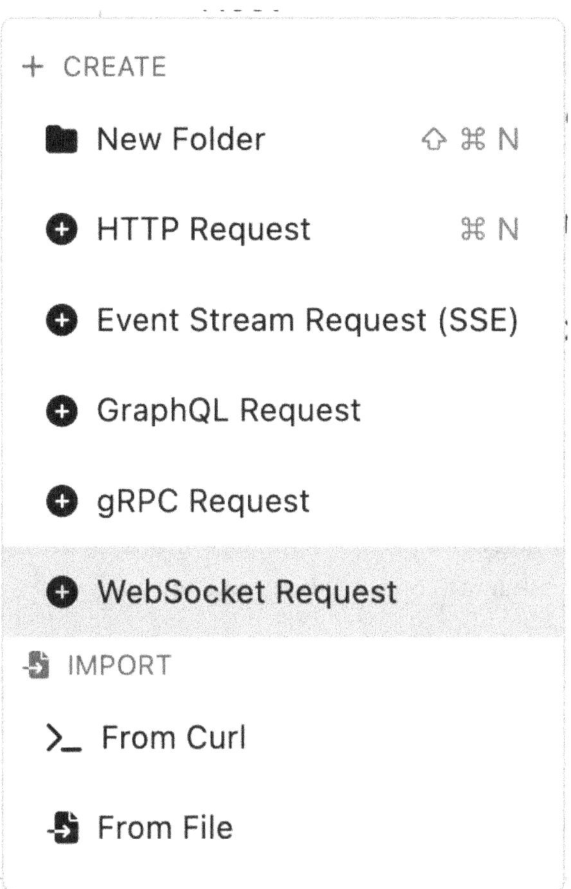

Figure 5-3. *Creating WebSocket Request*

Creating a request of this type automatically performs the process of upgrading the HTTP connection to WebSocket protocol later. If you send a request in Insomnia and receive a 400 Bad Request response, please make sure to check that the request type is WebSocket Request.

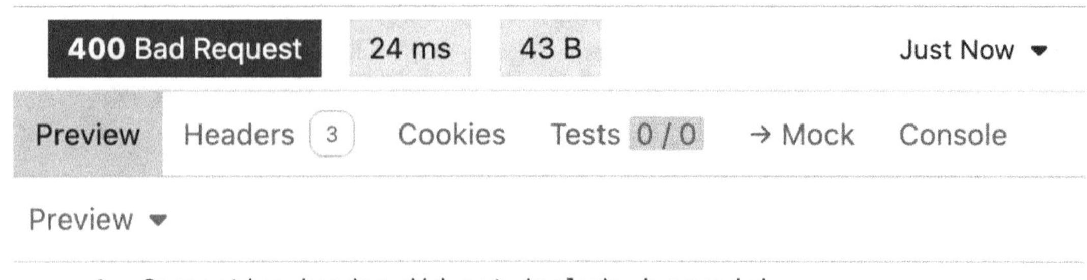

Figure 5-4. *Error Message When Creating Incorrect Request*

After correctly setting the protocol and endpoint, click the [Connect] button to enter the connected state as shown in Figure 5-5. The Events tab in the right panel shows the socket communication content. Upon initial connection, the message "Connected successfully" indicates that the connection started normally.

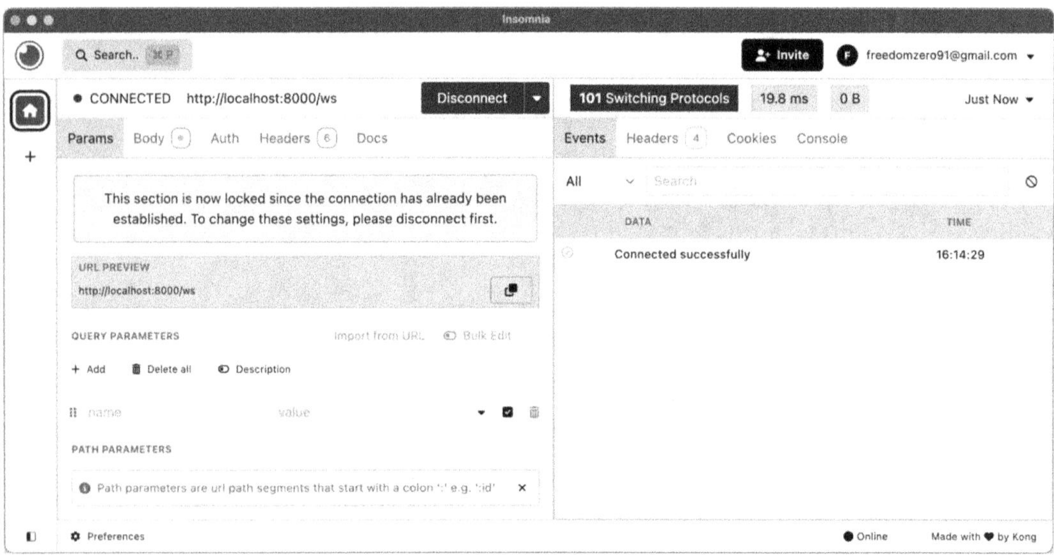

Figure 5-5. *Successful WebSocket Protocol Switch*

To send a new message to the server, write text in the Body tab of the left panel and click the [Send] button. Let's try sending the message "Hello Axum!".

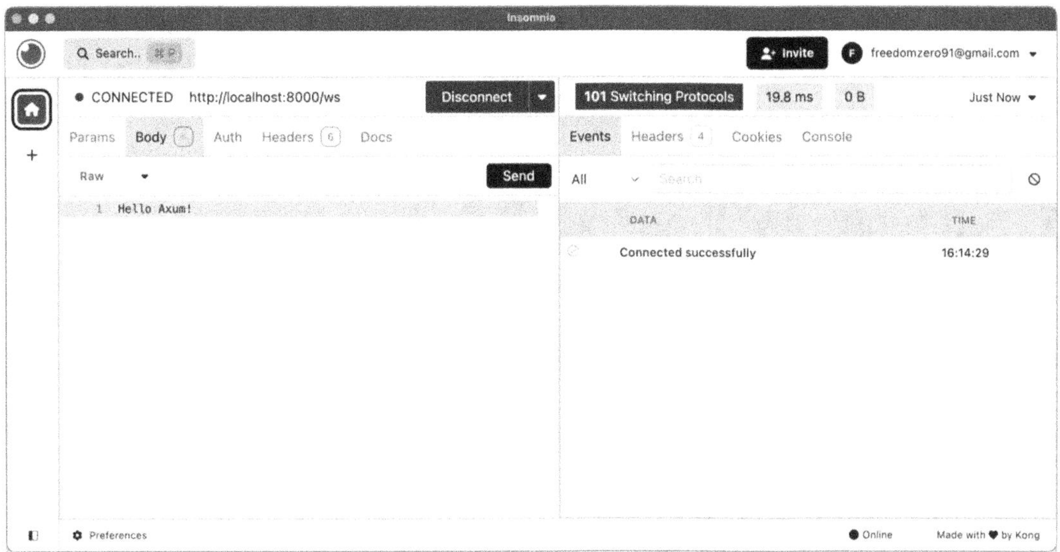

Figure 5-6. *Sending WebSocket Message*

The right panel displays your message along with an upward arrow indicating that the message is being sent to the server. The server receives the message and sends back the response "Message received: Hello Axum!".

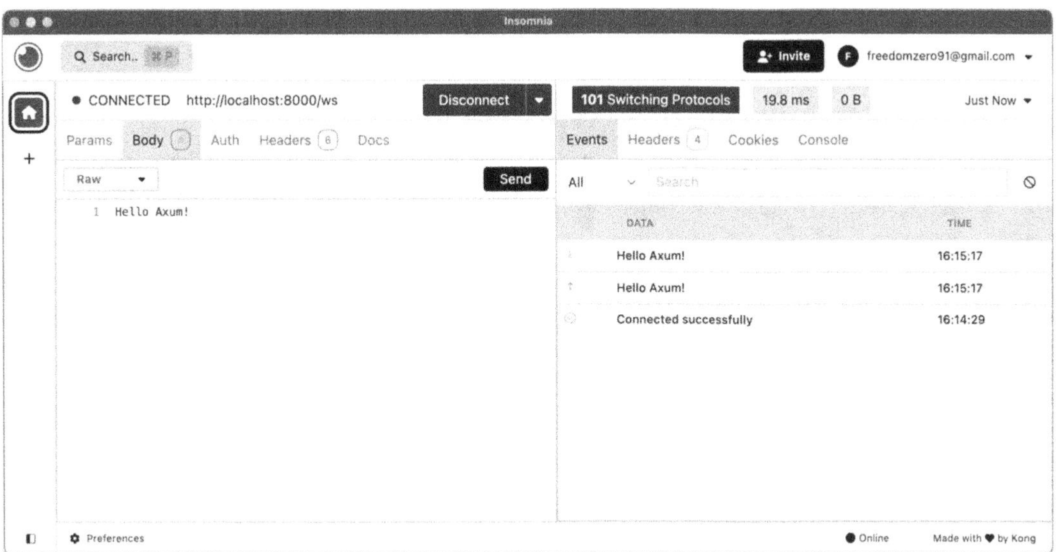

Figure 5-7. *Receiving WebSocket Message*

Now bidirectional communication continues unless either the server or client disconnects. To terminate the connection in Insomnia, click [Disconnect] at the top of the left panel.

5.3. Concurrent WebSocket Connections

In this section, let's consider a situation where multiple clients connect to the same server and exchange messages. Like chatting in a messenger program, we want to configure it so that when someone sends a message, everyone else can receive the same message. This situation involves multiple people sending messages and multiple people receiving messages, which can be easily implemented using tokio::sync::broadcast.

We create a communication channel using the broadcast::channel function. This function creates a multi-producer (Sender), multi-consumer (Receiver) channel where data sent by senders is delivered to all active receivers. These are used for different parts of a program to communicate with each other. Receivers receive messages, and Senders transmit messages. Note that the integer value represents the maximum number of messages that can be stored in the channel's buffer:

```
use tokio::sync::broadcast;

let (tx, mut rx1) = broadcast::channel(16);
```

The channel is divided into tx: Sender which can send messages, and rx1: Receiver which can receive messages. Here, through tx.subscribe(), we can create a new receiver rx2: Sender that will receive messages from that sender. In other words, both rx1 and rx2 will receive the same messages from tx:

```
let mut rx2 = tx.subscribe();
```

The tokio::spawn function creates and executes a new asynchronous task. rx1. recv().await.unwrap() asynchronously receives a value from the channel. Now the two asynchronous tasks will asynchronously wait for rx1 and rx2 to receive messages twice. The assert_eq! macro verifies that the first received value is 10 and the second received value is 20:

```rust
tokio::spawn(async move {
    assert_eq!(rx1.recv().await.unwrap(), 10);
    assert_eq!(rx1.recv().await.unwrap(), 20);
});

tokio::spawn(async move {
    assert_eq!(rx2.recv().await.unwrap(), 10);
    assert_eq!(rx2.recv().await.unwrap(), 20);
});
```

Now we transmit values using tx.send. After the receivers verify the sent values and find no issues, the main thread terminates and the program ends:

```rust
tx.send(10).unwrap();
tx.send(20).unwrap();
```

The complete code for creating producers and consumers from channels to transmit messages is as follows:

```rust
use tokio::sync::broadcast;

#[tokio::main]
async fn main() {
    let (tx, mut rx1) = broadcast::channel(16);
    let mut rx2 = tx.subscribe();

    tokio::spawn(async move {
        assert_eq!(rx1.recv().await.unwrap(), 10);
        assert_eq!(rx1.recv().await.unwrap(), 20);
    });

    tokio::spawn(async move {
        assert_eq!(rx2.recv().await.unwrap(), 10);
        assert_eq!(rx2.recv().await.unwrap(), 20);
    });

    tx.send(10).unwrap();
    tx.send(20).unwrap();
}
```

Note   assert_eq! is normally used in tests, not in the regular code.

Now let's write code so socket clients can send and receive messages transmitted via WebSocket protocol through this channel. It's important not to confuse the fact that sending and receiving through channels and the process of sending and receiving via WebSocket are completely separate.

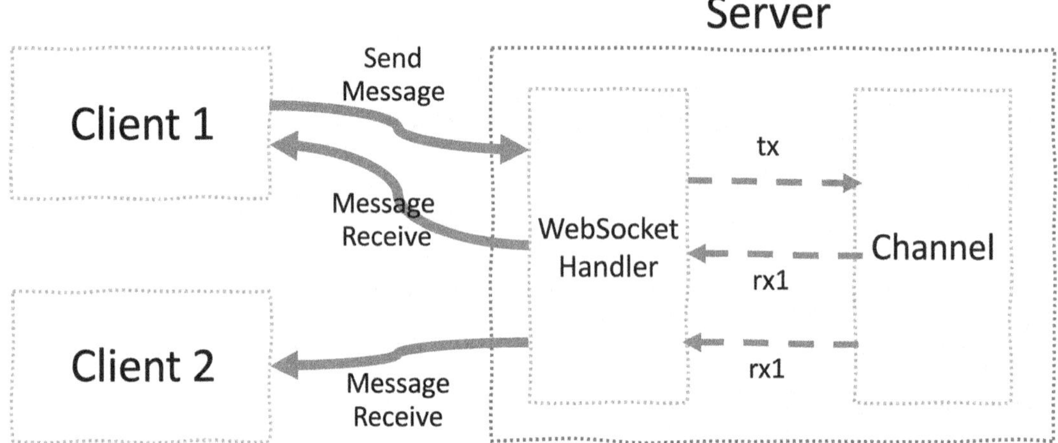

Figure 5-8. *Multi-message Reception Using WebSocket Handler and Channel*

When Client1 sends a message to the server via WebSocket, this message is sent to the channel through tx registered in the handler, and this message is received again through rx. The received message is sent to both Client1 and Client2 via WebSocket.

Now returning to Axum, let's write the main function as follows. We'll create a channel and share it between handlers as State. The reason we only create tx from broadcast::channel(32) is that even if we only share tx, we can create new receivers rx through tx.subscribe(). This tx is wrapped in Arc:

```rust
use std::sync::Arc;
use axum::{extract::ws::Message, routing::get, Router};
use tokio::sync::{
    broadcast::{self, Sender},
    Mutex,
};
```

```rust
#[derive(Debug, Clone)]
struct AppState {
    broadcast_tx: Arc<Mutex<Sender<Message>>>,
}

#[tokio::main]
async fn main() {
    let (tx, _) = broadcast::channel(32);
    let app = AppState {
        broadcast_tx: Arc::new(Mutex::new(tx)),
    };

    let app = Router::new()
        .route("/ws", get(websocket_handler))
        .with_state(app);

    let listener = tokio::net::TcpListener::bind("0.0.0.0:3000").await.
    unwrap();
    axum::serve(listener, app).await.unwrap();
}
```

Next is the handler function websocket_handler. Now the handler receives State as input and also passes this State to the callback function handle_socket registered in on_upgrade. This is because when the connection is actually established, the callback function handles the communication, so we need to enable sending or receiving messages transmitted via WebSocket to or from the channel. For this purpose, we've modified the callback function to be in closure form:

```rust
async fn websocket_handler(ws: WebSocketUpgrade, State(app):
State<AppState>) -> impl IntoResponse {
    ws.on_upgrade(|socket| handle_socket(socket, app))
}
```

In the handle_socket function, we create a new receiver broadcast_rx and execute an asynchronous task that uses this receiver to receive data from the channel. The recv_broadcast function is used in the asynchronous task. We also execute recv_from_client, which receives messages from WebSocket clients:

```rust
async fn handle_socket(ws: WebSocket, app: AppState) {
```

```
    let (ws_tx, ws_rx) = ws.split();
    let ws_tx = Arc::new(Mutex::new(ws_tx));

    {
        let broadcast_rx = app.broadcast_tx.lock().await.subscribe();
        tokio::spawn(async move {
            recv_broadcast(ws_tx, broadcast_rx).await;
        });
    }

    recv_from_client(ws_rx, app.broadcast_tx).await;
}
```

In recv_broadcast, we repeatedly receive messages from the channel using broadcast_rx.recv().await. If a new message arrives from the channel, we send that message via WebSocket using client_tx.lock().await.send(msg).await:

```
async fn recv_broadcast(
    client_tx: Arc<Mutex<SplitSink<WebSocket, Message>>>,
    mut broadcast_rx: Receiver<Message>,
) {
    while let Ok(msg) = broadcast_rx.recv().await {
        if client_tx.lock().await.send(msg).await.is_err() {
            return; // Disconnect on error
        }
    }
}
```

The recv_from_client function sends a message to the channel via broadcast_tx.lock().await.send(msg) whenever a message arrives from the WebSocket connection at client_rx.next().await:

```
async fn recv_from_client(
    mut client_rx: SplitStream<WebSocket>,
    broadcast_tx: Arc<Mutex<Sender<Message>>>,
) {
    while let Some(Ok(msg)) = client_rx.next().await {
        if matches!(msg, Message::Close(_)) {
            return;
```

```rust
        }
        if broadcast_tx.lock().await.send(msg).is_err() {
            println!("Failed to broadcast a message");
        }
    }
}
```

The complete code is as follows:

```rust
use std::sync::Arc;
use axum::{
    extract::{
        ws::{Message, WebSocket},
        State, WebSocketUpgrade,
    },
    response::IntoResponse,
    routing::get,
    Router,
};
use futures_util::{
    sink::SinkExt,
    stream::{SplitSink, SplitStream, StreamExt},
};
use tokio::sync::{
    broadcast::{self, Receiver, Sender},
    Mutex,
};

#[derive(Debug, Clone)]
struct AppState {
    broadcast_tx: Arc<Mutex<Sender<Message>>>,
}

#[tokio::main]
async fn main() {
    let (tx, _) = broadcast::channel(32);
    let app = AppState {
```

```rust
        broadcast_tx: Arc::new(Mutex::new(tx)),
    };

    let app = Router::new()
        .route("/ws", get(websocket_handler))
        .with_state(app);

    let listener = tokio::net::TcpListener::bind("0.0.0.0:3000").await.
unwrap();
    axum::serve(listener, app).await.unwrap();
}

async fn websocket_handler(ws: WebSocketUpgrade, State(app):
State<AppState>) -> impl IntoResponse {
    ws.on_upgrade(|socket| handle_socket(socket, app))
}

async fn handle_socket(ws: WebSocket, app: AppState) {
    let (ws_tx, ws_rx) = ws.split();
    let ws_tx = Arc::new(Mutex::new(ws_tx));

    {
        let broadcast_rx = app.broadcast_tx.lock().await.subscribe();
        tokio::spawn(async move {
            recv_broadcast(ws_tx, broadcast_rx).await;
        });
    }

    recv_from_client(ws_rx, app.broadcast_tx).await;
}

async fn recv_from_client(
    mut client_rx: SplitStream<WebSocket>,
    broadcast_tx: Arc<Mutex<Sender<Message>>>,
) {
    while let Some(Ok(msg)) = client_rx.next().await {
        if matches!(msg, Message::Close(_)) {
            return;
        }
```

```
        if broadcast_tx.lock().await.send(msg).is_err() {
            println!("Failed to broadcast a message");
        }
    }
}

async fn recv_broadcast(
    client_tx: Arc<Mutex<SplitSink<WebSocket, Message>>>,
    mut broadcast_rx: Receiver<Message>,
) {
    while let Ok(msg) = broadcast_rx.recv().await {
        if client_tx.lock().await.send(msg).await.is_err() {
            return; // disconnected.
        }
    }
}
```

Now let's restart the server and connect to it with Insomnia. This time we'll create two clients to verify that a message sent from one client arrives not only at the current client but also at the other client. Therefore, create two WebSocket requests in the left panel: one as client1 and the other as client2.

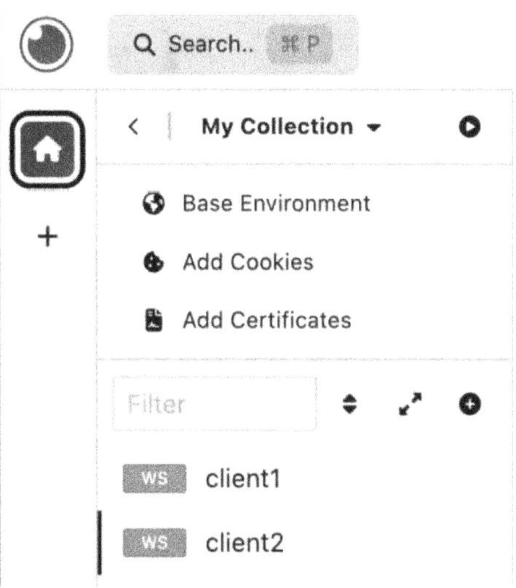

Figure 5-9. *Creating Two WebSocket Clients*

Connect both requests to the WebSocket server. If both are in connected state, a green circle appears to the right of the connection name as shown in Figure 5-10.

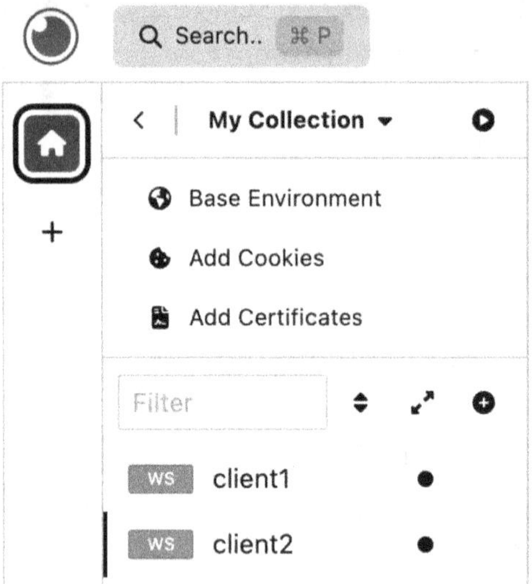

Figure 5-10. *How to Check Connection Status*

Now let's try sending the message "From Client 1" from client1. As you can see in the right panel, the message sent by client1 also comes back to itself as a response.

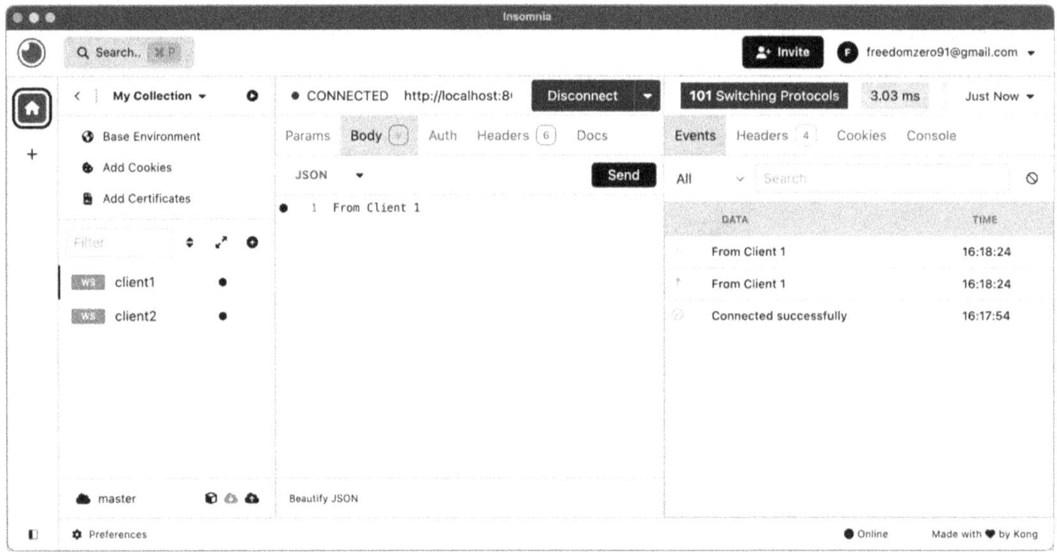

Figure 5-11. *Message Reception After Transmission from client1*

And when you go to client2, you'll see that the message "From Client 1" has arrived there as well. Similarly, when you send a message from client2, both client1 and client2 can receive the message.

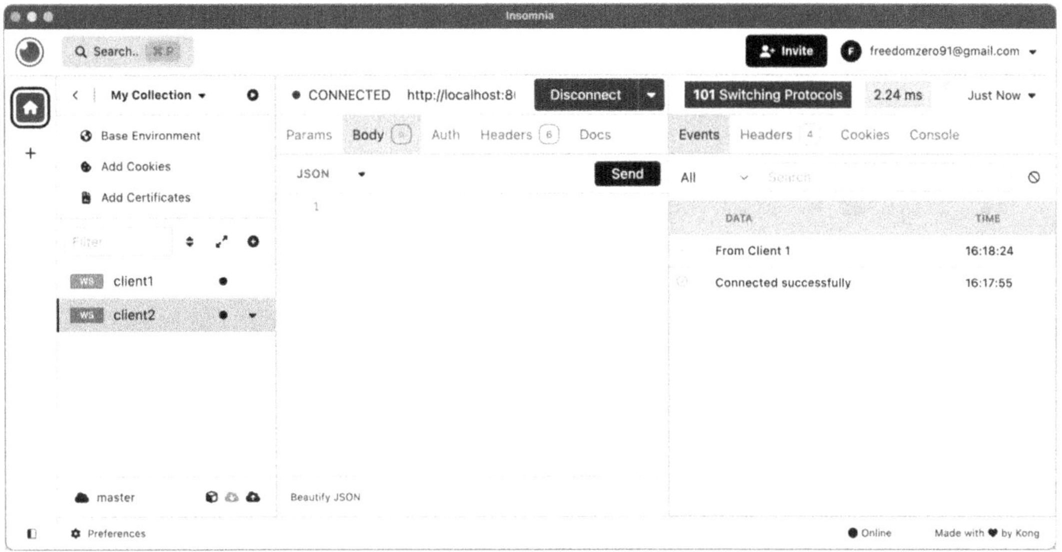

Figure 5-12. *Message Reception at client2*

In this way, by developing from multiple clients connecting to one server and simultaneously exchanging messages, you can implement a chat application.

5.4. Authentication Headers

The socket application we built earlier still has one problem. Namely, clients can connect to the server without any authentication procedure. We can easily implement authentication for WebSocket endpoints using middleware. Let's prevent connections without proper authentication headers by passing an authenticate function to axum::middleware::from_fn to handle authentication.

First, add a middleware layer to the main function as follows:

```rust
#[tokio::main]
async fn main() {
    let (tx, _) = broadcast::channel(32);
    let app = AppState {
        broadcast_tx: Arc::new(Mutex::new(tx)),
    };
```

```
    let app = Router::new()
        .route("/ws", get(websocket_handler))
        .route_layer(middleware::from_fn(authenticate)) // Added
        .with_state(app);

    let listener = tokio::net::TcpListener::bind("0.0.0.0:3000").await.
    unwrap();
    axum::serve(listener, app).await.unwrap();
}
```

The authenticate function is configured to process the request if the Authorization header value is "Bearer token", otherwise it rejects the request. In practice, you should add procedures to directly issue and verify tokens as we implemented the JWT authentication layer in Chapter 4, but here we've implemented it simply for convenience:

```
async fn authenticate(
    headers: HeaderMap,
    request: Request<Body>,
    next: Next,
) -> Result<Response, StatusCode> {
    if headers
        .get("Authorization")
        .map(|value| value == "Bearer token")
        .unwrap_or(false)
    {
        Ok(next.run(request).await)
    } else {
        Err(StatusCode::UNAUTHORIZED)
    }
}
```

The complete code excluding the WebSocket handler, which is common with the section "Concurrent WebSocket Connections," is as follows:

```
use std::sync::Arc;
use axum::{
    body::Body,
```

```rust
    extract::{
        ws::{Message, WebSocket},
        State, WebSocketUpgrade,
    },
    http::{HeaderMap, Request, StatusCode},
    middleware::{self, Next},
    response::{IntoResponse, Response},
    routing::get,
    Router,
};
use futures_util::{
    sink::SinkExt,
    stream::{SplitSink, SplitStream, StreamExt},
};
use tokio::sync::{
    broadcast::{self, Receiver, Sender},
    Mutex,
};

#[derive(Debug, Clone)]
struct AppState {
    broadcast_tx: Arc<Mutex<Sender<Message>>>,
}

#[tokio::main]
async fn main() {
    let (tx, _) = broadcast::channel(32);
    let app = AppState {
        broadcast_tx: Arc::new(Mutex::new(tx)),
    };

    let app = Router::new()
        .route("/ws", get(websocket_handler))
        .route_layer(middleware::from_fn(authenticate))
        .with_state(app);
```

```rust
    let listener = tokio::net::TcpListener::bind("0.0.0.0:3000").await.
    unwrap();
    axum::serve(listener, app).await.unwrap();
}

async fn authenticate(
    headers: HeaderMap,
    request: Request<Body>,
    next: Next,
) -> Result<Response, StatusCode> {
    if headers
        .get("Authorization")
        .map(|value| value == "Bearer token")
        .unwrap_or(false)
    {
        Ok(next.run(request).await)
    } else {
        Err(StatusCode::UNAUTHORIZED)
    }
}
```

Now restart the server and try connecting from Insomnia without including the Authorization header as before. As shown in Figure 5-13, you can see that the connection is rejected with 401 Unauthorized.

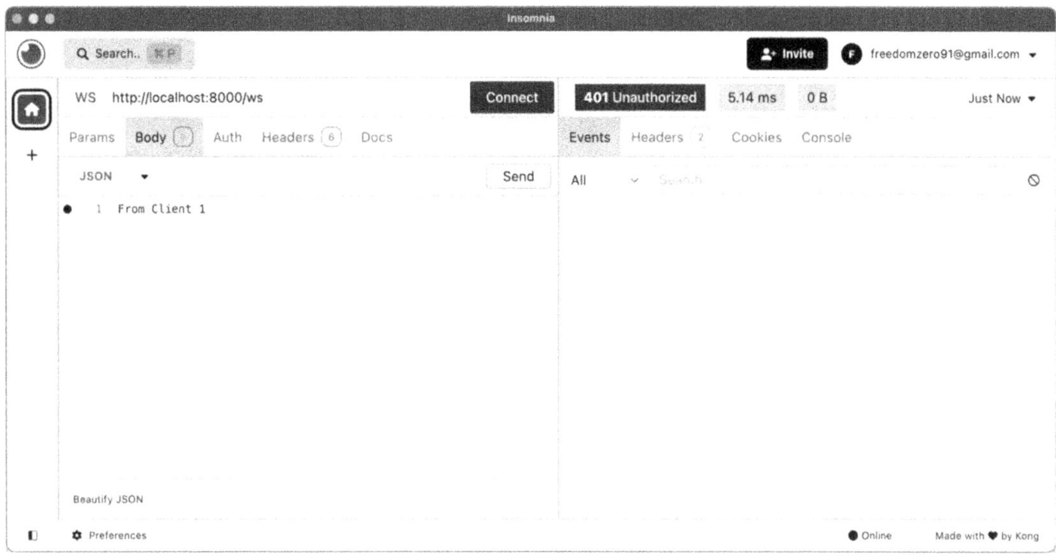

Figure 5-13. *Receiving 401 Status Code*

This time, let's add the authentication header as shown in Figure 5-14.

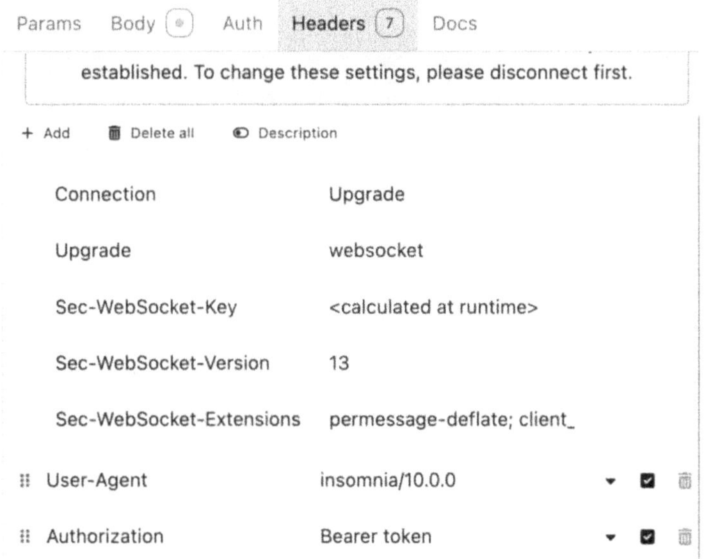

Figure 5-14. *Adding Authentication Header*

When you try connecting again, you can see that it switches to WebSocket protocol normally.

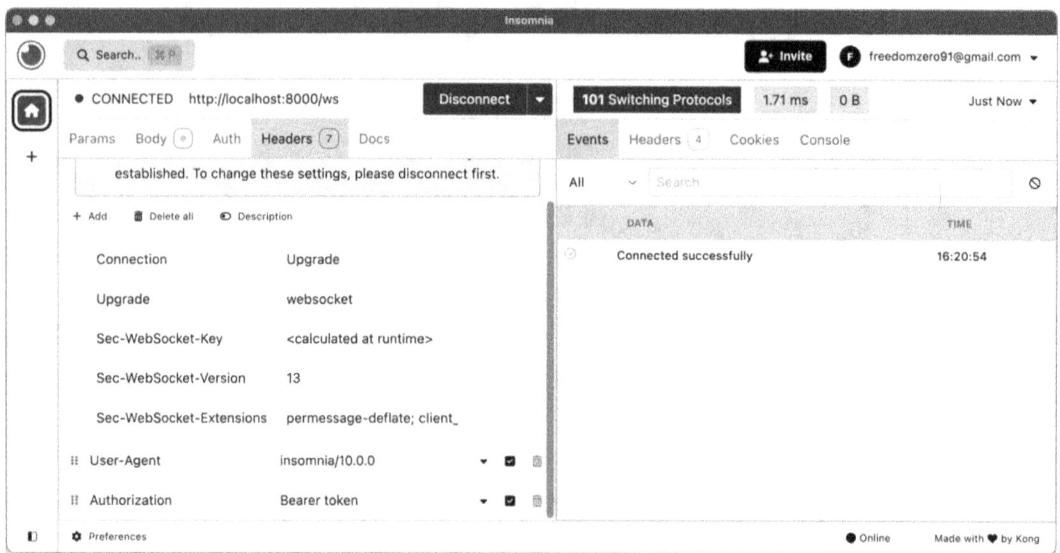

Figure 5-15. *Successful Protocol Switch After Adding Authentication Header*

Note   WSS is the secure version of the WebSocket protocol, which transmits data securely through encryption like HTTPS. In regular WebSocket connections, data is transmitted as unencrypted plain text, which poses risks of hacking or eavesdropping, but WSS minimizes these risks by using TLS (Transport Layer Security).

WSS uses port 443, the same as HTTPS, instead of HTTP's default port 80, and browsers automatically recognize WSS connections to establish secure connections.

To use WSS, both server and client must install TLS certificates. A TLS certificate is a digital certificate that verifies the web server's identity and provides keys used for data encryption. Using WSS allows developers to develop real-time web applications without worrying about data security issues.

5.5. Review

- We explored the characteristics of WebSocket protocol and handshaking.

- We learned how to establish connections with clients through WebSocket handlers and exchange messages through senders and receivers.

- We learned how to have multiple clients simultaneously exchange messages with the server through channels.

- We can configure authentication for WebSocket endpoints the same way as HTTP endpoints through authentication layers.

CHAPTER 6

Project: Building a Chat Service

6.1. Project Overview

In this chapter, we will build a chat service with both a frontend and a backend. After completing the code, we will also walk through the process of deploying it using Docker. The project is structured as follows: multiple clients access the service through a web browser, and the backend serves the frontend web pages. From the frontend, users can chat with others in real time by communicating with the backend. Chats take place within rooms, and users can create or delete new rooms. Rooms and chat messages are stored in a database.

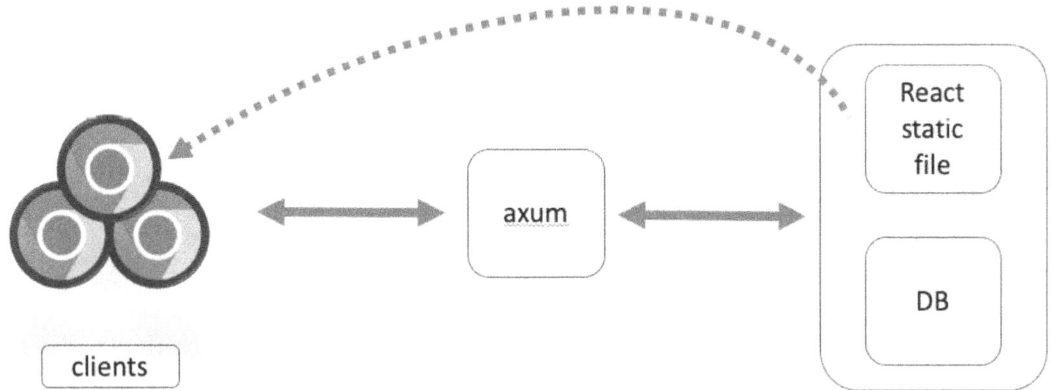

Figure 6-1. *Project Structure*

Here is what the completed chat service we will build in this chapter looks like.

When you first connect, a prompt appears asking you to enter a username. After entering a username and clicking the "Enter" button, you are taken to a page where you can see the list of chat rooms.

Figure 6-2. *Enter a Name for the Chat*

You can join an existing chat room. Alternatively, you can click the "Create new room" button to create a new chat room, or click the "Delete" button to delete one.

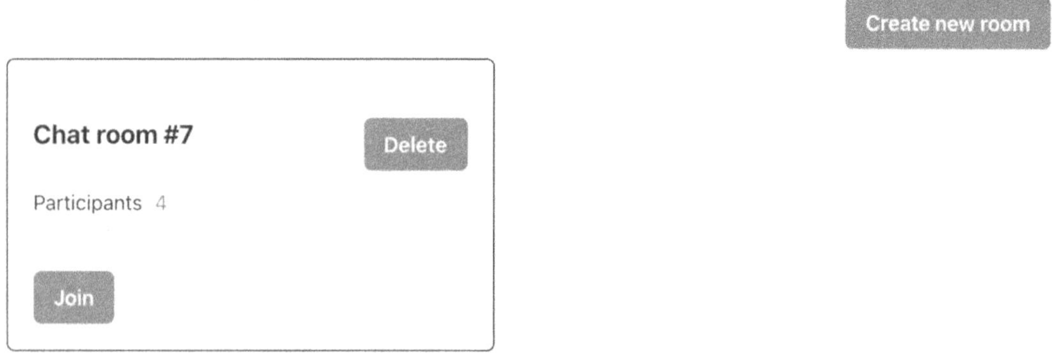

Figure 6-3. *Chat Room List*

When you click the "Join" button to enter a chat room, you can chat with other users. The sender's name, the chat message, and the time the message was sent are displayed.

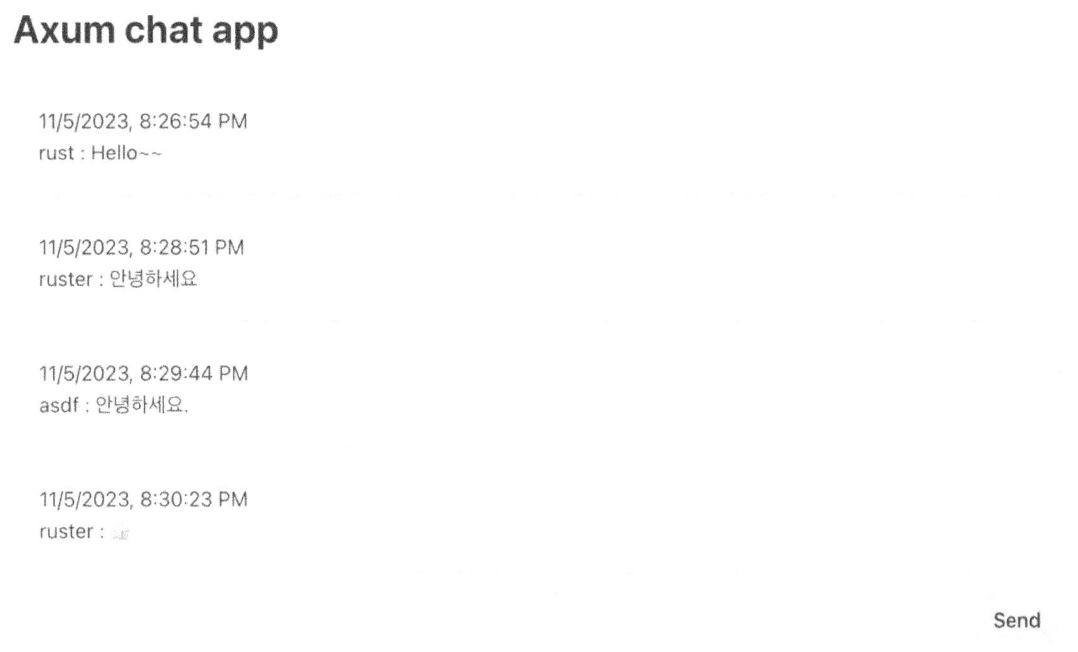

Axum chat app

11/5/2023, 8:26:54 PM
rust : Hello~~

11/5/2023, 8:28:51 PM
ruster : 안녕하세요

11/5/2023, 8:29:44 PM
asdf : 안녕하세요.

11/5/2023, 8:30:23 PM
ruster :

Send

Figure 6-4. *Chat Screen*

6.1.1. What Is SSE?

SSE (Server-Sent Event) is a technology for sending events from the server to the client. Instead of the client continuously asking the server whether new events have occurred, the server automatically sends events to the client when they happen. The client remains connected to the server and can receive events from it. Events are transmitted in JSON format. Since SSE is a built-in browser feature, the client can handle events using JavaScript when they are received.

SSE is similar to WebSocket, but unlike WebSocket, the client cannot send messages to the server. Messages can only be sent from the server to the client. However, since SSE uses HTTP, it is easier to implement a real-time server compared to WebSocket. In this project, the client does not send new chat messages via SSE. Instead, it sends them through a REST API, and the server then broadcasts the received messages to all connected clients via SSE.

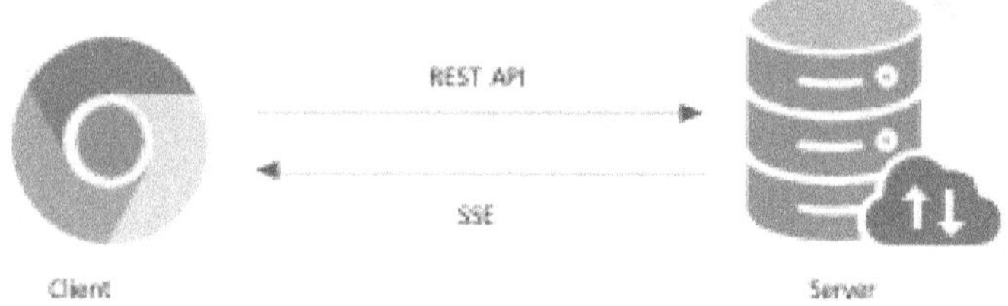

Figure 6-5. *How SSE Chat Application Works*

Table 6-1. *Summary of Client-Server Communication Methods*

Feature	Polling	Long Polling	WebSocket	SSE
Connection	Short-term	Long-term until new data or timeout	Persistent	Persistent
Direction	Unidirectional (client to server)	Unidirectional (server to client)	Bidirectional	Unidirectional (server to client)
Efficiency	Inefficient	More efficient than polling	Most efficient	Efficient
Support	Widely supported	Widely supported	Server-side support and compatibility issues with older browsers	Widely supported

6.1.2. Code Repository

The complete code for this project can be found in the GitHub repository below:

```
https://github.com/Indosaram/axum-react-chat-app
```

The project is organized into two main folders: a `frontend` folder containing the frontend code and a `backend` folder containing the backend code.

6.2. Hands-on

Now let's work through the project step by step as follows:

1. Project Setup

2. Creating SSE Endpoints

3. Configuration Management and Database Connection

4. Creating REST API Endpoints

5. Building the Frontend

6. Automated Testing

7. Production Readiness and Deployment

6.2.1. Project Setup

First, create a new project. Navigate to the folder where you want to create the project in the terminal, then run the following command.

```
cargo new axum-chat-app
cd axum-chat-app
```

Add the dependencies for the project to the `Cargo.toml` file. The full list of dependencies used in this project is as follows.

Note   This chapter uses Axum 0.8, which is a newer version than the 0.7.x used in previous chapters. While the core concepts remain the same, there are some API changes—most notably, path parameters now use {param} syntax instead of :param. Other dependencies like tower and tower-http have also been updated to their latest compatible versions.

```
[dependencies]
axum = { version = "0.8", features = ["json", "macros"] }
tokio = { version = "1", features = ["full"] }
tokio-stream = { version = "0.1", features = ["full"] }
tower-http = { version = "0.6", features = ["full"] }
tower = { version = "0.5", features = ["full"] }
futures-util = "0.3"
tracing = "0.1"
tracing-subscriber = { version = "0.3", features = ["env-filter"] }
sea-orm = { version = "1.0", features = [ "sqlx-postgres", "runtime-tokio-
native-tls", "macros" ] }
```

```
serde_json = "1.0"
serde = { version = "1.0", features = ["derive"] }
dotenvy = "0.15"
envy = "0.4"
chrono = "0.4"
```

The versions listed in the book are based on the time of writing. You are free to use the latest compatible versions available at the time you practice. Using the cargo add command will automatically install the latest versions.

Next, modify main.rs as follows to verify that a basic Axum server is working.

```rust
use axum::{routing::get, Router};

async fn hello_world() -> &'static str {
    "Hello, world!"
}

#[tokio::main]
async fn main() {
    let app = Router::new().route("/", get(hello_world));

    let listener = tokio::net::TcpListener::bind("0.0.0.0:3000").await.
    unwrap();
    println!("Server is running on port 3000.");
    axum::serve(listener, app).await.unwrap();
}
```

Run the project to confirm it works correctly.

```
cargo run
```

Alternatively, using cargo watch will automatically restart the server whenever the source code changes.

```
cargo watch -x run
```

In your local environment, navigate to http://localhost:3000 in a web browser, and you should see "Hello, world!" displayed.

Now let's start writing the actual code. First, create a `.env` file in the project root and enter the following content. The role of this file will be explained in detail when we cover configuration management in the section "Configuration Management and Database Connection."

```
RUST_LOG=debug
```

6.2.2. Creating SSE Endpoints

Next, we will create an SSE endpoint and connect to the server using Insomnia. Write `main.rs` as follows. We create a message queue to hold messages sent by clients and pass it as a `State`. `State` is a way to share data across the entire application (see Chapter 2). The created message queue is used in the `chat.rs` file to store messages sent by clients.

Here, we encounter a routing method that we haven't used before: nested routing. Nested routing means embedding one router inside another. Until now, our endpoint paths were simple addresses like "/users" or "/product", but the paths we want to add here, such as "/chat/subscribe" and "/chat/send", share the common prefix "/chat". In such cases, using nested routing means we only need to write the "/chat" path once, making the code more concise and flexible when paths change. The first argument to `.nest` is the path to nest under, and the second argument is the nested router. The nested router is written as follows.

```rust
let app = Router::new()
    .nest(
        "/chat",
        Router::new()
            .route("/subscribe", get(subscribe))
            .route("/send", post(send)),
    )
```

The code so far looks like this.

```rust
mod api;
use api::chat::{send, subscribe};
use axum::{
    routing::{get, post},
    Router,
};
```

```rust
use tokio::sync::broadcast;
use tracing_subscriber::{fmt, prelude::*, EnvFilter};

#[tokio::main]
async fn main() {
    dotenvy::dotenv().ok();

    tracing_subscriber::registry()
        .with(fmt::layer())
        .with(EnvFilter::from_default_env())
        .init();

    let message_queue: broadcast::Sender<String> =
    broadcast::channel(10).0;
    let app = Router::new()
        .nest(
            "/chat",
            Router::new()
                .route("/subscribe", get(subscribe))
                .route("/send", post(send)),
        )
        .with_state(message_queue);

    let listener = tokio::net::TcpListener::bind("0.0.0.0:3000").await.
    unwrap();
    println!("Server is running on port 3000.");
    axum::serve(listener, app).await.unwrap();
}
```

Now let's write the endpoints that communicate with clients to send and receive chat messages. Create the following folder structure and add files inside the /api folder.

```
src
├── api
│   ├── chat.rs
│   └── mod.rs
└── main.rs
```

The `mod.rs` file is as follows.

```
pub mod chat;
```

The `chat.rs` file consists of two functions: a `subscribe` function that provides clients with an SSE subscription connection, and a `send` function that allows clients to send messages to the server. First, the `subscribe` function is as follows. It converts the message queue received through `State` into a `BroadcastStream`. Since `BroadcastStream` implements the `Stream` trait, it can be passed to `Sse`. `Sse` maintains the connection and notifies clients when new messages arrive in the queue. The data is transmitted in JSON format through the `Event` struct contained in the `msg` variable.

```
use axum::{
    extract::State,
    response::{
        sse::{Event, KeepAlive, Sse},
        IntoResponse,
    },
};
use futures_util::stream::StreamExt;
use serde_json::json;
use tokio::sync::broadcast::{self};
use tokio_stream::wrappers::BroadcastStream;

pub async fn subscribe(
    State(queue): State<broadcast::Sender<String>>,
) -> impl IntoResponse {
    let stream = BroadcastStream::new(queue.subscribe()).map(|msg|
    match msg {
        Ok(msg) => Ok(Event::default()
            .event("message")
            .data(json!(msg).to_string())),
        Err(e) => Err(e),
    });

    Sse::new(stream).keep_alive(KeepAlive::default())
}
```

The send function is a REST API endpoint used when clients send messages to the server and is unrelated to SSE. This function sends new_message to the message queue received through State.

```
pub async fn send(
    State(queue): State<broadcast::Sender<String>>,
    new_message: String,
) -> &'static str {
    queue.send(new_message).expect("Error sending message");

    "Message sent"
}
```

Run the server and create a new request in Insomnia. Set the creation type to "Event Stream Request."

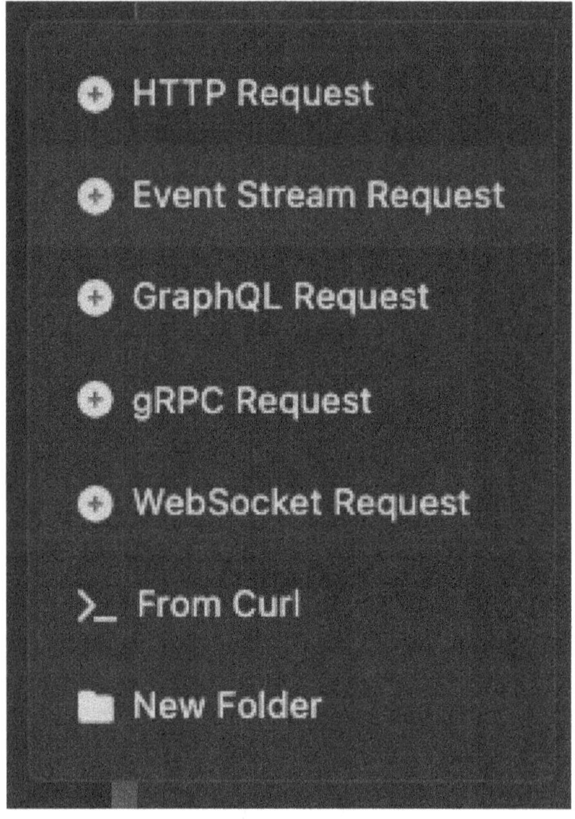

Figure 6-6. *Create SSE Request*

Connect to the following address. Click the Connect button to establish an SSE connection with the server.

```
http://localhost:3000/chat/subscribe
```

Once the connection is successfully established, "200 OK" appears on the right side of the screen, and messages sent from the server are displayed in real time. A green circle appears next to the request on the left side, indicating the current connection status.

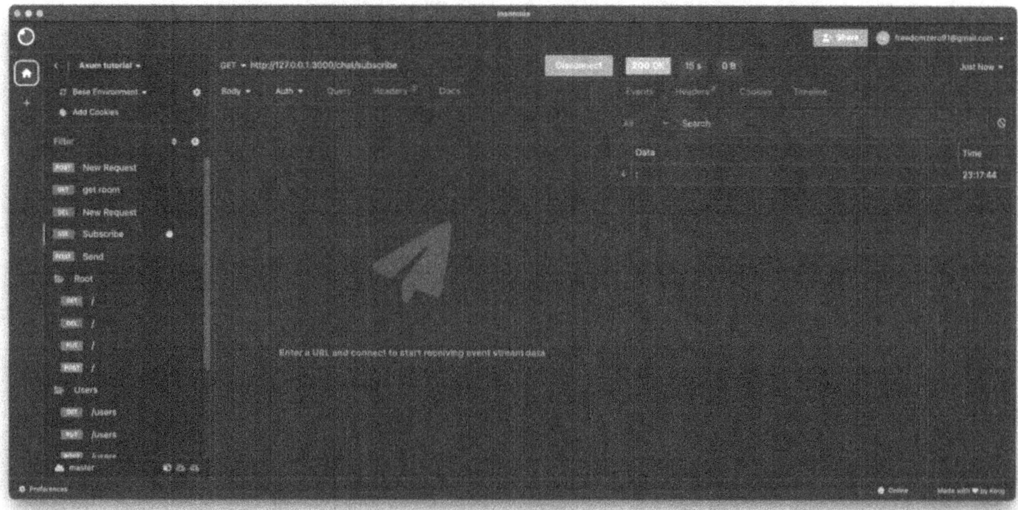

Figure 6-7. *Check Connection Status*

Let's send a message to the server. Create a new request in Insomnia. Set the creation type to "POST." We will send the string "Hello Axum!" to the following address.

```
http://localhost:3000/chat/send
```

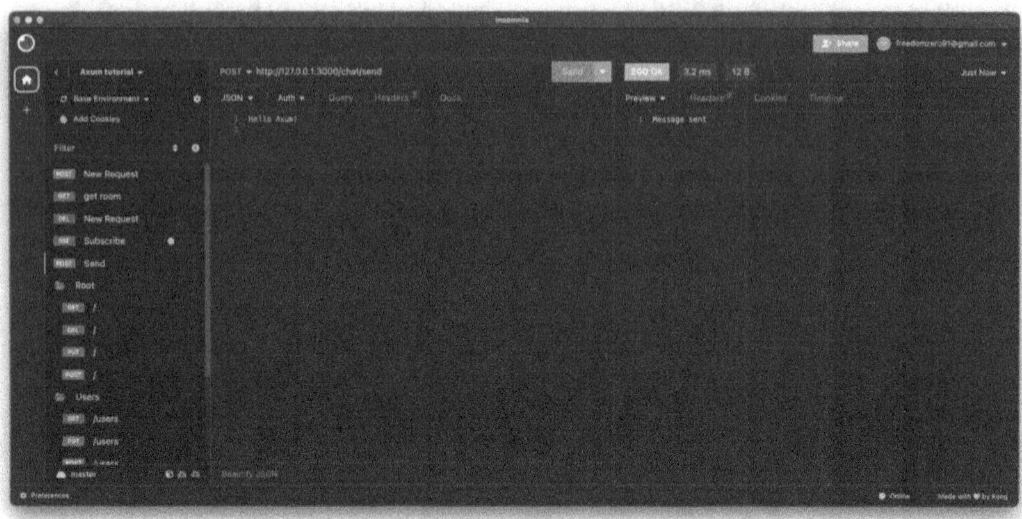

Figure 6-8. *Send SSE Message*

If you go back to the request we connected earlier, you can see that the message we just sent has been received successfully.

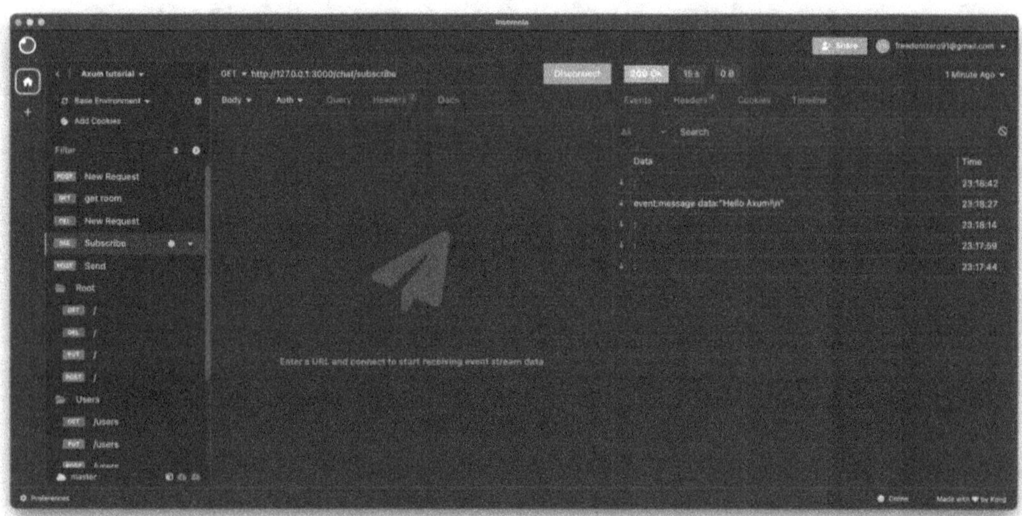

Figure 6-9. *Received SSE Message*

6.2.3. Configuration Management and Database Connection

In this step, we will learn how to manage configuration systematically and use it to connect to a database.

6.2.3.1. Configuration Management

One rule that must never be broken when operating a real service is **"strictly separating source code from configuration."** If database passwords or external API keys are hardcoded in the source code, a security incident will occur the moment the code is pushed to GitHub or a similar platform. Additionally, the code would need to be rebuilt every time the environment changes, which is inefficient.

Simply fetching environment variables as strings like `std::env::var("DATABASE_URL")` leads to the following problems:

1. **Runtime Errors**: Even if there's a typo in the environment variable name, you won't discover the error until after the program is running.

2. **Tedious Parsing**: Numeric data such as port numbers (`u16`) must be manually parsed every time.

3. **No Way to Check for Missing Values**: There is no explicit way to know which configuration values are required when the server starts.

To solve these problems, we use the `envy` crate. `envy` automatically maps the contents of system environment variables or `.env` files to Rust struct fields. We already added `dotenvy`, `envy`, and `serde` to `Cargo.toml` in the section "Project Setup."

Define a `Config` struct to hold the environment variables. Create a new file `src/config.rs` and write the following.

```
use serde::Deserialize;

#[derive(Deserialize, Clone)]
pub struct Config {
    pub database_url: String,
```

```rust
    #[serde(default = "default_port")]
    pub server_port: u16,
}

fn default_port() -> u16 { 3000 }

impl Config {
    pub fn from_env() -> Self {
        dotenvy::dotenv().ok();

        envy::from_env::<Config>()
            .expect("Required environment variables are not set. Please
            check your .env file.")
    }
}
```

Add the following content to the `.env` file in the project root.

```
# .env
RUST_LOG=debug
DATABASE_URL=postgres://axum_user:1234@localhost:5432/axum_chat_db
SERVER_PORT=3000
```

> 💡 *The `.env` file contains sensitive information, so it must be added to `.gitignore`. If the `.env` file gets pushed to a Git repository, it can lead to a security incident.*

When the server starts, dotenvy reads the `.env` file and registers its contents as system environment variables, and envy automatically maps those values to each field of the `Config` struct. Even numeric values like `SERVER_PORT` are automatically converted to u16 during serde's deserialization process, so no separate parsing code is needed.

In the Rust ecosystem, there are two crates for reading `.env` files: dotenv and dotenvy. Since dotenv has not been maintained since 2020, it is recommended to use its successor project, dotenvy.

6.2.3.2. Database Connection

Now let's use the `database_url` from `Config` to connect to the database. We use the same `Database::connect` method as covered in Chapter 3.

To share the database connection and message queue across handlers, create an api/state.rs module and enter the following. FromRef is used so that each field can be extracted individually.

```rust
use crate::entities::chat::Model as Chat;

use axum::extract::FromRef;
use sea_orm::DatabaseConnection;
use tokio::sync::broadcast;

#[derive(Clone, FromRef)]
pub struct AppState {
    pub conn: DatabaseConnection,
    pub queue: broadcast::Sender<Chat>,
}
```

Since the queue field of AppState is defined as broadcast::Sender<Chat>, the function signatures of subscribe and send in chat.rs that we wrote in the section "Creating SSE Endpoints" must also be updated. Change the existing State<broadcast::Sender<String>> to State<broadcast::Sender<Chat>>.

```rust
use crate::entities::chat::{self, Entity as ChatEntity, Model as Chat};

pub async fn subscribe(
    State(queue): State<broadcast::Sender<Chat>>,
) -> impl IntoResponse {
    let stream = BroadcastStream::new(queue.subscribe()).map(|msg|
    match msg {
        Ok(msg) => Ok(Event::default()
            .event("message")
            .data(json!(msg).to_string())),
        Err(e) => Err(e),
    });

    Sse::new(stream).keep_alive(KeepAlive::default())
}

pub async fn send(
    State(queue): State<broadcast::Sender<Chat>>,
    new_message: String,
```

```rust
) -> &'static str {
    let _ = queue.send(serde_json::from_str(&new_message).expect("Invalid
    chat JSON"));

    "Message sent"
}
```

Use `Config` in `main.rs` to connect to the database and create the `AppState`.

```rust
use api::state::AppState;
use sea_orm::Database;

#[tokio::main]
async fn main() {
    let config = Config::from_env();

    tracing_subscriber::registry()
        .with(fmt::layer())
        .with(EnvFilter::from_default_env())
        .init();

    let conn = Database::connect(&config.database_url)
        .await
        .expect("Failed to connect to the database.");

    let state = AppState {
        conn,
        queue: broadcast::channel(10).0,
    };

    ...

    .with_state(state);
}
```

6.2.3.3. Migration

Next, let's add database migration. The schema we will use in the chat project is as follows. The relationships between the tables are as follows:

- Room's Participants consists of a list of Users.

- Chat has one Room connected through the foreign key RoomId.

- Chat's Sender points to one User.

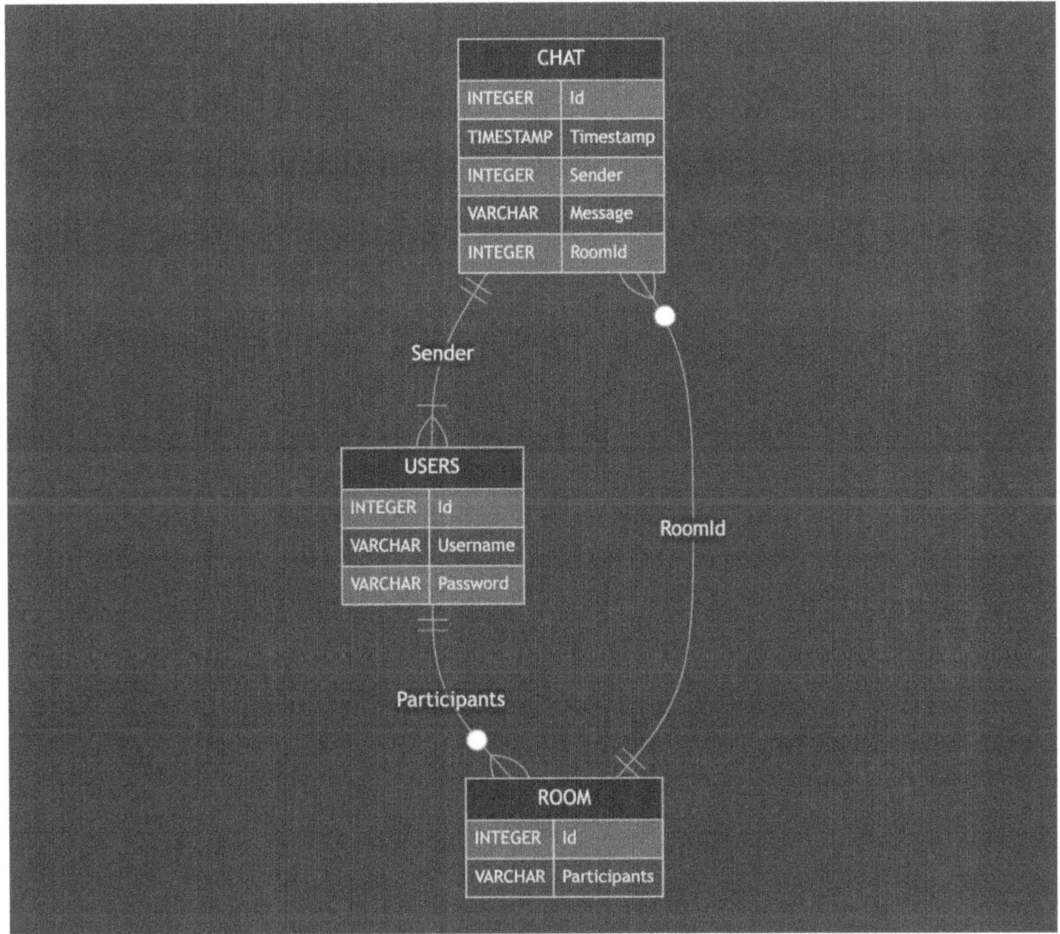

Figure 6-10. *Relationship of Tables*

Initialize the migration.

```
sea-orm-cli migrate init
```

In the up function, write the content for creating each table. The Users table is as follows.

```
manager
    .create_table(
        Table::create()
            .table(Users::Table)
            .if_not_exists()
            .col(
                ColumnDef::new(Users::Id)
                    .integer()
                    .not_null()
                    .auto_increment()
                    .primary_key(),
            )
            .col(
                ColumnDef::new(Users::Username)
                    .string()
                    .unique_key()
                    .not_null(),
            )
            .col(ColumnDef::new(Users::Password).string().not_null())
            .to_owned(),
    )
    .await?;
```

The Room table is as follows.

```
manager
    .create_table(
        Table::create()
            .table(Room::Table)
            .if_not_exists()
            .col(
```

```
                ColumnDef::new(Room::Id)
                    .integer()
                    .not_null()
                    .auto_increment()
                    .primary_key(),
            )
            .col(
                ColumnDef::new(Room::Participants)
                    .string()
                    .not_null(),
            )
            .to_owned(),
    )
    .await?;
```

The Chat table is as follows.

```
manager
    .create_table(
        Table::create()
            .table(Chat::Table)
            .if_not_exists()
            .col(
                ColumnDef::new(Chat::Id)
                    .integer()
                    .not_null()
                    .auto_increment()
                    .primary_key(),
            )
            .col(ColumnDef::new(Chat::Timestamp).timestamp().not_null())
            .col(ColumnDef::new(Chat::Sender).string().not_null())
            .col(ColumnDef::new(Chat::Message).string().not_null())
            .col(ColumnDef::new(Chat::RoomId).integer().not_null())
            .foreign_key(
                ForeignKey::create()
                    .name("fk_chat_room_id")
                    .from_tbl(Chat::Table)
```

```
                    .from_col(Chat::RoomId)
                    .to_tbl(Room::Table)
                    .to_col(Room::Id),
            )
            .to_owned(),
    )
    .await?;
```

Add this content to the up function in the code below. In the down function, write the content for dropping the tables created in the up function.

```
use sea_orm_migration::prelude::*;

#[derive(DeriveMigrationName)]
pub struct Migration;

#[async_trait::async_trait]
impl MigrationTrait for Migration {
    async fn up(&self, manager: &SchemaManager) -> Result<(), DbErr> {

        ...

        Ok(())
    }

    async fn down(&self, manager: &SchemaManager) -> Result<(), DbErr> {
        manager
            .drop_table(Table::drop().table(Users::Table).if_exists().
            to_owned())
            .await?;

        manager
            .drop_table(Table::drop().table(Room::Table).if_exists().to_
            owned())
            .await?;

        manager
            .drop_table(Table::drop().table(Chat::Table).if_exists().to_
            owned())
            .await?;
```

```
        Ok(())
    }
}
```

Finally, create the enums representing each table.

```
#[derive(DeriveIden)]
enum Users {
    Table,
    Id,
    Username,
    Password,
}

#[derive(DeriveIden)]
enum Room {
    Table,
    Id,
    Participants,
}

#[derive(DeriveIden)]
enum Chat {
    Table,
    Id,
    Timestamp,
    Sender,
    Message,
    RoomId,
}
```

Once the migration file is complete, apply the migration and generate `Entity` files using the CLI. This is the same method as covered in Chapter 3.

```
sea-orm-cli migrate up
sea-orm-cli generate entity -o src/entities
```

Define the `migration` folder as a separate workspace and add it as a crate.

```
[workspace]
members = [".", "migration"]

[dependencies]

...

migration = { path = "migration" }
```

Here is the full `main.rs` with the migration code added. Using `Migrator::up` ensures that migrations are applied automatically when the server starts. The second argument to the up function allows you to specify a particular version to migrate to. If set to None, the migration proceeds to the latest version.

```
mod api;
mod config;
mod entities;

use api::{
    chat::{send, subscribe},
    state::AppState,
};

use axum::{
    routing::{get, post},
    Router,
};

use config::Config;
use migration::{Migrator, MigratorTrait};
use sea_orm::Database;
use tokio::sync::broadcast;
use tracing_subscriber::{fmt, prelude::*, EnvFilter};

#[tokio::main]
async fn main() {
    let config = Config::from_env();
```

```rust
tracing_subscriber::registry()
    .with(fmt::layer())
    .with(EnvFilter::from_default_env())
    .init();

let conn = Database::connect(&config.database_url)
    .await
    .expect("Failed to connect to the database.");

Migrator::up(&conn, None).await.unwrap();

let state = AppState {
    conn,
    queue: broadcast::channel(10).0,
};

let app = Router::new()
    .nest(
        "/chat",
        Router::new()
            .route("/subscribe", get(subscribe))
            .route("/send", post(send)),
    )
    .with_state(state);

let addr = format!("0.0.0.0:{}", config.server_port);
let listener = tokio::net::TcpListener::bind(&addr).await.unwrap();
println!("Server is running on port {}.", config.server_port);
axum::serve(listener, app).await.unwrap();
}
```

6.2.4. Creating REST API Endpoints

Next, we will add the chat room API, chat list API, and user API code. The current src folder structure is as follows.

```
src
├── api
│   ├── chat.rs
│   ├── state.rs
│   ├── mod.rs
├── entities
└── main.rs
```

Add chat_room.rs and user.rs under the api folder and modify the mod.rs file as follows.

```rust
pub mod chat;
pub mod chat_room;
pub mod state;
pub mod user;
use std::collections::HashMap;

use axum::{
    extract::{Query, State},
    Json,
};
use serde::{Deserialize, Serialize};

use sea_orm::{
    ActiveModelTrait, ActiveValue, ColumnTrait, Condition,
    DatabaseConnection, EntityTrait,
    ModelTrait, QueryFilter,
};

use crate::entities::{
    chat::{self, Entity as ChatEntity},
    room::{ActiveModel, Column, Entity as RoomEntity, Model},
};

pub async fn get_room(
    State(conn): State<DatabaseConnection>,
    Query(params): Query<HashMap<String, String>>,
) -> Json<Vec<NewRoom>> {
    let mut condition = Condition::all();
```

```
    if let Some(id) = params.get("id") {
        condition = condition.add(Column::Id.eq(id.parse::<i32>().
        unwrap()));
    }

    let rooms = RoomEntity::find()
        .filter(condition)
        .all(&conn)
        .await
        .unwrap();

    let mut new_rooms: Vec<NewRoom> = Vec::new();

    for room in rooms {
        let participants: Vec<String> = serde_json::from_str(&room.
        participants).unwrap();

        new_rooms.push(NewRoom {
            id: Some(room.id),
            participants,
        });
    }

    Json(new_rooms)
}

#[derive(Serialize, Deserialize)]
pub struct NewRoom {
    id: Option<i32>,
    participants: Vec<String>,
}

pub async fn post_room(
    State(conn): State<DatabaseConnection>,
    Json(room): Json<NewRoom>,
) -> Json<Model> {
    let participants = serde_json::to_string(&room.participants).unwrap();
```

```rust
    let room = ActiveModel {
        id: ActiveValue::not_set(),
        participants: ActiveValue::Set(participants),
    };

    Json(room.insert(&conn).await.unwrap())
}

pub async fn put_room(
    State(conn): State<DatabaseConnection>,
    Json(room): Json<NewRoom>,
) -> Json<Model> {
    let result = RoomEntity::find_by_id(room.id.unwrap())
        .one(&conn)
        .await
        .unwrap()
        .unwrap();

    let mut participants: Vec<String> = serde_json::from_str(&result.
participants).unwrap();
    participants.push(room.participants[0].clone());

    let new_room = ActiveModel {
        id: ActiveValue::Set(result.id),
        participants: ActiveValue::Set(serde_json::to_string(&participants)
        .unwrap()),
    };

    Json(new_room.update(&conn).await.unwrap())
}

pub async fn delete_room(
    State(conn): State<DatabaseConnection>,
    Query(params): Query<HashMap<String, String>>,
) -> Json<&'static str> {
    let id = params.get("id").unwrap().parse::<i32>().unwrap();
```

```
    let chats = ChatEntity::find()
        .filter(chat::Column::RoomId.eq(id))
        .all(&conn)
        .await
        .unwrap();

    for chat in chats {
        chat.delete(&conn).await.unwrap();
    }

    let room = RoomEntity::find_by_id(id)
        .one(&conn)
        .await
        .unwrap()
        .unwrap();

    room.delete(&conn).await.unwrap();

    Json("Deleted")
}
```

The user.rs file is as follows.

```
use std::collections::HashMap;

use axum::{
    extract::{Query, State},
    Json,
};

use sea_orm::{
    ActiveModelTrait, ActiveValue, ColumnTrait, Condition,
    DatabaseConnection, EntityTrait,
    ModelTrait, QueryFilter,
};

use crate::entities::users::{ActiveModel, Column, Entity as
UsersEntity, Model};
```

```rust
pub async fn get_user(
    State(conn): State<DatabaseConnection>,
    Query(params): Query<HashMap<String, String>>,
) -> Json<Vec<Model>> {
    let mut condition = Condition::all();

    if let Some(id) = params.get("id") {
        condition = condition.add(Column::Id.eq(id.parse::<i32>().
        unwrap()));
    }

    if let Some(username) = params.get("username") {
        condition = condition.add(Column::Username.contains(username));
    }

    Json(
        UsersEntity::find()
            .filter(condition)
            .all(&conn)
            .await
            .unwrap(),
    )
}

#[derive(serde::Deserialize)]
pub struct UpsertModel {
    id: Option<i32>,
    username: Option<String>,
    password: Option<String>,
}

pub async fn post_user(
    State(conn): State<DatabaseConnection>,
    Json(user): Json<UpsertModel>,
) -> Json<Model> {
    let new_user = ActiveModel {
        id: ActiveValue::NotSet,
        username: ActiveValue::Set(user.username.unwrap()),
```

```rust
        password: ActiveValue::Set(user.password.unwrap()),
    };

    let result = new_user.insert(&conn).await.unwrap();

    Json(result)
}

pub async fn put_user(State(conn): State<DatabaseConnection>, Json(user):
Json<UpsertModel>) -> Json<Model> {
    let result = UsersEntity::find_by_id(user.id.unwrap())
        .one(&conn)
        .await
        .unwrap()
        .unwrap();

    let new_user = ActiveModel {
        id: ActiveValue::Set(result.id),
        username: ActiveValue::Set(user.username.unwrap_or(result.
        username)),
        password: ActiveValue::Set(user.password.unwrap_or(result.
        password)),
    };

    Json(new_user.update(&conn).await.unwrap())
}

pub async fn delete_user(
    State(conn): State<DatabaseConnection>,
    Query(params): Query<HashMap<String, String>>,
) -> Json<&'static str> {
    tokio::time::sleep(tokio::time::Duration::from_secs(3)).await;
    let mut condition = Condition::any();

    if let Some(id) = params.get("id") {
        condition = condition.add(Column::Id.eq(id.parse::<i32>().
        unwrap()));
    }
```

```rust
    if let Some(username) = params.get("username") {
        condition = condition.add(Column::Username.contains(username));
    }

    let user = UsersEntity::find()
        .filter(condition)
        .one(&conn)
        .await
        .unwrap()
        .unwrap();

    user.delete(&conn).await.unwrap();

    Json("Deleted")
}
```

Add an endpoint to chat.rs that takes room_id as a query parameter and retrieves the list of chat messages for that chat room.

```rust
pub async fn get_chat(
    State(conn): State<DatabaseConnection>,
    Query(params): Query<HashMap<String, String>>,
) -> Json<Vec<Chat>> {
    let room_id = params.get("room_id").unwrap();

    Json(
        ChatEntity::find()
            .filter(Column::RoomId.eq(room_id.parse::<i32>().unwrap()))
            .all(&conn)
            .await
            .unwrap(),
    )
}
```

All handlers are now complete. Let's add the routing to main.rs.

```rust
let app = Router::new()
    .nest(
        "/chat",
```

```
    Router::new()
        .route("/", get(get_chat))
        .route("/subscribe", get(subscribe))
        .route("/send", post(send)),
)
.route(
    "/room",
    get(get_room)
        .post(post_room)
        .put(put_room)
        .delete(delete_room),
)
.route(
    "/user",
    get(get_user)
        .post(post_user)
        .put(put_user)
        .delete(delete_user),
)
.with_state(state);
```

6.2.5. Building the Frontend

The fifth step is building the frontend. To run the frontend, you need the NodeJS runtime and the yarn CLI tool. The frontend was built using React and Vite, and the UI system uses Chakra UI. If you are not familiar with React, you don't need to build the frontend yourself—you can simply copy the pre-built files from the backend/static folder in the code repository. If you want to run the frontend yourself, use the following commands to install the dependencies and start the development server.

```
cd frontend
yarn
yarn run dev
```

Or, to create a new build, use the following command. The build will be automatically generated in the backend/`static` folder.

```
yarn run build
```

Since the backend serves the files directly from that folder, there is no need to make additional changes to the backend code just because the frontend was rebuilt. When the frontend is built, the following folder structure is created.

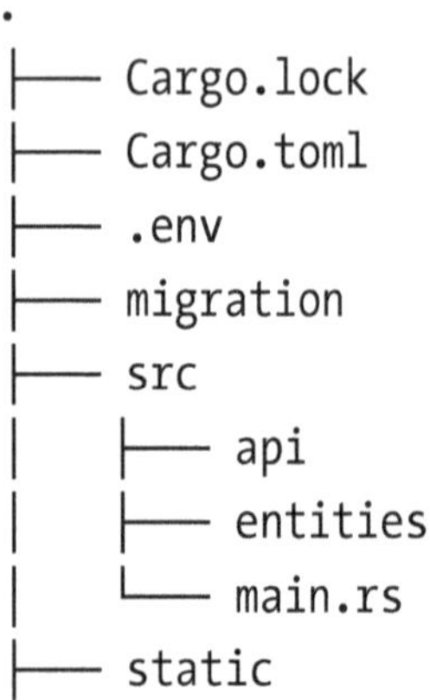

```
.
├── Cargo.lock
├── Cargo.toml
├── .env
├── migration
├── src
│   ├── api
│   ├── entities
│   └── main.rs
├── static
```

To serve the `static` folder from the backend, we use the `ServeDir` and `ServeFile` middleware services from `tower_http`.

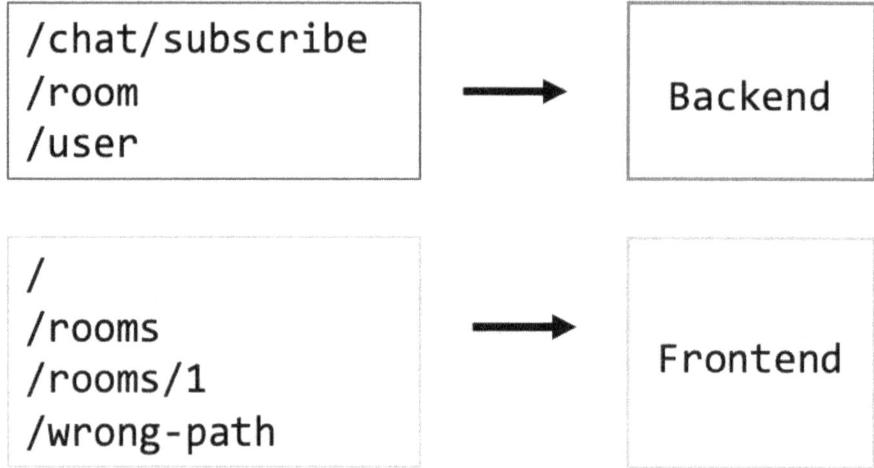

Figure 6-11. *Serve Static Files*

This code uses Axum's `nest_service` method to route any requests that don't match the API routes defined above to the frontend.

```
let app = Router::new()
    ...

    .nest_service(
        "/",
        ServeDir::new("static").not_found_service(ServeFile::new("static/
        index.html")),
    )
```

`.nest_service("/", ...)` connects the root path to a service that serves static files. The `ServeDir::new("static")` part creates a new service that serves files from the "static" directory. The `not_found_service` method specifies a fallback service `ServeFile::new("static/index.html")` to use when the `ServeDir` service cannot find the requested file. In this case, it is configured to serve the "index.html" file from the "static" directory.

In summary, this code sets up a service that serves static files from the "static" directory when accessed at the root path ("/"). If a file cannot be found, it falls back to serving the "index.html" file from the "static" directory. This is a common pattern when serving SPAs (Single-Page Applications). An SPA is a web application that can display multiple pages using a single HTML file. React is the most popular and widely used SPA library. The intent is to serve the SPA's static files and fall back to the index file for unknown paths, allowing the SPA to handle routing on the client side.

To verify that everything we've built so far works correctly, use `cargo run`. If the frontend page appears, you can enter a name to navigate to the chat room list page, create or delete chat rooms, and enter chat messages, then everything is working.

6.2.6. Automated Testing

Now that all features are complete, let's verify that our API works as intended using automated tests. As features grow, it becomes nearly impossible to manually test using Insomnia every time. Especially after refactoring or library updates, the only way to guarantee that "existing features still work correctly" is through automated tests.

6.2.6.1. tower::Service and Oneshot Testing

Axum's Router fully implements the `tower::Service` interface internally. Why does this matter? Because it means **"you can send HTTP requests directly to the router object itself without opening an actual port."** This is called `oneshot` testing. Since this approach doesn't go through an actual network, execution speed is overwhelmingly fast, and there is absolutely no risk of port conflicts with other test processes.

To make tests easy to write, it's a good practice to extract the router creation logic from the `main` function into a separate function.

```rust
// Dedicated function for creating the router
pub fn create_app(state: AppState) -> Router {
    Router::new()
        .nest(
            "/chat",
            Router::new()
                .route("/", get(get_chat))
                .route("/subscribe", get(subscribe))
                .route("/send", post(send)),
        )
        .route(
            "/room",
            get(get_room)
                .post(post_room)
                .put(put_room)
                .delete(delete_room),
        )
        .route(
            "/user",
            get(get_user)
                .post(post_user)
                .put(put_user)
                .delete(delete_user),
        )
        .with_state(state)
}
```

6.2.6.2. Integration Test Implementation

```rust
#[cfg(test)]
mod tests {
    use super::*;
    use axum::{
        body::Body,
        http::{Request, StatusCode},
    };
    use tower::ServiceExt; // Required import for using the oneshot method

    #[tokio::test]
    async fn test_create_room_endpoint() {
        // 1. Set up the test environment
        let config = Config::from_env();
        let conn = Database::connect(&config.database_url).await.unwrap();
        let state = AppState {
            conn,
            queue: broadcast::channel(10).0,
        };
        let app = create_app(state);

        // 2. Create a mock HTTP POST request object
        let request = Request::builder()
            .uri("/room")
            .method("POST")
            .header("Content-Type", "application/json")
            .body(Body::from(r#"{"participants": ["alice", "bob"]}"#))
            .unwrap();

        // 3. Send the request directly to the router (no actual server
        //       required)
        let response = app.oneshot(request).await.unwrap();

        // 4. Verify the response
        assert_eq!(response.status(), StatusCode::OK);
    }
}
```

Running `cargo test` in the terminal produces the following results.

```
$ cargo test

   Compiling axum-chat-app v0.1.0
    Finished `test` profile [unoptimized + debuginfo] target(s) in 3.42s
     Running unittests src/main.rs

running 1 test
test tests::test_create_room_endpoint ... ok

test result: ok. 1 passed; 0 failed; 0 ignored; 0 measured; 0 filtered out;
finished in 0.15s
```

Notice that the test execution time is very short because no actual network was used.

oneshot *literally means firing "just one shot" at the router. Therefore, if you need to send multiple requests within a single test function, you should use a combination of* ready *and* call *methods instead of* oneshot. *For more details, refer to the tower official documentation.*

6.2.6.3. Test File Structure

In Rust, there are two main locations for writing tests:

1. **Unit Tests (Same File)**: As shown in the example above, write a
   `#[cfg(test)]` module at the bottom of the source file.

2. **Integration Tests (tests/ Directory)**: Create a `tests/` directory in
   the project root and write independent test files.

```
axum-chat-app/
├── src/
│   ├── main.rs
│   └── api/
│       └── chat.rs      # #[cfg(test)] unit tests at the bottom
├── tests/
│   ├── room_api.rs      # Integration tests
│   └── health_check.rs
├── .env
└── Cargo.toml
```

When developing an API server, focusing on integration tests (in the `tests/` directory) is more effective in practice.

6.2.6.4. Practical Advice: Test Database Strategies

The most challenging part of integration testing is database management. In practice, the following strategies are used:

1. **Transaction-Based Isolation**: This is the most recommended approach. Open a transaction at the start of the test and perform a `Rollback` when the test ends. In SeaORM, this can be easily implemented using `db.begin()`.

2. **Unique Schemas**: Generate a unique schema name for each test run to use completely physically isolated spaces.

3. **Test-Specific .env Configuration**: Configure `Config::from_env()` to read `DATABASE_URL_TEST` in test environments to completely prevent accidentally touching the production database.

6.2.7. Production Readiness and Deployment

In this final step, we will prepare our service for stable operation in a production environment.

6.2.7.1. Graceful Shutdown

Shutting down a running server should not be as simple as just cutting the power. If you forcibly terminate the server process with `kill -9` to restart it for deploying new code, users' requests that were in the middle of saving important data will be cut off.

Graceful Shutdown refers to the process of safely exiting when the server receives a signal saying "I'm about to shut down, so just finish what you're doing."

Using Tokio's signal functionality, we write an asynchronous function that waits for both `Ctrl+C` (SIGINT) and `SIGTERM`.

```rust
use tokio::signal;

async fn shutdown_signal() {
    let ctrl_c = async {
```

```rust
    signal::ctrl_c()
        .await
        .expect("Failed to register Ctrl+C handler");
};

#[cfg(unix)]
let terminate = async {
    signal::unix::signal(signal::unix::SignalKind::terminate())
        .expect("Failed to register SIGTERM handler")
        .recv()
        .await;
};

#[cfg(not(unix))]
let terminate = std::future::pending::<()>();

tokio::select! {
    _ = ctrl_c => println!("Received manual shutdown (Ctrl+C)
    signal."),
    _ = terminate => println!("Received system termination (SIGTERM)
    signal."),
}

println!("Finishing in-progress requests and beginning safe
shutdown...");
}
```

Now register the function we just created when running axum::serve in main.rs.
The final server execution portion of main.rs looks like this.

```rust
let addr = format!("0.0.0.0:{}", config.server_port);
let listener = tokio::net::TcpListener::bind(&addr).await.unwrap();

println!("Server is running on port {}.", config.server_port);
axum::serve(listener, app)
    .with_graceful_shutdown(shutdown_signal())
    .await
    .unwrap();

println!("Server has been fully shut down.");
```

If you actually run the server and press Ctrl+C, you can see the following output.

```
$ cargo run

Server is running on port 3000.
^C
Received manual shutdown (Ctrl+C) signal.
Finishing in-progress requests and beginning safe shutdown...
Server has been fully shut down.
```

> *In production environments, it is common to set a **timeout** for graceful shutdown. If a request being processed takes infinitely long, the server might never shut down. It is recommended to add defensive logic using* `tokio::time::timeout` *to forcibly terminate the process if it doesn't shut down within a certain period (typically 30 seconds).*

6.2.7.2. Create a Docker Image

Let's write a Dockerfile to build a Docker image. In the Dockerfile, we'll go through multiple stages to build the frontend and backend separately and combine them into one.

First, there's the frontend stage. In this stage, we use the node:20-alpine image as the base image. Then we copy the frontend code to the container. We install dependencies using yarn. And we build the output to the dist folder using vite.

Next, there's the backend stage. In this stage, we use the rust:1.73 image as the base image. Then we copy the backend code to the container. We build a binary crate named docker.

Finally, there's the production stage. In this stage, we use a new rust:1.73 image as the base image. Then we copy the built frontend assets to the static folder. We set the backend binary as the entrypoint.

In summary, we build the frontend and backend separately, then copy the artifacts and combine them into a single production image. Building using stages has the advantage of keeping the Docker image size small because you don't need to include dependencies or intermediate outputs needed to create each artifact in the production environment.

```
# Frontend build
FROM node:20-alpine AS frontend
```

```
COPY frontend .
RUN yarn install
RUN yarn run vite build --outDir dist

# Rust build
FROM rust:1.73 AS backend
COPY backend .
RUN cargo build --release --bin docker

# Production stage
FROM rust:1.73

COPY --from=frontend dist static
COPY --from=backend target/release/docker app
COPY --from=backend .env .env

ENTRYPOINT ["./app"]
```

> 💡 *The Dockerfile above includes the* `.env` *file in the image for convenience, but in production environments, it is recommended to inject environment variables at runtime for security, such as using* `docker run --env-file .env` *or* `docker run -e DATABASE_URL=....`

6.2.7.3. Build the Docker Image

To build a Docker image based on the Dockerfile you wrote, use the following command:

```
docker build -t axum-chat-app .
```

We specified the Docker image tag as `axum-chat-app`, but modify this part to fit your situation. For example, if you're using an image repository like Docker Hub, you can use the repository name and version as `<repository-name>:<version>` for the image tag. For example, in the case of a Docker image I built and uploaded myself, I built it using the following tag and then pushed it to the repository:

```
docker build -t indosaram/axum-chat-app:latest .
docker push indosaram/axum-chat-app:latest
```

Since this Docker image is public, you can also download and run it.

6.2.7.4. Run the Docker Image

To run the created Docker image, use the following command. Don't forget to open port 3000 for our application:

```
docker run -p 3000:3000 axum-chat-app
```

Now when you access `http://localhost:3000`, the web app should work correctly. If you get a database connection error, check whether Postgres is running and whether the connection information is correct. Using this Docker image, you can run an Axum server on server hosting platforms like AWS.

6.3. Review

- We learned how to manage configuration by separating code and settings using `dotenvy` and `envy`.

- We learned how to write automated tests using `tower::Service` and the `oneshot` method.

- We learned how to implement Graceful Shutdown for safe server termination.

- We learned how to build and run a Docker image for Axum.

6.4. Closing

Rust is truly a language with unlimited potential. Based on convenient syntax like high-level languages while safely achieving performance like low-level languages, it's no coincidence that global IT companies like Microsoft, Google, and Amazon are actively adopting Rust. Rust will become the language of the future, and learning Rust is an investment in your future.

Likewise, backend servers written in Rust will become highly acclaimed. The fact that it's simply fast doesn't end with just fast processing speeds—it leads to reduced computing costs. The reason AWS is providing ARM architecture-based servers through the Graviton project is because it can significantly reduce costs in large-scale computing environments. Therefore, Rust backends will become essential in fields requiring large-scale, high-performance computing in the future. I hope this book increases your interest in Axum and Rust backends. I look forward to more people using Rust backends and creating services that use Rust backends in the future.

For code conciseness, error handling in this chapter uses .unwrap() for brevity. For production-quality error handling patterns using AppError and Result types, refer to Chapter 3.

Index

© Indo Yoon 2026
I. Yoon, *Beginning Axum*, https://doi.org/10.1007/979-8-8688-2631-3

I

J

K

L

M

N

O

P

Q

R

S

PostgreSQL database, 10–13, 42
query execution, 156
in SeaQuery (*see* SeaQuery)
SQLite, 14
table declarations, 107
SQLite, 14
State management
configuration files, 79
database connections, 79
extension, 89
internal state, 80
shared state, 80
value changes, 82, 83, 85–87
Status codes, 73–76, 78
StreamExt trait, 191
SurrealDB, 103

T

Token, 208
tokio::spawn function, 198
Tower middleware
adding layers, 161
asynchronous functions, 160
compression methods, 167–169,
171, 172
features, 159, 160
JWT authentication layer (*see* JWT
authentication layer)
logging layer, 163–166
operating principles, 159, 168
timeout layer, 162

U

UpsertModel, 138
UTF-8, 59
Utility crates, 190

V

validate_token function, 179, 180
verify_password function, 177, 182
Visual Studio Code (VSCode), 2, 8–10

W, X, Y, Z

Warp, 5
WebSocket
authentication headers, 207–212
channels, 191, 198–200, 202
concurrent websocket connetions, 198,
200–202, 204–207
creating request, 195
definition, 187
error message, 196
futures, 190
handshake, 188, 189, 191, 192
Insomnia, 194
message, 191
multiple connections, 198, 207
principles, 188
receiving message, 198
text variant, 193
tokio, 190
upgrade, 191

GPSR Compliance
The European Union's (EU) General Product Safety Regulation (GPSR) is a set
of rules that requires consumer products to be safe and our obligations to
ensure this.

If you have any concerns about our products, you can contact us on

ProductSafety@springernature.com

In case Publisher is established outside the EU, the EU authorized
representative is:

Springer Nature Customer Service Center GmbH
Europaplatz 3
69115 Heidelberg, Germany

www.ingramcontent.com/pod-product-compliance
Lightning Source LLC
Chambersburg PA
CBHW060558120726
48002CB00010B/2728